Contingent Figure

CONTINGENT FIGURE

CHRONIC PAIN AND QUEER EMBODIMENT

MICHAEL D. SNEDIKER

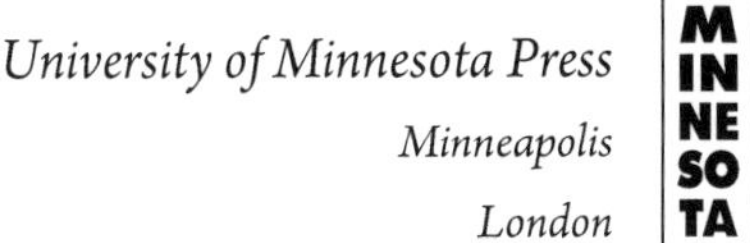

The University of Minnesota Press gratefully acknowledges the financial assistance provided for the publication of this book by the Department of English at the University of Houston.

Published by the University of Minnesota Press
111 Third Avenue South, Suite 290
Minneapolis, MN 55401–2520
http://www.upress.umn.edu

ISBN 978-0-8166-9188-3 (hc)
ISBN 978-0-8166-9190-6 (pb)

A Cataloging-in-Publication record for this book is available from the Library of Congress.

Printed in the United States of America on acid-free paper

The University of Minnesota is an equal-opportunity educator and employer.

UMP BmB 2021

for EC and EKS

Discharged you are discharged.
Not a sound.
Not so sense. Silence.
Little silence.
So painful, so ill visible, so necessary.
That is a tender that is a tender circumstance.
Suppose he had a friend.
What is too listen.
Begin a blessing.
Just begin it.

—GERTRUDE STEIN, "FINISHED ONE"

Spinelit sunwave. Newton said space is as it were God's sensorium and we say time is as it were God's spine. A fish swims in a cube of water like at a black obsidian obelisk. Now I should as it were not be alone I am only strange. I am now wise.

—KEVIN HOLDEN, "SKY-ALGORITHM PROSOID"

Contents

Preface: Crasher xi

Introduction: "So Much for My Figurative Self"; or, Aesthetic Duress (*Plein Air,* in Parts) 1

1. Melville's Iron Crown of Lombardy: Phenomenology beyond the Phantom Limb 35
2. Queer Philology and Chronic Pain 61
3. "The Vision – pondered long": Chronic Pain and the Materiality of Figuration 85
4. Inveterate Pagoda: Late James, Ongoingness, and the Figure of Hurt 125
5. Is the Rectangle a Grave? Floating Attention, Betweenness in Relief 155
6. Weaver's Handshake: The Aesthetics of Chronic Objects 183

Acknowledgments 213

Notes 215

Index 249

Preface

Crasher

Luxury: lasciviousness; the habitual use of what is choice or costly; refined.

Luxate: to put out of joint.

Lux: a unit of illumination:

let there be light or, as Alexander Pope's translation of *The Odyssey* puts it,

Lux'd the neck joynt—my soul descends to hell.[1]

Sumptuary: lavishness.

Sumpture: beast of burden;

as in (Lear to Goneril):

Returne with her, Perswade me rather to be slaue and sumter / To this detested groome.[2]

"Sex," writes Foucault, "is not that part of the body which the bourgeoisie was forced to disqualify or nullify in order to put those whom it dominated to work. It is that aspect of itself which troubled and preoccupied it more than any other, begged and obtained its attention, and which it cultivated with a mixture of fear, curiosity, delight, and excitement. The bourgeoisie made this element identical with its body, or at least subordinated the latter to the former by attributing to it a mysterious and undefined power; it staked its life and its death on sex by making it responsible for its future welfare. . . . [I]t subordinated its soul to sex by conceiving of it as what constituted the soul's most secret and determinant part."[3]

By this account, the history of my sexuality is commensurate with if not indistinguishable from my life with chronic pain.

At twenty, late-blooming (relatively speaking), I came to relish a queerness I'd until that point been living in the terrified margin of. Between a rock and a hard place, lamella deliberating equally and oppositely inoperable nothings: portrait of the artist as Henry James's ungovernably precocious (weak-hearted) schoolboy, Miles. As in: *miles to go before I sleep,* Aida buried alive. That was then, the childhood and adolescent dormancies. Flash forward to twenty-two, solitary in Venice. My first trip alone, first taste of the lonesomeness a life with chronic pain became. *Aida* was my first experience of opera. In the aftermath of La Fenice's ruinous arson, staged at a temporary site, some nearby lagoon, spotlights held a sky-long tarp of blue in unending twilight.

Those solitary, late-December afternoons, flaneuring with *baicoli* and a net bag of clementines, I wandered Venice's vividly sunstruck alleys ravished but also deeply worried about paralysis, of the neck cracked inadvertently past repair. It hurt constantly, and cracking it felt allaying and exacerbating all at once, exacerbating what it allayed.[4] Ominous comfort in the creak of crepitus acoustically confirming a solidity for which the eyes couldn't vouch—bone on bone, like a stone being ground into one of those ancient red Venetian bricks. Sun-struck: as Barthes might say, fingering the wound. And downhill we go.

"Resistances . . . are the odd term in relations of power; they are inscribed in the latter as an irreducible opposite. Hence they too are distributed in irregular fashion: the points, knots, or focuses of resistance are spread over time and space at varying densities, at times mobilizing groups or individuals in a definitive way, inflaming certain points of the body, certain moments in life."[5]

Flash back. I was a gangly boy. Well intentioned, best to their ability, my parents took me to a psychologist, fearing I wanted to be a girl. Perhaps I did. What I mostly wanted (proto-Jamesian kindergartner) was to be less afraid. Proleptic poetic justice, the psychologist and I played Old Maid. Haunted by the hand in hand.

Although the neck at that point didn't hurt, not in the way it would, its ridiculous Parmigianino elongation preoccupied all the same. I wore turtlenecks into summer, vain suburban stratagem of concealment (wishful object permanence loophole). Reflected in the bathroom mirror, thumb and index finger pinching either side where the electrodes of Frankenstein's monster might protrude, I stretched my neck wide, reveled in the fantasy that this ersatz girth was its own. If, those years before coming out, the neck (disavowing work of the definite article) was the focalizing object of my contempt, if it came to bear all that psychical freight of expectation and embarrassed disappointment, how could its low, imperceptible crumble not come to feel like fate?

Back (unless it's forward) to twenty, time spiraling through itself: I came out flagrantly, reconciled myself, incorrigible ectomorph, to the body I had. The neck, perhaps, was the remainder of that reconciliation, what rapprochement couldn't metabolize or contain. Like Bartleby, I gorged on the writing set before me, early touchstones articulating a way of being if not belonging (illuminating that longing) for which as yet I had so scarce vocabulary of my own. Queer theory showed a way toward myself (I found it, lost it, there). At the same time, I was fumbling with an interiority no less engrossed in the neck's painful efflorescence. I had no idiom for this nor schoolroom and for a long time lived, wishful preterit, in that fumbling like a second closet.

Synecdoche for twenty years' conviction of insufficiency and aggrieved locus of the body's burgeoning unreliability, queerness and chronic pain felt incompatible and interchangeable. The neck persisted with an intensity all but eclipsing desire, its shape guessed by corona. Uncloseted, libido let off-leash chomped at the bit where the bit had been, and the neck a second leash (around libido's very neck): the chaperone as unappeasable infant. In that pre-Truvada era, the neck cruised the euphemizing vestibule of "safe sex" with its own pamphleteering cautions. How to disappear in the calculus of a desire warped with fear of the neck being thrown ever further out of whack? Search me, smithereens. This is what queer failure felt like: not knowing if I would have been freer with myself, more devil-may-care, if the pain were less a part of the equation. There was never time, so it felt, to find out.

If I wasn't malingering, then why did this dovetail of sex and pain, even from its center, feel so conveniently legible? I don't mean to toggle between queerness/chronic pain and sex/chronic pain as though their synonymousness were confirmable or self-evident. But in those first fitful years of queer self-realization, the formidable confluence of their respective Image Repertoires seemed unimpeachable. Whether or not I expected chronic pain to feel like a crash course in the variously mercurial and sedimentous fault lines between queerness and sex, it mostly just felt like the crash, the crasher.

Between then and now were too many doctor visits to tally, too many stopgap diagnoses, semi-triage ministrations. But the prescriptions and counsel proffered by Western and non-Western practices alike trafficked in argots of treatment and care that never took. What I envisioned needing was a vocabulary of living *with,* to be acquired piecemeal, improvisatory, over time. The pain wasn't addressed, I waited for it to be addressed. And when *it* responded to the writing set before it, I honored the decisive attention of affinity where it came, however strange.

It's in the shadow of the neck's degenerative transfixion that *Contingent Figure* has been written. The essays collected here obliquely chronicle what happened when the neck entered the picture, when it called the shots, where it recognized itself dilating past recognition. As with *Queer Optimism,* the theory and practice of this present undertaking are unthinkable apart from their devotion to close reading, the temporality of which—or, at least, one of multiple temporalities presiding within the rhythm of what George Poulet calls the phenomenology of reading—is beautifully described by Elizabeth Freeman in her preface to *Time Binds: Queer Temporalities, Queer Histories*:

> To close read is to linger, to dally, to take pleasure in tarrying, and to hold out that these activities can allow us to look both hard and askance at the norm. . . . Thus what I'd like to identify as perhaps the queerest commitment of my own book is also close reading: the decision to unfold, slowly, a small number of imaginative texts rather than amass a weighty archive . . . and to treat these texts and their formal work as theories of their own.[6]

Pain, like interest or desire, is a divining rod (however each through either end of binoculars resolves itself from the other). Consider the following instances of its mimetic foraging, how its noise cuts a swath of attention between itself and prospective solidarity forms, commensurate patterns of extemporized solid substance: In the penultimate scene of

Henry James's early novel *Roderick Hudson,* Rowland Mallet scrambles to the bottom of a cliff where the ruin of Roderick's own lost body lies. Rowland's "marvel[ing]" that "he had not broken his neck" dreams a solidarity with Roderick modeled on if not quite surpassing the latter's aesthetic frangibility—"an attempt to move him would show some hideous fracture, some horrible physical dishonour"[7]—echoing, in turn, Roderick's earlier, ironic confession to Rowland, "I was not afraid of breaking my neck then, but I feel in a devil of a tremor now."[8]

Almost thirty years later, James revisits Roderick's calamity and its foreshadowings in a portentous late scene in *The Golden Bowl.* Walking the terrace in the pitch of a "moonless and starless" hour, Maggie is horrified to find herself face-to-face with Charlotte Stant, her husband's mistress and father's wife:

> By the time she was at her companion's side, for that matter, by the time Charlotte had, without a motion, without a word, simply let her approach and stand there, her head was already on the block, so that the consciousness that everything had gone blurred all perception of whether or no the axe had fallen. Oh the "advantage," it was perfectly enough, in truth, with Mrs. Verver; for what was Maggie's own sense but that of having been thrown over on her back with her neck from the first half-broken and her helpless face staring up? That position only could account for the positive grimace of weakness and pain produced there by Charlotte's dignity.[9]

Like the twinned necks of Roderick and Rowland, Maggie's sensational fantasy of a broken neck finds its asymmetrical match in Charlotte's "handsome head and long straight neck," which "testified through the dusk to their inveterate completeness and noble erectness" (493). The nobility of Charlotte's neck is the precondition for its ultimate debasement at the hands—"such sharp, imagined things"[10]—of Maggie and her father, Adam:

> [Charlotte] stopped when her husband stopped . . . and the likeness of their connexion wouldn't have been wrongly figured if he had been thought of as holding in one of his pocketed hands the end of a long silken halter looped round her beautiful neck. He didn't twitch it, yet it was there; he didn't drag her, but she came; and those betrayals that I have described the Princess as finding irresistible in him were two or three mute facial intimations which his wife's presence didn't prevent

> his addressing his daughter—nor prevent his daughter, as she passed, it was doubtless to be added, from flushing a little at the receipt of. They amounted perhaps only to a wordless, wordless smile, but the smile was the soft shake of the twisted silken rope, and Maggie's translation of it, held in her breast till she got well away, came out only, as if it might have been overheard, when some door was closed behind her. "Yes, you see—I lead her now by the neck." (523–24)

I offer these examples of the neck's navel-gazing to underscore at outset a circuitry of reading that *Contingent Figure* actively resists. At the heart of this resistance lies an interest in giving an account of chronic pain apart from the mutual cottoning of narrativity and mimesis. As Leo Bersani observes, "narrativity sustains the glamour of historical violence. . . . A coherent narrative depends on stabilized images; stabilized images stimulate the mimetic impulse."[11] By contrast, the texts examined in the following pages tend toward mobilities both errantly fugal and deceptively equilibrious, inseparable from the excrescence of their fomentingly figurative substance.[12] The frisson of this textual movement amounts to the difficulty of knowing where affect ends and figuration begins. "And so it comes about," Erich Auerbach writes of Lucretius, "that he often calls [atoms] 'forms,' *figurae,* and that conversely one may often translate *figurae,* as Diels has done, by 'atoms.' The numerous atoms are in constant motion; they move about in the void, combine and repel one another: a dance of figures."[13]

When it comes to disability theory's entanglement with a phenomenology of chronic pain, the frequency with which critical interventions depend on narrative's tendency toward mimetic exempla reflects the lasting impact of Elaine Scarry's *The Body in Pain: The Making and Unmaking of the World*. Scarry's indispensable insights gravitate to narrative form and the experience of story. "In the long run," Scarry writes, "we will see that the story of *physical pain* becomes as well a story about the expansive nature of human *sentience* . . . just as the story of *expressing* physical pain eventually opens into the wider frame of *invention*."[14] Scarry's framing of pain along these lines inscribes her interest in "the way other persons become visible to us, or cease to be visible to us," as though pain were something experienced by others and we implicitly its afflictionless witness.

Even, however, as pain is expressed, retold, and repeated as story, it is being felt in nonnarrative terms. Mel Y. Chen has noted that "toxicity incontrovertibly meddles with the relations of subject and object."[15] That the same could be said of pain's meddling effects complicates what it would mean to think about the object of chronic pain as a subject in its own right—to insist, in Fred Moten's approximate terms, upon the subjectivity of the object[16]— not least when it comes to the frequency with which the grammar of subject and object on which conventions of narrative depend so thoroughly affect (and are affected by) our sense of the perceptible at the often unspoken expense of the imperceptible. *Contingent Figure*'s meditation on the receptivity of inner experience reckons with the imperceptible impressments of what Chen might describe as the perplexing animacy of duress. Figuration constitutes both language and field not of an interiority interrupted by pain but of the porousness of pain's own quotidian interior.

This project has been lived with longer than I'd have predicted. Five years into it, the original manuscript was scrapped and rewritten in its entirety. Five years after that, beyond even a writer's invariable taste for self-sabotage, I've clung to its solace in the absence of other viable therapies. If this book on chronic pain came to feel interminable, I fear it's because on some level I couldn't envision (wishful subjunctive) living with the pain without the book's immersions and surface menisci, the queer pleasure of not knowing at any given moment if I were diving into the wreck of the neck or coming up at last however long for air.

Introduction

"So Much for My Figurative Self"; or, Aesthetic Duress (*Plein Air,* in Parts)

> To the contrary, life itself—nothing other than the incessant process of figuration—is now understood as writing
>
> —BRANKA ARSIĆ, "POETRY AS FLOWERING OF LIFE FORMS: RANCIÈRE'S READING OF EMERSON"

This is a book written in the vicinity of chronic pain; even more so, the peculiar relation between chronic pain and figuration, a word, as I've come to understand it, that isn't so easily defined. It is my contention that the slight unfamiliarity of this latter terrain helpfully disorients what in the matter of pain has grown, grows, deceptively familiar, not least when it comes to introducing some breathing room between pleasure and pain, whose codified pairing seldom does either any favors. The title of this chapter alludes to Nathaniel Hawthorne's wry pivot in "The Custom-House" upon being terminated by the Whigs between three accidious years as "Loco-foco Surveyor"[1] and his eventual return to a life of writing, "rusty through long idleness" (33), that will eventually yield *The Scarlet Letter.* If figuration names an interval between public service and the retreating labor of enthrallment, it also binds Hawthorne to those insufficiently historical, characterologically credulity-straining, fascinatingly resistant first denizens of *The Scarlet Letter*—"My imagination was a tarnished mirror. It would not reflect, or only with miserable dimness, the figures with which

I did my best to people it. The characters of the narrative would not be warmed and rendered malleable, by any heat that I could kindle at my intellectual forge" (27)—and to Hester Prynne herself, who doesn't exceed this account of figuration so much as embody it, the intensity of its vitiation, to the hilt.

Contingent Figure's study of chronic pain involves an effort to better understand the felt rhythms of a chronicity akin to the queer temporality of cruising.[2] In *The Grain of the Voice,* Roland Barthes writes of cruising that the "body is . . . on the lookout for its own desire. And then, cruising implies a temporality that accentuates the meeting, the 'first time.' As if the first meeting possessed an unheard-of privilege: that of being withdrawn from all repetition."[3] It is cruising's implacable magnetization to the first seductive cusp of an encounter that ironically propels the engine of repetition by which it realizes the seriality of its constitution. Cruising, that is, occupies at least two coterminous temporal fields: the lavender-lit purposiveness of erotic astonishment momentarily allowed the fiction of temporal independence, and the gloaming lassitude of so many cruising overtures not reciprocated, politely and not so politely demurred, the unabating debasement and poisonous lonesomeness that often inform the no less persistent desire for a clean slate.

Whether one's experience of chronic pain worsens or improves (or, perchance, miraculously vanishes), there remains in it a Barthesian element of cruising's first-time seriality. Like the accretion of singular interactions by which cruising's irresistible habit, drip by drip, is built, chronic pain contributes to a temporalizing form that grazes tangentially past its own simultaneously oneiric and drudging, flooding and emptying, substance. In calling this substance figurative, I don't mean that it approximates or recalls literal solidity without quite achieving it, without crossing the literal's threshold. I don't, that is, mean "figurative" as it's ordinarily taken as a form of erasure or disqualification: *this is how it feels,* this conception of "figurative" declares, *but not what it is.* By contrast, *Contingent Figure* speculates that the substance of chronic pain is substantively, even accretively, figurative in both its movement and work. Less solid, so to speak, than the cartilage it infests or the nerves it havocs yet putatively less abstract than emotion or memory, and so forth, figuration has for some time seemed most plausible to me as transitional matter. To amend the above formula, entertaining the possibility that chronic pain *is* how it *feels* differently formulates the relation between pain and figuration as an echo of Poe's claim in "Philosophy of Composition" that a poem will be known by its effect.

As I hope to make clear, *Contingent Figure*'s somewhat idiosyncratic notion of figuration only occasionally lines up with the conventionally ordered apparatus of allegory or metaphor. Recall I. A. Richards's now canonical conception of the latter in terms of vehicle and tenor: some known entity (implicitly, its mundanely recognizable substance) luminously brings within our orbit an element or thing otherwise obscurely withdrawn past the empirical. Figuration, as pertains to these present pages, arrives and unfolds without this promise of—without the notarizing need for—vehicular complement. To think of the false etymological relationship between luxury and subluxation, the expense of figuration departs from the prosaic in a manner that renders the departure its own unsettling mundanity. *Contingent Figure* reports from those scenes of aesthetic duress whose suspended interruption disturbs aspects of reading and embodiment otherwise at risk of disappearing, one way or another, into the demands of proper use; it seeks to describe the vigor of their fugues, digressive elaborations, and impinging compressions with the patience of empirical observation and the fidelity of bearing witness. What is beheld there often feels like the closest I can get to my pain, its strangeness, its elusion of vanishing point or horizon. Leaning chronic pain and figuration against each other in hopes of scrying their crystallizing relation, we may note that neither term is tethered exclusively to either the mundanity of metaphor's vehicle or the abstraction of its tenor. Variously nebulous and teeming, the interfulgent stuff of *Contingent Figure*'s operative terms is difficult to specify. It is my belief that our underestimation of figuration's thingness continues to limit our modes of conceptualizing, corresponding with, attending to, chronic pain.

In his introduction to *Herculine Barbin,* Foucault speaks of pleasure as though it were neither strictly phenomenological nor discursive. "One has the impression," he writes, "that everything took place in a world of feelings—enthusiasm, pleasure, sorrow, warmth, sweetness, bitterness—where the identity of the partners and above all the enigmatic character around whom everything centered, had no importance. It was a world in which grins hung about without the cat."[4] Foucault's vision of dissolving apparatus and the nongenealogical presentation of feeling hovering in its wake presents more questions than it finds. It's unclear how readers might think through this experience of pleasure without bodies without betraying its deliverance from those categories—identities, partners, characters—it is hailed as exceeding. Somewhat differently put, Foucault's text leaves the interstice between corporal vanishment and unimportance as tantalizingly open as that between the indelible and the eschewable. It's within these fissures that figurative language conducts itself, closer in quality to affect itself than the conventional figures of narrative and illustration from which Francis Bacon and Marcel Proust work, writes Deleuze, to free their own work: "a kind of Figure, torn away from figuration and stripped of every figurative function."[5] The figurative language that is *Contingent Figure*'s concern moves between the residuum of somatic disturbance and the threatening stasis of normatively figurative constraint. Like affect more generally, the difference between these homonymous elements is first known through feel. We find an analogous affective hydraulic in the posthumous speech of Dickinson, in which the persuasiveness of a singular, continuous-seeming voice has less to do with its collation with any one form of subjectivity than with the intensity of feeling it articulates from the smudge of where a person capable of such feeling has been surrendered. The question of where this voice stops and the work of figuration begins is never far from the phenomenological heart of her poems.

Consider the last stanza of a poem to which these pages will return, "After great pain a formal feeling comes –":

> This is the Hour of Lead –
> Remembered, if outlived,
> As Freezing persons, recollect the Snow –
> First – Chill – then Stupor – then the letting go –[6]

That we may imagine the penultimate line's "Freezing persons" as coextensive with the voice that seeks to make sense of them doesn't mean we can assume this latter voice issues from a person recognizable to itself or us as such. On the contrary, the experience of being a person seems as distant from the poem as the experience that these persons are trying to rescue. Dickinson's quatrain asks us to imagine persons trying to recollect snow while they are freezing; our inability to think about persons remembering a condition inseparable from the one they are in means that persons so stringently defined through their efforts at recollection are themselves in the poem's insistently limiting terms all but unimaginable. The difficulty of recollecting what one so intransigently is experiencing—even as the latter so defies experience that we are asked to imagine it in terms of analogy—suggests that there is in such saturating pain something only verging on the phenomenological. We are thus asked to construe affective immediacy as subjectivity hollowed out, at best indirectly commensurate with that of the characters we vicariously, inadequately remember (being), let alone, in pain's blinding presence, understand.

The need to disarticulate chronic pain from character may strike some as counterintuitive. After all, isn't character precisely where one would expect to look for a literary representation of chronic pain or disability, more generally? Although the answer is yes, our temptation to take this alignment for granted should give pause, not least because the self-evidence of characterology as a site of somatic disappointment and distress presumes an understanding of embodiment's legibility that delimits the subject before it's broached. Lest the "depopulated and decontextualized space"[7] of Dickinson's poetry seem on its own an odd place for testing characterological constraint, Samuel Otter's introduction to an issue of *Leviathan* devoted to Melville and disability proves a helpful supplement. The point of departure for Otter's remarks is an early set of Melville sketches, "Fragments from a Writing Desk" (1839). In the second of these fragments, our chauvinist narrator's riverine reverie is interrupted by the gliding appearance of a "figure effectually concealed in the ample folds of a cloak,"[8] who leaves at his feet a love letter, "an elegant little, rose-coloured, lavender-scented billet-doux" (197). Written, so the narrator infers from its "femininely delicate" handwriting, by the messenger's mistress, the billet is signed only Inamorata: less name than amorously generalizing placeholder. And so, "plunging ahead like an infuriated steed," the narrator pursues this mysterious harbinger along the river until he is brought to a strange villa in a strangely embowering grove, a place of "singular and grotesque beauty" (199). Hoisted alongside the messenger—*by basket*—through one of the villa's lofty windows, the narrator finds himself face-to-face with a lavish fever-dream of an odalisque—Inamorata, we are led to believe—who had "apparently been lost in some melancholy revery" of her own (203).

Otter's introduction cites the narrator's first glimpse of this "creature": this "lovely being . . . lay reclining upon an ottoman; in one hand holding a lute, and with the other lost in the profusion of her silken tresses, she supported her head" (202). The description continues, conjuring less a woman than a confectionary pornograph whose Liberace effusiveness can't help but challenge what might otherwise be adduced as a strictly heterosexual gaze:

> She was habited in a flowing robe of the purest white, and her hair, escaping from the fillet of roses which had bound it, spread its negligent graces over neck and bosom and shoulder, as though unwilling to reveal the extent of such transcendant charms.—Her zone was of pink satin, on which were broidered figures of Cupid in the act of drawing his bow; while the ample folds of her Turkish sleeve were gathered at the wrist by a bracelet of immense rubies, each of which represented a heart pierced thro' by a golden shaft. Her fingers were decorated with a variety of rings, which as she waved her hand to me as I entered, darted forth a thousand coruscations, and gleamed their brilliant splendors to the sight. Peeping from beneath the envious skirts of her mantle, and almost buried in the downy quishion on which it reposed, lay revealed the prettiest little foot you can imagine; cased in a satin slipper, which clung to the fairy-like member by means of a diamond clasp. (203)

So far so good, our narrator oglingly thinks, "mute, admiring and bewildered in her presence." His "heart dissolving away like ice before the equinoctial heats" of Inamorata's dark eyes, the nameless narrator "seize[s] the passive hand" of "this glorious being," exclaiming, "I feel my passion is requited: but, seal it with thy own sweet voice, or I shall expire in uncertainty!" But when "her lips moved—my senses ached with the intensity with which I listened,—all was still,—they uttered no sound; I flung her from me, even though she clung to my vesture, and with a wild cry of agony I burst from the apartment!—She was dumb! Great God, she was dumb! DUMB AND DEAF!" (204). Thus concludes this biliously interesting little sketch, whose final violence not only recalls Poe's "Ligeia," as Otter observes, but looks ahead to the acidulous close of Kristen Roupenian's much-celebrated 2017 *New Yorker* story "Cat Person":

> "When u laguehd when I asked if you were a virgin was it because youd fucked so many guys"
>
> "Are you fucking that guy right now"
>
> "Are you"
>
> "Are you"
>
> "Are you"

"Answer me"
"Whore."[9]

To be sure, the flabbergasting awfulness that Roupenian ventriloquizes is differently discomfiting when it comes from Melville, whose abusive relation to his wife is well documented.[10] How, then, to cull from the invectively capitalized last words of Melville's text some sense of his profound and provoking explorations of disability?

Otter's reading of the above is instructive. "At the climax of the second sketch," Otter writes, "muteness and deafness are left to stand as capitalized signs of monstrous defect. . . . 'Inamorata,' who at first sight appears more than human, is ultimately revealed as only a sight, without access to sound or speech, and thus less than human. Her objectification is symbolized by her muteness and deafness, or, in the telling diction that then and now conflates the absence of conventional speech with cognitive impairment, by her 'dumbness.'"[11] At the same time, however, the narrator's exclamation of Inamorata's "defect" does not treat dumbness and deafness as the mar of an otherwise ontologically credible subject so much as reinforces the purely optical extravagance by which her characterological vitiation is from the outset defined. In other words, it's not quite that Inamorata is "ultimately revealed as only a sight," since this is how she's been presented all along. The static image of Inamorata, with its "broidered figures of Cupid," has less in common with any imaginable person than with the boudoir's densely allusive decor, those "luxurious couches, covered with the finest damask, on which were likewise executed after the Italian fashion the early fables of Greece and Rome. Tripods, designed to represent the Graces bearing aloft vases, richly chiseled in the classic taste, were distributed in the angles of the room, and exhaled an intoxicating fragrance" (*PT,* 202). Until that last sentence's final clauses, one would be forgiven for thinking those Grace-depicting tripods were themselves wrought in the damask, even as their "intoxicating exhalation" comes closer to breath than anything rising or falling, coming or going, from Inamorata. With her lute and silken tresses, Inamorata is less a character much less a person than the sort of emblem (from *emblema,* "inlaid ornamental work") depicted in her surroundings in "threads of crimson silk and gold . . . pictures illustrative of the loves of Jupiter and Semele,—Psyche before the tribunal of Venus, and a variety of other scenes, limned all with felicitous grace" (202).

Elizabeth Renker notes the impatient vehemence with which the narrator ultimately "flung [Inamorata] from me" as deliberate echo of the text's opening line: "'Confusion seize the Greek!' exclaimed I, as wrathfully rising from my chair, I flung my ancient Lexicon across the room, and seizing my hat and cane, and throwing on my cloak, I sallied out into the clear air of heaven" (197). In Renker's concise account, "The violence directed at a book with which the sketch opens is converted into the violence directed at a woman with which it closes, reinforcing the association between pages and women and presenting both as objects to be 'flung' from him."[12] Conceiving Inamorata as a woman treated like an object asks, however, that we suspend our readerly disbelief regarding her elaborate textual flatness; it's along similar lines, I think, that Otter's account of Inamorata's objectification depends on a version of the text—one at least minimally gesturing toward the rudiments of realism—that is not the one before us, much as the latter might inspire our desire for the verisimilitude that "Fragments" thoroughly resists.

After all, repellent as he is in those moments when he comes asymptotically closest to seeming human, the narrator is no more characterologically persuasive than the object of his dubious desire. If the text's revelation of Inamorata's muteness expressively repeats a holographic nonhumanness not wholly distinguishable from the textuality that surrounds her (not unlike the moot, ontological equivalence between the "prettiest little foot" and the "downy quishion" in which it's "almost buried"), recall how the sight of Inamorata leaves the narrator correspondingly "mute, admiring and bewildered" (203). And indeed, when something like desire—what the text designates "the wild expression of . . . love"—"ren[ds]" the narrator's "bosom like a whirlwind, and tore up [his] past attachments as though they were but of the growth of yesterday" (203), his heart and its investments rip like so much paper. Although desire may not credibly attach to either of these nominal characters, it moves through them the way desire, after all, moves through writing. For lack of a better word, desire names the vigor by which the narrator flings not only the lexicon and Inamorata but himself: "flinging myself upon the grassy turf, I was soon lost in revery, and up to the lips in sentiment" (197). Up to the lips, which is to say, "immured in his fantasies," as Otter characterizes Inamorata's Poe-like entrapment in textual misogyny, as Inamorata herself.

It's in this disembodied choreography of seizing and flinging that we arrive at the appeal of Foucault's Cheshire smile, suspended in the air more credibly, tenaciously, than the bodies or persons that beget or feel it. Otter's introduction seems to intuit this strangeness, as though to suggest disability's presence, even in this early Melville text, as an unsettlingly figurative phenomenon. An interesting tension exists, then, between Otter's characterization of Inamorata as "the first . . . in a series of figures across Melville's prose and poetry whose physical or psychic difference is often stigmatized and whose ways of being in the world are explored" and his claim, one sentence earlier, that "these slight, intricate sketches inaugurate Melville's career-long pursuit of issues attached to bodies: the presence of human physical and cognitive variation, the impulse to interpret human difference, the relationships between the material and the metaphorical, the response to 'disability,' the pressures of the 'normal'" (9). Succinctly put, the figures that populate "Fragments from a Writing Desk" urge us to imagine Melvillean corporeality and the intricacy of the texts in which they appear as mutually generative, since when it comes to disability in Melville, the material *is* metaphorical, or, at least, figurative. Otter's predilection for characterology's promise of access to the real comes at the cost of attention to just this figurative lavishness, as in his assertion that "critics too often have overlooked the disabilities represented in Melville's texts or restricted their understanding to the figurative: disability 'as metaphor,' to use Susan Sontag's influential phrase. That is, they have interpreted disabilities as signifying moral or spiritual deformity or psychic distress and viewed them as providing the key to the characters of Melville's characters" (10–11). But this latter version of the figurative, what Otter associates with a didacticism that too often distorts the particularity of the Melvillean text, pertains to an *external* operation: projected onto Melville's writing. While I too distrust this version of the figurative, I'm endlessly drawn to the figurative principle of disability that animates Melville's own production, internal to it.

Otter's conception of Melville's "stigmatized" figures warrants further consideration. More precisely, his understanding of stigma's imbrication with our "ways of being in the world" posits stigma as the thread by which a figure's way of being appears, in turn, for us to follow, as though stigma named both the becoming-legible of "physical or psychic difference" for the world and the figure's experience of that legibility. Erving Goffman is similarly drawn to the multiple layers of textuality that stigma imparts, to which our attention is sharpened, in the opening remarks of his eponymous study. "The Greeks," Goffman writes, "originated the term *stigma* to refer to bodily signs designed to expose something unusual and bad about the moral status of the signifier."[13] That the textual abundance of this scene troubles any assumed equivalence between stigmatic inscription and a figurative body's capacity for signification may be gleaned from the difficulty of mapping the sentence's sundry indices of reading onto "the signifier" at its end. Far from delimiting a single readerly event or perceptual surface, Goffman's remarks treat stigma as a sheaf of textual variance whose irresoluble internal relations suggest the difficulty of saying to what (much less how) stigma hails our feel for literacy. "The signs were cut or burnt into the body," Goffman continues, "and advertised that the bearer was a slave, a criminal, or a traitor—a blemished person, ritually polluted. . . . Later, in Christian times, two layers of metaphor were added to the term: the first referred to bodily signs of holy grace that took the form of eruptive blossoms on the skin; the second, a medical allusion to this religious allusion, referred to bodily signs of physical disorder. Today the term is widely used in something like the original literal sense."[14] If this blossoming of metaphor, of allusion upon allusion, orients us toward a hermeneutic practice that treats the figurative as a vital if ghostly aspect of our social field, this present undertaking attempts an empiricism adequate to the surprise of figuration's eruptive ecology.[15]

When it comes to both its theoretical and practical underpinnings, disability studies isn't alone in its disciplinary trust in the visible world's epistemological sufficiency, even as the more strenuously the gap between theory and praxis is argued, the more the inner life of the imperceptible—along with the figurative forms it houses—is made to seem far afield. This subordination of figurative interest to more demonstrably exigent forms of the literal, the actual—the statistical, graphical, and narrative, and so forth—feels all the more worrisome when the displacement of the former occurs in the name of urgency itself. And yet the allure of the literal isn't so easily jettisoned. For example, when David T. Mitchell and Sharon L. Snyder note that "disabilities bear the stigma of a reminder that the body proves no less mutable or unpredictable than the chaos of nature itself,"[16] disability isn't, as in Goffman, synonymous with a person's shortcoming or handicap. Rather, it is personified as a body in its own right, if we may imagine inscribability—inseparable, here, from questions of the bearable and unbearable—in terms of its retroactive conferral of a body's inscriptive surface. At the same time, the relative straightforwardness of a disability made to bear the disabling weight of the prospective meaning by which its own promise of meaning fades into the background (the figure of a figure, albatross of an albatross) is thrown off-balance by the second clause's characterization of the "chaos" of the body's mutability. Both the body that is disability's metaphorical vehicle and the body of which disability's own stigma is the spectral remnant prove unable, it would seem, to bear the comparable legibility of disability's mark. Recalling the ontological hinterlands voiced across Dickinson's "As Freezing persons, recollect the Snow," the at once blistering and deliquescent precariousness of this only nominally somatic scene clarifies the difficulty of knowing what we are looking *at,* much less *for,* when the textual profundity of a character like Ahab collapses into the "of course" of the peg leg he is made to stand on.

Ellen Samuels's account of nonvisible disability complicates Mitchell's sense that, "in literature as in life, people with disabilities arrive with their limitations openly on display."[17] Samuels writes that "the focus on specularity and visible difference that permeates much disability theory creates a dilemma not only for nonvisibly disabled people who wish to enter the conversation but for the overarching concepts of disability and normalization themselves. Passing, closeting, and coming out become vexed issues that strain at the limitations of the discourse meant to describe them."[18] More specifically, Samuels's meditation on what it means to come out as disabled involves a theorization of analogy, the ways in which coming out as disabled both are and are not like coming out as African American or queer. In her readings of disability's analogic relation to race and sexual orientation, Samuels suggests that these shifting narratives of visibility coincide with the pulsing of our awareness (or lack thereof) of analogy itself. That is, analogy's illumination of the nonvisible allows us to "see" what isn't empirically available so much as abstractly suggestive.

Todd Carmody cites Samuels's work in his essay, "Rehabilitating Analogy." "After all," Carmody writes, "when one claims that 'race is like disability' or that 'disability is like race' emphasis need not fall on the verb *is.* If we instead stress the descriptor *like,* our focus shifts from social identity to the discursive *forms* that shape social identity."[19] Taken together, Samuels and Carmody offer an arresting counterpoint to a field that has emphasized the ontology of *is* at the expense of the no less phenomenal aesthetics of *like*. Their accounts of analogy—its conception of likeness as nonsubordinate to being—reconfigure disability studies as formalism. At this juncture, it no less behooves us to hear in the appellation of disability studies the capacity of disability theory to render what is in front of us interesting through the rigor of its attention to what is not. The last sentence of Carmody's essay is a call for openness to a textual density not unlike the kind described in the next chapter's meditation on "like." Indeed, Carmody's remediation of analogy gravitates to the very word, noting that "the possibility that legal discourse around disabling workplace accidents would have provided a formal precedent or discursive analogue for a conciliatory project of racial accommodation encourages us to think anew about how race might have been 'like' disability in the late nineteenth century."[20]

Carmody's engagement with disability's figurative logic counters disability study's long-standing and indeed often justified wariness of metaphor, albeit I'm more inclined in this context to name the majority of these metaphors what they are: *clichés*. To give a few examples: in their essay on fantasies of deafness in early modern England, Jennifer L. Nelson and Bradley S. Berens critically note that "deafness is metaphorized and the deaf themselves are reduced to metaphor in a process that is played out in sermons, royal proclamations, and a rogue pamphlet, as well as in plays and poems";[21] Samuels similarly writes that "most Melville critics, even those who specifically focus on the body, have tended to ignore disability altogether. Those who do address it usually treat it as a metaphor. . . . Cameron, for example, discusses the theme of dismemberment in Melville as a sign of philosophical alienation from the body and its boundaries rather than in terms of actual physical disability";[22] Robert McRuer, in turn, worries that "recogniz[ing] disposable domestics . . . as disabled" might run "the risk of merely metaphorizing, or perhaps of spectralizing, disability."[23] Rosemarie Garland Thomson concisely addresses this resistance to the metaphorical in her groundbreaking 1997 book, *Extraordinary Bodies: Figuring Physical Disability in American Culture and Literature*. As she argues, "if we accept the convention that fiction has some mimetic relation to life, we grant it power to further shape our perceptions of the world. . . . Because disability is so strongly stigmatized and is countered by so few mitigating narratives, the literary traffic in metaphors often misrepresents or flattens the experience real people have of their own or others' disabilities."[24] Despite its subtitle's nominal investment in figuring, *Extraordinary Bodies* has little to say about figuration per se, not because its preference is for "real disabled people" (11) but because it understands realness and figuration as mutually exclusive.

To accede to demarcations of disability skewed toward the metaphorical is indeed sometimes to find oneself complicit in the substitution of hackneyed abstraction for the textures of embodied experience. Critical resistance to such unscrupulous readings of disability as trope is understandable, to say the least. At the same time, the knowingness of formulations like "reduced to metaphor" and "merely metaphorical" preemptively risk suggesting that the realness of "actual physical disability" is imperiled by the errant nonphysicality of figuration *tout corps.* After all, often as questions of metaphor seem to distance us from what in disability seems most vitally compelling, there are as many instances where figuration brings us closer to the bafflements of phenomenal intensity than otherwise possible. Throughout *Contingent Figure* the case will be made for considering metaphor and figuration as nonequivalent, however else they're otherwise treated as approximately synonymous. In the spirit of Eric Auerbach's essay "Figura," I understand the field of figuration in terms of a generalized substance from which metaphor and other distinct elements of the rhetorician's repertoire are derived. As Auerbach cautions:

> The distinction between trope and figure proves to be difficult. Quintilian himself often hesitates before classifying a turn of speech as one or the other; in later usage *figura* is generally regarded as the higher concept, including trope, so that any unliteral or indirect form of expression is said to be as figurative. . . .
>
> . . . The system that he set forth was a very elaborate one; yet it seems likely that for a rhetorician Quintilian was relatively free in his thinking and as disinclined to excessive hairsplitting as the spirit of the times permitted. The art of the hinting, insinuating, obscuring circumlocution, calculated to ornament a statement or to make it more forceful or mordant, had achieved a versatility and perfection that strike us as strange if not absurd. These turns of speech were called *figurae.*[25]

Whereas Auerbach's account of Quintilian invokes expressive directness and literality as connate, *Contingent Figure* maintains that in the case at least of its particular dossier, there is no more direct or accessible form of what figuration expresses than that which it presents. Auerbach suggests as much in his turn to figurative ornaments' "forceful[ness] or mordan[cy]."

From the Latin meaning "to bite," *mordant* initially denoted the bejeweled, hooked fastening of a girdle and, later, the movable part of a crab's pincer. The word attests to figuration's hook, the means by which we find ourselves caught in and on the text before us, tirelessly biting[26] in both directions (try and persuade the fish on a hook of the latter's indirectness). Looking ahead to the book's last chapter, mordancy also names the corrosive, etching fluid of an engraver; an adhesive compound for fixing gold leaf; a substance that binds a textile to its dye. In each of these cases, that the mordant ultimately appears less materially perceptible than that which is engraved, gilded, or stained does not diminish its own curious materiality. Both corrosive and adhering, the mordancy of figuration comes to resemble the very substance of relation.

While literary analyses abound that recount textual scenes of disability as the loss of the latter's integrity to the pablum of cliché, the following chapters trace encounters with or adjacent to disability that feel figurative from the get-go—or, rather, that reckon with the peculiar density of disability's figurative medium unmoored from whatever physicality, if any, to which it otherwise corresponds. At its simplest, *Contingent Figure* insists not on figuration's independence from physicality so much as on the physicality *of* figuration. If, as I will argue, the figurative potency of Melville's or Dickinson's writing expresses something vital about or in the vicinity of chronic pain, this is because chronic pain exists on and through the body no less than on the page as the excrescent movement of figuration. After all, much as I imagine *Contingent Figure* as a contribution to disability theory, it's not "about" disability per se. As a subject, chronic pain conjures a phenomenal field at once more specific than disability and differently spacious. Recalling metaphor's sub-special relation to figurative substance, chronic pain names one specific range of debilitating experience among countless others. It also, however, describes an exasperating coloring of pain that imbues and accompanies all manner of other diagnoses. As salient to this present study is the extent to which chronic pain denotes the pain of chronicity by which nearly every day of disability and debility is marked. More simply, however, the subject of this book is chronic pain because the earliest item in its case study was the ongoing despair of living decades and counting with the pain of a degenerative neck at the center of my life. Writing about it has often seemed as difficult as living with it, more or less. That it's always there even through the Salomé veils of the book's wandering has come to feel like the daily field of a *plein air* painter. Under clouds, at dusk, tinted by the weather of the painter's dejection and, sometimes, surrender: the field remains the same (changing at a rate too slow for these improvised experiments quite to catch).[27]

Metaphor's intrusion on textual scenes of disability is frequently inseparable for critics from its interference with their presumption that characters with disabilities either correspond or can be made to correspond to "real disabled people." This bias underlies Garland Thomson's frustration with metaphor's "flatten[ing] [of] the experience [of] real people" or, more generally, the extent to which "representation tends to objectify disabled characters by denying them any opportunity for subjectivity or agency."[28] Garland Thomson notes that if "disabled characters acted, as real people with disabilities often do, to counter their stigmatized status, the rhetorical potency of the stigma would be mitigated or lost. If Hawthorne's Chillingworth made many friends, for instance, or appeared lovable to Hester, his role in *The Scarlet Letter* would be diminished."[29] Not only would Chillingworth's role be diminished; *The Scarlet Letter* would all but cease to exist. Notwithstanding its strange careen into counterfactual, Garland Thomson's observation entertains the emendation of Hawthorne's text with an almost mercenary blitheness whose unilateral vision of recuperation-as-correction treats those textual inventions deemed deficient (i.e., least tolerable) to the wishful antihermeneutic procedure of treatment or extirpation. Let us then make our own return to *The Scarlet Letter* for what it can otherwise teach us about the aesthetic duress of chronic pain and figuration as mutually expressive mordancies.

The fifteenth chapter of *The Scarlet Letter,* "Hester and Pearl," begins with a depiction of Chillingworth that slips from the narrator's deceptively modest estimation to the more pensive speculations of Hester Prynne:

> So Roger Chillingworth—a deformed old figure, with a face that haunted men's memories longer than they liked—took leave of Hester Prynne, and went stooping away along the earth. He gathered here and there an herb, or grubbed up a root, and put it into the basket on his arm. . . . Hester gazed after him a little while, looking with a half fantastic curiosity to see whether the tender grass of early spring would not be blighted beneath him. . . . Did the sun, which shone so brightly everywhere else, really fall upon him? Or was there, as it rather seemed,

> a circle of ominous shadow moving along with his deformity, whichever way he turned himself? (119)

Hawthorne assigns deformity to Chillingworth with the regularity of an epithet. Just following the novel's introduction of Hester at the scaffold—a phantasmagoric stream of memories of her life to that point "c[o]me swarming back"—she beholds "another countenance, of a man well stricken in years, a pale, thin, scholar-like visage, with eyes dim and bleared by the lamp-light that had served them to pore over many ponderous books. Yet those same bleared optics had a strange penetrating power, when it was their owner's purpose to read the human soul. This figure of the study and the cloister, as Hester Prynne's womanly fancy failed not to recall, was slightly deformed, with the left shoulder a trifle higher than the right" (43). Directly following the apparition of this "well-stricken" man in the montage of Hester's memory, he resurfaces in the crowd before the scaffold in terms indistinguishable from this preceding paragraph's description. In drawing us through this second characterization—of the "slight deformity of [Chillingworth's] figure," the way "one of [the] man's shoulders rose higher than the other" (44)—Hawthorne revises the notional persistence of Hester's memory as our own experience of a figure's flickeringly repetitive presence. Such mimetic disturbances counter "Lucretius' doctrine of the structures that peel off things like membranes and float round in the air, his Democritean doctrine," as Auerbach writes, "of the 'film images'" through which "we first find the word [*figura*] employed in the sense of 'dream image,' 'figment of fancy,' 'ghost.'"[30] If Chillingworth the person is given to seem diaphanous as Hester's dream image of him—a material substance (such in this case as it is) spectrally peeling off the ghost form—Hawthorne will go on to suggest he is more so, since "under the appellation of Roger Chillingworth . . . was hidden another name, which its former wearer had" . . . "chose[n] to withdraw" . . . "from the roll of mankind," just as he himself had chosen to "vanish out of life as completely as if he indeed lay at the bottom of the ocean" (79). Chillingworth will never seem so persuasive a character let alone person than he quasi-posthumously does as a figure's figure.

It's with similarly jarring persistence that *The Scarlet Letter* semaphores Chillingworth's disfigurement in terms of his "penetrating" acumen in the business of reading souls. Bracketing the text's more general exposition of obsolesced enfleshment, the avidity with which his bleared vision courts the luxuriant textuality of Dimmesdale's self-beratement (an old New England strain of spiritual manspreading), both the theatricalized intimacy and vocational rigor of Chillingworth's practice suggest an American psychoanalysis *avant la lettre.* The legibility of Dimmesdale's interior under this scrutiny amplifies its susceptibility to itself, an unabating pain spurred by a guilt sharp enough to prove afflictive but too depleted to be exercised toward any end besides its own. Less guilt than figure of guilt, the literal or nonliteral constitution of Dimmesdale's self-castigation proves beside the point, since knowing "in Mr. Dimmesdale's secret closet, under lock and key, there was a bloody scourge" won't resolve beyond doubt whether the substance of scourge and closet isn't figurative in the ways we've been tracing (99–100). If we know anything about the substance of the scourge, it is the chronicity of its accretive power over time: "his form grew emaciated; his voice . . . had a certain melancholy prophecy of decay in it; he was often observed . . . to put his hand over his heart, with first a flush and then a paleness, indicative of pain" (83), since on his own breast, echoing Hester's own embroidered A, "in very truth, there was, and there had long been, the gnawing and poisonous tooth of bodily pain" (102).

As the novel's sense of interior and exterior substance increasingly blurs, Dimmesdale's perverse analysis and its effects come to seem less an inversion of the scarlet letter's disciplinary alchemy than a metonymic variation of the same. That the examples of Dimmesdale and Chillingworth equally portend the deep structural impaction of figurative being and chronic pain form the background against which Hester's shame at the pillory gets ingeniously distributed across time, in the scarlet ampersand between Foucauldian discipline and punishment, as its own trial in chronicity. However unbearable the punitive spectacle of the scaffold may be—even as, in fact, its queasiness seems also to register as the discomfiting absence of excruciation—it has nothing on the self-sustaining incessance of the scarlet letter's injuriousness, a docilizing force so fused in the fiber of living that one would be hard pressed to say where one stopped and the other began. For all of its textual overdetermination, the catalyzing work of the scarlet letter is felt by Hester from the beginning as nothing less than a specifically interminable anguish. "To a sensitive observer," Hawthorne writes (an ascription to which we readers answer no less than Chillingworth), "there was something exquisitely painful in it" (39). It "transfigure[s] the wearer," has "the effect of a spell, taking her out of the ordinary relations with humanity, and inclosing her in a sphere by herself" (39–40). Unlike her initial term of prison confinement, specified as "a separate and insulated event, to occur but once in her lifetime," Hester's "walk from her prison-door" begins what Hawthorne calls her "daily custom" (55). If the disfigured figure of Chillingworth projects a fast-drawn sketch of how chronic pain might look in a lineup (however keenly or ambiently it crosses that threshold of visibility), the interface between scarlet letter and what of Hester has yet to be transfigured gives voice to how chronic pain feels: the bruising and abrading distress of violent circumscription where it rubs the postpenal life's deceptive promise of freedom raw:

> She could no longer borrow from the future, to help her through the present grief. To-morrow would bring its own trial with it; so would the next day, and so would the next; each its own trial, and yet the very same that was now so unutterably grievous to be borne. The days of the far-off future would toil onward, still with the same burden for her to take up, and bear along with her, but never to fling down; for the accumulating days, and added years, would pile up their misery upon the heap of shame. (55)

Were it possible to disarticulate the external, etiological question from the inner, phenomenological one, we might more readily respond to the matter of chronic pain posed as when "continually, and in a thousand other ways, did [Hester] feel the innumerable throbs of anguish . . . so cunningly contrived . . . by the undying, the ever-active sentence of the Puritan tribunal" (60). Continually, undying, ever-active: Hawthorne's final estimation hits close to home: "From first to last, in short, Hester Prynne had always this dreadful agony in feeling a human eye upon the token; the spot never grew callous; it seemed, on the contrary, to grow more sensitive with daily torture" (60).

To play devil's advocate, one could note that Hawthorne doesn't suggest Hester suffers from chronic pain so much as turns to the latter to analogize the strangeness of her Romantic condition, as when the repelled terror of Hester's neighbors "was often brought before her vivid self-perception, like a new anguish, by the rudest touch upon the tenderest spot," or when "a coarser expression" falls "upon the sufferer's defenceless breast like a rough blow upon an ulcerated wound" (59–60). For me, though, the most remarkable aspect of these appositions—like an anguish, like blowing on an unhealing wound—is just how little their figurative specificity distinguishes them from any *other* aspect of Hester's world. Pearl, Dimmesdale, and Chillingworth are, like Hester, so consistently described as figurative that it would be more surprising if there existed in relation to any of them a physicality that *weren't* immediately susceptible to the queer gravity of figuration. In *What Is Posthumanism?,* Cary Wolfe exhorts us toward a "new and more inclusive form of ethical pluralism that it is our charge, now, to frame. That project would think the ethical force of disability and nonhuman subjectivity as something other than merely an expansion of the liberal humanist ethnos to ever newer populations."[31] Despite lying beyond the scope of Wolfe's call to arms, Hawthorne's investigation of figurative substance posits a salutary, mid-nineteenth-century model of what posthumanism *was,* articulating a phenomenal language for duress with which contemporary theories of posthumanism would do well to grapple. "Then, what was he?," Dimmesdale inquires of himself, "—a substance?—or the dimmest of all shadows?" (98). Hester, meanwhile, is said to stand "apart from mortal interests, yet close beside them, like a ghost that . . . can no longer make itself seen or felt" (59). In the figurative economy of *The Scarlet Letter,* Hester's inability to make herself felt is inseparable from her newfound, implacable capacity for feeling everything—erethistically, synesthetically—in the tenderly sore spot marked by the letter. At the same time, her inability to be seen or felt is displaced by the irresistible lure by which she "find[s] herself the text of the discourse" (60). If to be read and responded to less like a plaque or institutional address than in terms of the figurative concentration and discomfiture of a difficult poem is to be made to feel like a ghost, the eventual reunion of Dimmesdale and Hester could hardly be conceived otherwise than as "a ghost . . . awe-stricken at the other ghost": "So strangely did they meet . . . that it was like the first encounter, in the world beyond the grave, of two spirits . . . now stood coldly shuddering, in mutual dread" (129).

Like so many scenes within this novel's parsing of figurative ontology felt as chronic pain (the chronic pain of figuration), the thermodynamics of this "coldly shuddering" exchange—"Dimmesdale put forth his hand, chill as death, and touched the chill hand of Hester" (129)—communicates to Hawthorne's star-crossed specters how they "now felt themselves, at least, inhabitants of the same sphere" (129). Readers of the "The Custom-House" will recognize the language of this last sentiment in Hawthorne's own plangent "effort [to . . .] recall the figures and appellations" of his own prior time, just "six months ago," in Salem. "Soon, likewise, my old native town will loom upon me through the haze of memory, a mist brooding over and around it; as if it were no portion of the real earth, but an overgrown village in cloud-land, with only imaginary inhabitants to people its wooden houses. . . . Henceforth, it ceases to be a reality of my life. I am a citizen of somewhere else" (34).[32]

Melville's "Bartleby" affords an exquisitely modest correlative to Hawthorne's more melodramatic staging of characterological deficiency. Like the atonic crookedness of Dimmesdale's shoulders, I feel Bartleby's salience to disability theory in my neck. "In plain fact," the story's lawyer narrator observes, "[Bartleby] had now become a millstone to me, not only useless as a necklace, but afflictive to bear" (*PT*, 32). It is not incidental that the "plain fact" of the millstone which Bartleby is imagined as resonates with Mitchell and Snyder's notion of the "physical *fact* of Ahab's prostheticized difference."[33] *Contingent Figure* in many ways is my attempt to describe how twenty-five years of chronic neck pain not only could be described as a millstone but also could be experienced *as* that millstone's fact, commensurate in a fashion with the manner in which Bartleby's subsistence as a figure of disability represents, in fact, the most literal thing about him. Along these lines, I'm riveted by something the lawyer says that is as grammatically enigmatic as Bartleby's own utterance: "I am pained, Bartleby" (*PT*, 35). Michael Bérubé has written that "any of us who identify as 'non-disabled' must know that our self-designation is inevitably temporary, and that a car crash, a virus, a degenerative disease, or a precedent-setting legal decision could change our status in ways over which we have no control whatsoever."[34] It is with this seeming suddenness that Bartleby appears at the lawyer's door, without warning and only coincidentally lining up with the lawyer's retroactive narrative effort to frame Bartleby's constitutive contingency.[35] It's not, then, inaccurate to say alongside Garland Thomson and others that the lawyer searches fruitlessly for a cure. My sense, however, is that the cure—more elusive than anything in the lawyer's extemporaneously ordered universe—is for his, not Bartleby's, chronic condition. Bartleby, in this reading, *is* (not a character but) that chronic condition. What the text has to tell us about pain has less to do with the pain that

Bartleby does or doesn't feel than with the intractable, humiliating perversity with which Bartleby, like a pain, is felt.

CHRONICITY OF FORMS: CLAUDIA RANKINE AND THE LONELINESS OF ATTRITION

In *Don't Let Me Be Lonely,* Claudia Rankine elaborates "a sharp pain in my gut" that she's had "all my life" as "not quite a caving in, just a feeling of bits of my inside twisting away from flesh in the form of a blow to the body."[36] Interfacing between how the pain doesn't quite feel and how it does, that lone adverb "just" autopoetically performs the burden of the line's figurative work no less than the accounts of pain on either side of it. In so doing, the line's surgical theater contracts to the pathological radius of the adverb's mediation between modes of pain whose surface discrepancies strain the sense of near resemblance to which "just" otherwise attests. John Ashbery writes of Gertrude Stein's *Stanzas in Meditation* that "these austere 'stanzas' are made up almost entirely of colorless connecting words such as 'where,' 'which,' 'these,' 'of,' 'not,' 'have,' 'about,' and so on."[37] Suspended between without directly participating in the algetic proscenium of Rankine's lines, the word "just" might recall Stein's colorless connectives were it not that both *Don't Let Me Be Lonely* and *Citizen* insist on revisioning the American fiction of racial colorlessness in terms of inveterately chromatic—or, at least, chronically inveterate—substance. The work of polite compression that "just" ordinarily enacts renders all the more striking the uncompromising sinuousness insisted upon by the clauses that follow, this "feeling of bits of my inside twisting away from flesh in the form of a blow to the body."

How, one wonders, does the extent of injury thus disclosed amount to so much less than "not quite a caving in" as to answer to the understating labor of "just"? The answers posed by Rankine's text depend on the word's operation as a quilting point of sorts between multiple grammatical and political registers, its participation in an aesthetics of injury that calibrates our attention to the specifically figurative dimensions of pain and justice alike. Somatically arresting as its description is, the speaker's "sharp pain in [the] gut" resists easy characterization as either somatic or psychical per se. At the same time, the quality of the text's auto-attention exposes the tendency in a catchall term like "psychosomatic" to hypostasize each of the compromise-portmanteau's respective halves. "And I am not exactly a crying person," Rankine writes, "though my eyes / tear up frequently because of my allergies. In any case, / the other tears, the ones that express emotions, the / ones that recognize and take responsibility for the soul / don't come. Instead I get a sharp pain in my gut. And / though heart disease is the leading killer of American / women, the pain has nothing to do with that. I have / had it all my life. Not quite a caving in," Rankine continues, returning us to where we, where she, had already been (56). What counts, we are led to ask, as *my* allergies, *my* gut? In both cases, what is one's own is felt, lived, as what it isn't: allergies, whose tears might otherwise be taken from the outside as the exposing ratification of individual feeling, turn out instead to confess the self's encounter with some alterior substance: the "wash[ing] away," so an earlier passage in the text defines it, "of foreign bodies" (43). The generic texture of "And I am not exactly a crying person" is all the more thrown by the text's distinction between tears spurred by environment, expressive perhaps of an impersonal sensitivity to the world's imperceptible traffic, and tears "that express emotions." Thrice conjured in Rankine's book, this idiom originates in Frederick Douglass's 1844 meditation on the slave songs of his childhood. "I did not, when a slave," Douglass writes, "understand the deep meaning of those rude and apparently incoherent songs. I was myself within the circle; so that I neither saw nor heard as those without might see and hear. . . . The mere recurrence to those songs, even now, afflicts me; and while I am writing these lines, an expression of feeling has already found its way down my cheek."[38] That the logic of lachrymal sentiment at the heart of Douglass's autobiography appears in Rankine under erasure, as what is *not* conveyed, leaves the allusion as uncannily vacated as the advertising boilerplate of "heart disease" as "the leading killer of American women." Chronic pain finds its way into Rankine's poetry with all the confidingly fraught impersonality of Jenny Holzer's *Truisms.*

The aesthetics of confession traced in the above lines illuminates the force of the subtitle carried by both *Don't Let Me Be Lonely* and *Citizen,* "An American Lyric." We may infer from the hydraulic of the speaker's oscillant presence the technology by which lyric poetry in the Trayvon era sustains its subject as nothing so much as in the act of vanishing, refracted in the withdrawal of an authorial voice whose outline all the more acutely only sometimes lines up with those to which it bears witness. To live in and as an American Lyric is to live chronically with the violence of the self's foreclosure. And so, on the heels of this episode, *Don't Let Me Be Lonely* chronicles a televised event, preceding 9/11 by several weeks, though the matter of weeks, months, and years irregularly dissolves in the propensity for such events (a category to be left purposefully open) to go on repeatedly. Having twisted in their own way from the putative flesh of the real, these events haunt themselves. Rankine writes:

> Sometimes I look into someone's face and I must brace myself—the blow on its way. For instance, I go into my bedroom to put on socks because my toes could be cold and on the TV is Abner Louima. . . . It's been four years since he was sodomized with a broken broomstick while in police custody. It was two months and three surgeries before he could leave the hospital. He has just agreed to a settlement with the city and the police union for 8.7 million dollars . . . . A reporter asks him how it feels to be a rich man. Not rich, says Louima. Lucky, lucky to be alive. Instinctively my hand braces my abdomen. (56)

It's not quite that the appalling incarnation of Louima's attack could go without saying, but that the text's re-creation of the speaker's absorption of its televised aftermath—what jurisprudence with either withering irony or acumen calls a "settlement"—is invested in the difficulty of saying where one form of trauma ends and, almost impervious to questions of scale, another begins. The text presses us to reckon with the disconcerting continuity of unremitting pain through and across bodies, tearing through the ordinary discreteness of literal and figurative fields. The interlocking symmetry formed between "brac[ing] myself—the blow on its way" and "instinctively my hand braces my abdomen" frames the Louima case as an interiority that feels inaccessible not only because its traumatizing brutality defies depiction but because the porousness of interiority shared between victims and witnesses (an unmaintainable distinction, as Douglass makes searingly clear) renders articulation's furthering access all but gratuitous, even as the grisly sadism of Louima's attack literalizes Douglass's vision of seeing the unseen. In the words of the state prosecutor's opening remarks—and let me say that what follows is upsettingly graphic and potentially triggering—after shoving the broken broomstick up Louima's rectum so forcefully it rips his rectum and ruptures his bladder, NYPD officer Justin Volpe holds "the stick . . . up to Abner Louima's mouth. He wanted Abner Louima to see what he and Charles Schwarz had just done to him. He wanted Mr. Louima to see the blood and the feces that he just pulled out of him."[39] It's in the context of this brutality that the reporter's question of "how it feels to be a rich man" proves so grotesquely feckless. And so "my hand braces my abdomen" as though a lifelong pain in the gut belonged exclusively to neither of them. And not just to both or neither, since the next sequence of the book cites the forty-one shots fired into Amadou Diallo, how they "never add up, never become plural, and will not stay in the past" (57).

In the face of forty-one shots fired infinitely like the Angel of History from the future, nearness to being alive is made to feel as contingent as any correlative nearness to death. As in Dickinson, that other poet of American Lyrics, the difference between the two is only sometimes sustainable. This equivocation informs the subjunctive oddity of Rankine having gone "into [the] bedroom to put on socks because my toes could be cold": as though the bedroom—less safe haven than portal, via television, to all the acrimony and heartache of a commons-in-disarray—were always already double exposed as the steel mortuary tray of a poet's deathbed. The chronicity of visceral feeling that Rankine's poetry so vividly explores suggests an entelechy in relation to which literal and nonliteral being seem at best vitiated corruptions: psychosomatic as a euphemism for affliction awful enough to feel incapacitating for years on end, but able no less frequently to be lived with, survived, challenging fatality as sole measure of an ailment's ontic weight. The regularity with which persons experience the incessance of chronic illness as incapacitating in its own right illuminates a congruence between this demographic and the populations at the heart of Jasbir Puar's *The Right to Maim,* even as Puar rightly insists that we subject this perceived convergence to scrutiny. Derrida observes in an interview just following 9/11 what amounts to Puar's own thesis,[40] though it's Puar who brings this insight explicitly to bear on disability studies. She writes:

> It is this tension . . . between being and becoming, this is the understated alliance that I push in this project. The first presumes a legitimate identification with disability that is manifest through state, market, and institutional recognition, if not subjective position: I call myself disabled. But this cannot be the end of the story, because what counts as a disability is already overdetermined by "white fragility" on one side and

> the racialization of bodies that are expected to endure pain, suffering, and injury on the other.[41]

I call myself disabled: Puar's reflexive *je m'appelle* only up to a point resembles interpellation's ordinarily authoritative address, catalyzing an indeterminate interval between its predicate, "subjective position," and subjectivity. Where does this call of disability originate, and how does its psychic life of power differ from the fictions of capacity on which Foucauldian docility otherwise depends? At the same time, "I call myself" connotes interpellation misexecuted, that is, infelicitously disabled. After all, Althusser's interpellative scene minimally requires that the subject recognize its subordination, answer to its call, whereas Puar's formulation only guarantees the call is made. This reflexive self-seduction (*se + ducere,* to lead away) contains the germ of its own failure, as though the fate of not being able to lead oneself from the dead approached the cruel optimism of wooing oneself, trying to, without end. Such a myth of Orpheus as Sisyphus nevertheless amounts to its own form of wishfulness no less than that of the dream of self-interpellation. Whereas the latter would perhaps hope to reclaim an identity, however broken, from the regime of an institutional apparatus, the former prospectively imagines inhabiting a broken-enough interpellative zone as to occupy its dis-ease as a form if not of resistance than at least possibly finer sentience. This, in part, is how I understand Puar's "I call myself disabled," in whose pathos I somewhat warily recognize my condition, what Puar invokes as the "white fragility" in whose problematic and incontestable folds of privilege my condition subsists. Except that I don't call myself disabled, though for two decades my neck has housed the degenerative stenosis and spurs of someone more than twice my age. If, in this treatment of Dante, we wore such statements as sandwich boards across our respective spines' disintegrations, mine instead would read, "I have chronic pain." What locutionary import can be gleaned in the syncope between these claims?

The above passage from Puar's *The Right to Maim* goes on to describe the racialized experience of "endur[ing] pain, suffering, and injury" as an "understanding of biopolitical risk: to extrapolate a bit from Claudia Rankine's prose: 'I am in death's position.' And to expand," Puar continues, "I am in debility's position."[42] If Puar's mode is one of extrapolation and expansion, my own winnowing instinct has been to synthesize an account of textuality's enigmatic capacity for fostering the grudging endurance of pain from within those textual fibers where it lodges. To compare the former utterance, "I call myself disabled," with "I am in death's position" is to note in the latter a textual embeddedness distinct from the former's performative work. "I am in death's position" appears in the opening pages of *Don't Let Me Be Lonely,* within a temporal no-man's-land binding debility to the phenomenology of chronic pain we've been charting. The passage is striking for its articulation of time if not as the material of our affective lives then the weather in which those—"our"—lives appear:

> There was a time I could say no one I knew well had died. This is not to suggest no one died. When I was eight my mother became pregnant. She went to the hospital to give birth and returned without the baby. Where's the baby? we asked. Did she shrug? She was the kind of woman who liked to shrug; deep within her was an everlasting shrug. (5)

Although the baby isn't "kn[own] well," its nearness to the lives of both the speaker and her mother illuminates "knew" as a condensation of asynchronous modes of knowing: that of the speaker as an eight-year-old, and as an adult in an apprehensive end time approximately coextensive with our own. Somewhere between knowledge, death, and the vastness of time, "eight" marks an encroaching awareness at odds with the analepsis of "There was a time." The speaker recounts, as it were, an age she associates not only with her childhood self but with the adjacent numerical puzzle of that self's having expected her pregnant mother to return from the hospital not as one person, but two. The mathematics of the text leaves unspoken the extent to which the lost infant "counts" as someone or "no one," just as it leaves unspoken whether the would-be siblings' counterfactual rapport passes for knowing someone, much less knowing someone well. These at once alluring and retreating relational possibilities conjure another poem spoken by an eight-year-old in the midst of a similar predicament. The "Lyric" in the subtitle of *Don't Let Me Be Lonely,* that is, invariably references "We are Seven," Wordsworth's curious dialogue between an adult speaker and "a little cottage Girl":

> She was eight years old, she said;
> Her hair was thick with many a curl
> That cluster'd round her head.[43]

Each time the girl's interlocutor asks "how many [sisters and brothers] may you be," she responds that they are seven, despite two of the siblings having already died, and two others "gone to sea." Frances Ferguson notes that "in the preface to *Lyrical Ballads,* Wordsworth distances himself from the personification of abstract ideas . . . and he goes on to assert that he wishes to keep his reader 'in the company of flesh and blood.' But, of course, the interest of 'We are Seven' lies in the girl's being able by counting to personify persons—which in this case represent neither abstract ideas nor flesh and blood."[44]

In both Wordsworth and Rankine, the otherwise discrete border between "abstract" and "flesh and blood" is recalibrated through a temporizing system generated in the confusion of numbers loosed from the quotidian, crystallizingly reabsorbed in the felt conviction of a self's interior. This hinterland between the actual and the imaginary—the twilight indistinctness of Hawthornian Romance—no less foreshadows an intersection between the trials of twenty-first-century racial survival and the brutalizing quiet of the latter's own perverse logic of weathered duress. "Did she shrug? She was the kind of woman who liked to shrug; deep within her was an everlasting shrug." The gesture's holographic triplicate proliferates in the present of Rankine's lines the serial accretions of a shrug that might iterate itself indefinitely, even as each iteration occupies its own approximate ontological plane in relation to the tableau's proceedings. The first iteration is hypothetical—did she shrug?—a question that might alight in memory (or come close to alighting) whether faithful or not to an original, "flesh and blood" referent. The second iteration, "She was the kind of woman who liked to shrug," seems at least initially fixed in the past. At the same time that the shrug defines or names some element specific to the speaker's mother's constitution, its gesture participates in the performatively generalizing invention of this "kind of woman," projecting a militia of similarly predisposed women across the fraying canvas of hard knocks. At this point in the poem's recollection, Rankine herself shrugs off our own readerly expectations, insofar as "the kind of woman who likes to shrug" supplies the answer to a question we may not have had, displacing all those other occasions and outcomes to which the shrug may bear witness if not assuage with the simple statement of "lik[ing] to shrug." In the motoring hum of chronicity that steals good and seeds hurt, the evacuating rise and release of the gesture enough finds itself in the vicinity of what was lost to serve provisionally as its own object of loose attachment. Lastly, "deep within her was an everlasting shrug" all but realizes this isolated and ingrained choreography as an unsettling instance of Emersonian correspondence. The serialized shrug comes to populate the world while synecdochically supplanting any sense of interiority not touched by the intensity of its quiet. As Emerson writes in *Nature,* "It is easily seen that there is nothing lucky or capricious in these analogies, but that they are constant, and pervade nature. These are not the dreams of a few poets, here and there, but man is an analogist, and studies relations in all objects."[45] Analogists would do well, of course, to include in their objects of study the grammatical quality of their own vantage, however easily or dis-easily its coordinates give way to the recognitions of a self. The opening susurrus of the compound syllable *shrug* rounds into a sort of bowdlerized expletive bafflement, involving the word's definitiveness in a strain of systemic chronicity hinted at in Emerson's notion of pervasive constancy. It's not just that the analogies we live in proceed uninterrupted: their porousness analogously means they pour through us.

Writing of *Don't Let Me Be Lonely,* Anthony Reed suggests that "Rankine puts forward a post-lyric sense of literary time that emphasizes the mediality of the letter against the materiality of the phenomenal world."[46] I would somewhat differently propose that in lines such as the above, the "literary time" of Rankine's text is galvanized by a lyric substance for which the textual *is* materially phenomenal, and that the mediality of the text is nothing less than material. Even as the interruptions and shudders of these compulsive efforts at communication simulate the belated arc of bearing witness, the shape of witnessing as both juridical apparatus and act of intimacy is as often the poetry's object of critique as it is its praxis. In the book's next movement, the prospect of witnessing collides with the pathos of *nothing to see* in regard to the fruitless enterprise of witnessing one's own loneliness:

> Or one begins asking oneself that same question differently. Am I dead? Though this question at no time explicitly translates into Should I be dead, eventually the suicide hotline is called. You are, as usual, watching television, the eight-o'clock movie, when a number flashes on the screen: 1-800-SUICIDE. You dial the number. Do you feel like killing yourself? the man on the other end of the receiver asks. You tell him, I feel like I am already dead. When he makes no response

> you add, I am in death's position. He finally says, Don't believe what you are thinking and feeling. Then he asks, Where do you live? (7)

Am I dead? As a conversation more or less between the speaker and herself, this inquiry into whether one has already for some time not been living is suspended in the text's specification of chronicity as the temporal medium of her speculative posthumousness. The horizon of wondering one's death feels prospectively limitless, an expression resonant with the eight-year-old speaker's prior observation that the look on her father's face upon the death of his own mother "was flooded, so leaking . . . like someone understanding his aloneness. Loneliness" (5). And so "I am in death's position" stands midway between the speaker's unrest and the apparently formulaic solicitude of "the man on the other end of the receiver," an effort on the former's part to elaborate the spatiotemporal experience of "feel[ing] already dead." In its own way, "I am in death's position" is impenetrable (arguably from both sides of the receiver) in the same way that "Am I dead?" is untranslatable. Like Glenn Ligon's stencil rubbings, these jarringly impervious formulations are and aren't communicable. Hypostatically withdrawn from the quotidian they interrupt, they ask to be contemplated rather than understood. One is left with a sense of self-displacing reflexiveness; staring at no less than from one's self, death's position (everywhere and nowhere) describes a feeling of everlasting nearness to a life understood as having once been able to be taken for granted. I think about this scene of saturating disruption in terms of Maurice Blanchot's account of the cadaverous image, and our return through this image to the irreparability of an "esthetic object," in André Breton's words quoted by Blanchot, "those outmoded objects, fragmented, unusable, almost incomprehensible, perverse."[47] For Blanchot, this image's interminability is elemental: "In this absence of here and now what happens does not clearly come to pass as an event based upon which something solid could be achieved. Consequently, what happens does not happen, but does not pass either, into the past; it is never passed. It happens and recurs without cease" (238). Throughout *The Space of Literature,* the chronicity of the aesthetic object—that "shifty point from which indetermination condemns time to the exhausting futility of repetition" (241)—is defined by the object's exile from the sphere of use, "banished," Blanchot writes, from "capability" (240). The interface of Rankine's telephone receiver mediates a corresponding dialectic of textual utility and disrepair, holding open the glitch between "Do you feel like killing yourself?" and its lyrically withdrawn reply, "I feel like I am already dead." That the counselor at the hotline has no response to the speaker's statement touches on the latter's spectral kinship with Blanchot's conception of cadaverousness as both example of and figure for the image's profound abandonment. In turn, the counselor's implied stupefaction opens onto our own encounter with lyric reading, an experience, writes Blanchot, of being "taken: to pass from the region of the real where we hold ourselves at a distance from things the better to order and use them into that other region where the distance holds us—the distance which then is the lifeless deep," rendering "our intimacy an exterior power which we suffer passively. Outside of us, in the ebb of the world which it causes, there trails, like glistening debris, the utmost depth of our passions" (261–62).

BREAKING POINT, PREMISE, AND DEPARTURE

The following chapters put forward partial aspects of the chiastically fluctuant relation between chronic pain and figurative substance to which Rankine's recent poetry has been drawn. From a certain remove, their readings move sequentially across the x-axis of a long American nineteenth century. At the same time, the project's attunement to the less predictable gravitational pull of chronic pain's temporal universe—and its concomitant wariness when it comes to the fictions of narrative momentum—admits a fidelity to incessance as a counter-principle of accumulating density. To take seriously the queer shadings and self-involutions of chronicity has meant ceding certain traditional forms of development and sequence to slighter patterns of setback, lurch, and absorption: to repetition as an active practice in if not strategic method of what Agnes Martin calls the development of sensibility.[48] The work of *Contingent Figure* has entailed an immersion in the study of resonance as a subject's blinking surrender to its environment, and vice versa. My hope is that the readerly and writerly decisions I've made on behalf of this enterprise will justify the time, in turn, you spend with it.

Chapter 1, "Melville's Iron Crown of Lombardy: Phenomenology beyond the Phantom Limb," elaborates a correspondence between figurative vibrancy and the phenomenal complexity of a pain suspended, as often as not, between the Actual of physical substance and the Imaginary of abstraction. In this light, chronic pain posits an education in the moonlit vitalism of Hawthornian Romance. The chapter moves outward in scope to the great beyond that is the lavish style of Melville's novels *Pierre* and *Moby-Dick.* Seduced by deceptive surface recognitions in the nominal person of Ahab or the eponymously absent center at the heart of Melville's "Bartleby the Scrivener," disability theorists have for some time strained to map a reality of lived affliction onto the vitiated substance of Melvillean characterology. Try as they might, such readings erroneously treat the latter as though its compulsory promise of approximately human substance were our only access to the world of chronic pain. By contrast, this chapter charts those moments where characterological insufficiency gives way to a text's devotional excrescence, keenly drawn to and of the strange acuities of chronic pain's inner life.

Chapter 2, "Queer Philology and Chronic Pain," opens on the granular level of neither pain per se nor poetics so much as the import for both of the philological undertow of a single word, "like." Incidental if not uneventful as the word may often seem, the frequency with which it tends to disappear into the affective and analogical industry it substrates belies both the strange profundity of its usefulness and our capacity to take this utility for granted. Beginning with the revolutionary opening observation of Leo Bersani's 1987 essay, "Is the Rectum a Grave?"—"There is a big secret about sex: most people don't like it"[49]—these pages reflect on a constellation of queerness, queer theory, and chronic pain across the likes of Melville's "Bartleby" and "Benito Cereno," Stein's *Stanzas in Meditation,* and Moon Unit Zappa's "Valley Girl," revolving those moments where "like" catches on itself or otherwise malfunctions, rendering newly, textually perceptible something like the un-inurable quotidian of chronic pain, its persistent unsettlement.

Chapter 3, "'The Vision – pondered long': Chronic Pain and the Materiality of Figuration," considers chronic pain's profoundly recalibrative impact on the writing life of Emily Dickinson. If the radical vision of Dickinson's poetry depends on the storied, unabating sharpness of her perceptual attention, long spells of apparently irresolvable optical distress suggest the harrowing commensuration of her lyric perspicacity with the impeding pain of vision as its own implacable object. In light of New England mythology's distorting reduction of the poet's radius to Amherst and its environs, it's all the more remarkable that the longest and farthest of her travels consisted of two prolonged visits in 1864 to a

Boston ophthalmologist. Routinely as the power of Dickinson's lyric output is associated with its capacity to bear witness to grief, loss, and other forms of affliction, a tendency among critics to understand the latter in terms of its jolting interruption of the quotidian has given short shrift to her poetry's testament to incessant pain as the quotidian's own abiding texture.

Chapter 4, "Inveterate Pagoda: Late James, Ongoingness, and the Figure of Hurt," revisits a scene in Henry James's late autobiographical text, *Notes of a Son and Brother,* notorious among Jamesians for its depiction of (or more precisely, so critical consensus suggests, its failure to depict) the circumstances of a traumatic injury James suffers at the start of the Civil War. Over this past Jamesian century, the mystery of the injury—what the passage in question terms James's "obscure hurt"—has been variously understood as a metonym, euphemism, and even physical cause for the no less enigmatic matter of James's queerness. At the same time and not unrelated, the obscure hurt has served for biographers as James's catechism from a privileged childhood of ambient potential into his first nascent sense of becoming a writer of note, capable ultimately of fitting the scruples of Dickinsonian interiority with all the long, figurative spaciousness of Melvillean prose. This chapter sinks into the textual shadowland of James's autobiography for the sake of tracing from within its late style an aesthetic of chronic pain no less perceptible in James's New York Edition prefaces and final novels.

Taken together, Dickinson's and James's explorations of the vicissitudes of lived duress form a verso to *Contingent Figure*'s earlier examination of characterological strain's buckling under an affective force whose suffusive porousness troubles criticism's too-fast divvying of figurative from phenomenal life: as noted in the first chapter, figuration isn't external to the variable experience of lived embodiment: it *is* lived embodiment. As Dickinson and James suggest, the affinity between the figurative difficulty of an author's corpus and that author's coterminous vanishing into the lived medium of affliction supplements one of the founding premises of Elaine Scarry's *The Body in Pain,* a text that continues, rightly, to shape contemporary accounts of disability and chronic pain. In its conviction that we experience another person's pain as irremediably inaccessible and beyond language, *The Body in Pain* risks reducing readerly or critical intervention to the work of bearing witness *on behalf,* in a manner that effectively disavows the frequency with which the pain one labors to inhabit is, in fact, one's own. The Dickinson and James chapters, like *Contingent Figure* more generally, seek to rehabilitate pain's idiom from the vantage of the subject who weathers it, notwithstanding the extent to which this subjectivity is experienced as the jeopardized expression of an object subjected to pain's own inscrutable terms.

Lastly, chapters 5 and 6, "Is the Rectangle a Grave? Floating Attention, Betweenness in Relief" and "Weaver's Handshake: The Aesthetics of Chronic Objects," test the ability of the critical repertoire culled from preceding pages to illuminate the lyric mettle of two distinct queer theoretical encounters with aesthetic chronicity: Bersani's fascination with the paintings of Mark Rothko, and Eve Kosofsky Sedgwick's twained practice as both poet and textile artist. Bersani's fastidious chronicling of Rothko's rectangles amounts to a sustained reflection on a form of psychical relationality earlier charted in his seminal reading of Henry James's *The Golden Bowl,* "as if the geometry of human relations *implied* what we call human feelings into existence."[50] This rumination on so expressly aesthetic a geometry of relations informs Bersani's decades-long attraction to an erotics of abstracted expressionism to which the literalism of sex so often gives way. The surprising dispensability of erotic literalism finds its most incisive expression in Bersani's exploration of characterological incredulity in *Moby-Dick*'s treatment of Ishmael's nubile serenity in the tattooed arms of Queequeg. In the wake of our prospective freedom from the unbearable lightness of characterological mimesis and subjectivity alike, this chapter ultimately considers Bersani's ravishment less with either one of the two rectangles by which the majority of Rothko's compositions are vertically comprised than with the shimmeringly interstitial line by which any given pair of rectangles is variously held at once together and apart. Developed across a wide swath of his oeuvre, Bersani's attention to the enigmatic and mercurial cleavage of this line vitally contributes to the specifically aesthetic account of duress to which *Contingent Figure*'s meditations on chronic pain are magnetized.

In its movement from Bersani's exquisite concentration to the candor and figurative largesse of Sedgwick's shifting affiliations across medium and genre, *Contingent Figure* once again asks us to ponder a particular rhythm of implosion and impingement: the centrifugal and centripetal curves of formal feeling at the heart of the project's speculative theorization of and exercise in chronic sensibility. At the same time, however, this final chapter on Sedgwick turns in on itself, to the granular, intransigent resistance of substance that liaises and expresses our effort to survive ourselves and those systems of incessant duress to which however ambivalently we find ourselves in thrall. Following a line of rapport between Sedgwick's shifting vocations as poet, literary theorist, and textile artist, "Weaver's Handshake" attends to her investment in the chronicity of figuration, those moments where her work achieves a level of ontological liveliness unthinkable apart from the former's capacity as uniquely chronic substance. At the heart of this analysis is an experience of somatic incessancy articulated in Sedgwick's *Tendencies* as the analogy of gravestone-rubbing for the production of the "sexual," posthumously echoed in *The Weather in Proust* as what Sedgwick denominates the weaver's handshake, a shibboleth-like salutation between lovers of textile meant to replicate—thumb to tip of forefinger, rubbed back and forth—the gesture by which one assesses the quality and feel of fabric. The charisma of this iterative figure illuminates a queer materiality present across Sedgwick's corpus, from *Fat Art, Thin Art* and related accounts of poetics to that which *Touching Feeling* describes as a pedagogy of Buddhism, and ultimately, to both her practice and written consideration of the Japanese textile crafts *shibori* and *suminagashi*. Taken together, the resonance between these scenes suggests an important link between the queerness of Sedgwick's textual and textile investments and the nineteenth-century radical empiricism of Emerson's "theory of nature."

1. Melville's Iron Crown of Lombardy

Phenomenology beyond the Phantom Limb

Unlike many Melvillean explorations of disability studies, this chapter is only incidentally about Ahab's prosthetic leg. It is about Moby Dick only insofar as the whale's relation to Ahab figures the impossible ontology of chronic pain. These pages hypothesize the obscure labor of that verb, "figures." Not quite verb of being and not quite transitive, it is a transformative selvage, stitching itself repeatedly to itself from the outer edges. Chronic pain's relation to the figurative recalls (however fractiously headlong or disassembled) the fictively normalized body's relation to constative language. If the latter's aspirational clarity opens onto external reference or disappears into the efficiency of its execution, chronic pain's figurative repertoire efflorescingly presses against syntax, hovers and spools: performative, rhetorically saturated, libidinously dilatory. The scene of this encounter isn't mystical (albeit where in the midst of extremity the mystical appears remains necessarily an open question, especially when it comes to travail's erosion of one's accustomed radii). It's Purell and long-expired magazines in a pain doctor's waiting room; it's examination rooms decorated with promotional pharmaceutical swag and plastic models of vertebrae. And it's everywhere one passes as a pain-free person. Such transfiguring episodes of somatic distress recall Judith Butler's sense of a body that is "never fully given [through language] . . . given, when it is given, in parts—it is, as it were, given and withheld at the same time."[1] The back-and-forth of "given and withheld," like the rhetorical pivot of "as it were," is the mark not only of "language," but also of figurative language. This chapter will suggest that the literally quintessential, figurative lavishness of a text like *Moby-Dick* or *Pierre* can teach us something elemental about the experience of chronic pain, both ours and the "sharp shooting pains in his bleeding stump"[2] to which Peleg attributes Ahab's singular rancor.

It's not clear if Peleg's account of "shooting pains" quotes Ahab's own telling of the injury suffered in his first encounter with Moby Dick or if this is how Peleg has pieced together those threads of narration that have survived past that opening era of Ahab's crisis. Peleg tells Ishmael:

> I know Captain Ahab well; I've sailed with him as mate years ago; I know what he is—a good man—not a pious, good man, like Bildad, but a swearing good man—something like me—only there's a good deal more of him. Aye, Aye, I know that he was never very jolly; and I know that on the passage home, he was a little out of his mind for a spell; but it was the sharp shooting pains in his bleeding stump that brought that about, as any one might see. I know, too, that ever since he lost his leg last voyage by that accursed whale, he's been a kind of moody—desperate moody, and savage sometimes; but that will all pass off. (79)

With each of the five assertions of what Peleg purportedly "know[s]," the fact of knowledge gives way to an epistemological foundering, as though the perseverating self-certainty of "Aye, Aye, I," furrowed deep enough, might be mistaken for the *aiaiai* of Greek ululation. Peleg may be more or less correct when it comes to his narration of Ahab's pain—although veridical compunction can hardly be assumed when it comes to his motives for imparting to Ishmael one version of their captain over another—but his assumption that "any one might see" either Ahab's pain or the madness it spurs wishfully skirts the degree to which both the causes and effects of Ahab's suffering are internal phenomena, eluding view. At the same time, the idiomatic inflection of Peleg's assertion that anyone (including us) "might see" the link between Ahab's pain and his ensuing derangement doesn't depend on the empirical availability of Ahab's condition so much as enjoin us to treat our capacity for imagining pain as though it were loosely coextensive if not commutable with what remains optically withdrawn. Thinking about what Peleg has told him, Ishmael, in turn, tells us, "As I walked away, I was full of thoughtfulness; what had been incidentally revealed to me of Captain Ahab, filled me with a certain wild vagueness of painfulness concerning him" (79). Before laying eyes on the Pequod captain, Ishmael comes to experience Ahab's splintering noncoincidence as interpretive opacity, the gulf between "thoughtfulness" and "a certain wild vagueness of painfulness" suggesting Ishmael's capacity for the form of thought without necessarily a guarantee of its content. This shape of thought, this cavalet,[3] is repeated in the myriad hollows that carve Ahab, sea, and text alike into a series of haunted negative space: "There stand his trees, each with a hollow trunk, as if a hermit and a crucifix were within" (4). More locally, however, Ishmael's conversion of Peleg's terms into his own invites us to ponder the difference between "sharp shooting pains" and a "wild vagueness of painfulness," the latter's translation of the former's narrative definitude into the doubled suffix of abstraction twice removed—vagueness of painfulness—bound to no object so much as the wild swale of its own vagary. By contrast, Peleg's reportage of Ahab in advance of Ahab's actual appearance—anticipating in miniature our corresponding reliance on Ishmael's narration—is prosaic if not *pedestrianizing*: landlubber language, compared to the sea legs of the text's more pervasively hollowing narration, shooting through itself like harpoons or stars.

On the first page of *The Body in Pain,* Elaine Scarry writes that "when one hears about another person's physical pain, the events happening within the interior of that person's body may seem to have the remote character of some deep subterranean fact, belonging to an invisible geography that, however portentous, has no reality because it has not yet manifested itself on the visible surface of the earth."[4] Ishmael's "certain wild vagueness of painfulness" corresponds to Scarry's "subterranean fact" insofar as a fact so far removed from the surface of our ken persists as abstractly factual at best. Can a fact exist for itself? Does pain exist when the body it's in goes anesthetic? At the bottom of the sea, the fact may well be a dream, the route from "vagueness" to "painfulness" as gratuitiously innavigable as a ship through fog. How then for Ahab? Throughout the book, the captain all but disappears. As much as he is driven to search the pain out, he is already alone with it. If pain is a subterranean fact, this is where Ahab lives: "the isolated subterraneousness of the cabin made a certain humming silence to reign there, though it was hooped round by all the roar of the elements" (514). The sea, in turn, portends the inexorable fantasy of the body hyperbolically flayed. When one suffers chronic pain, one answers to (and sometimes, so it seems—*so it feels?*—is ontologized by) the very thing one can't see. And so the sea's hyperbole subtends the sufferer's fantasy of seeing of what the agony consists: "And now abating in his flurry, the whale once more rolled out into view; surging from side to side; spasmodically dilating and contracting his spout-hole, with sharp, cracking, agonized respirations. At last, gush after gush of clotted red gore, as if it had been the purple lees of red wine, shot into the frighted air; and falling back again, ran dripping down his motionless flanks into the sea" (286). Such scenes from Melville bleed into each other, a rhythm of activity and quiet corresponding to the quotidian of how pain looks from the outside (the calm, the withdrawing) and how it might feel *from the inside.* Usually, however, how it feels looks like nothing at all, a Misrach sea. Or rather: *how it feels like it looks,* these subtle distinctions overlaying each other like a diaphanous tissue.

And so, with all the havoc of an asymptote broached, the boat's final encounter with Moby Dick realizes the impossible moment when both the external world and our words for it prove devastatingly adequate to both one's imagination and the pain that fills it:

> Suddenly the waters around them slowly swelled in broad circles; then quickly upheaved, as if sideways sliding from a submerged berg of ice, swiftly rising to the surface. A low rumbling sound was heard; a subterraneous hum; and then all held their breaths; as bedraggled with trailing ropes, and harpoons, and lances, a vast form shot lengthwise, but obliquely from the sea. Shrouded in a thin drooping veil of mist, it hovered for a moment in the rainbowed air; and then fell swamping back into the deep. Crushed thirty feet upwards, the waters flashed for an instant like heaps of fountains, then brokenly sank in a shower of flakes, leaving the circling surface creamed like new milk round the marble trunk of the whale. (567)

On January 8, 1852, Melville famously writes to Sophia Hawthorne (Nathaniel Hawthorne's wife): "I shall not again send you a bowl of salt water. The next chalice I shall commend, will be a rural bowl of milk."[5] Traditionally, critics take for granted that the bowl of milk refers (whether sincerely or not) to *Pierre.* I'd like to hold onto the possibility, however, that the milk bowl no less compulsively looks backward to this extraordinary scene. The above lines feature neither Ahab nor his crew; everyone is reduced to pronouns. The whale himself is reduced if not to figuration then to form: "Shrouded in a thin drooping veil of mist, it hovered for a moment in the rainbowed air; and then fell swamping back into the deep." For all the words churning around it, the text's lactiform substance nearly evades nouns altogether, its participial and gerund forms registering the smiting energy of depth's interior as it moves through and becomes the sea's exterior surfaces. *Swelled, upheaving, sliding, submerged, rumbling, hum, bedraggled, trailing, obliquely, shrouded, drooping, hovered, rainbowed, swamping, crushed, flashed, brokenly, leaving, circling:* the substance of these lines is a series of gestures left by the whale like a thread through the eye of a monstrous needle. Incommensurate but nearly synchronic, blooming out of each other: an instance of figurative vitality that *Pierre* will further refine.

The newly creamed surface of the text belongs to neither sailor nor sea, an agitation of whiteness all the more staggering alongside the "dead, blind wall" (336–37) that the novel's white whales bring to mind. It's neither metaphorical nor allegorical, although it's also not "merely" descriptive. What makes it figurative is its movement, its strange autonomy. If trying to think about Ahab's pain leaves Ishmael feeling filled with the "vagueness of painfulness," I want to suggest that perhaps the closest *we* can get to *how Ahab feels* are these such moments of disastrous animacy. As Melville writes, "subsided not, but deepeningly contracted" (185), as though the irruption impressed a scene of disorder we were being trained not to follow but to trust in after it had vanished (as if it could be forgotten)—vanished, at least, for us. The figurative intensities of *Pierre* and these later passages from *Moby-Dick* invite our further attention to phenomenologies of chronic pain from the "peculiar sideway position" (330) of the person feeling them—how pain looks as it's being felt, how it feels. Ahab's "madness" offers a figure for our chronic suffering. *My* suffering. In the vanity of chronic pain, that Ahab can't remember a time before the whale figures my own inability to remember a time before the pain. This discovery feels less dramatic than tedious but no less escapable. Ahab's amnesia is prosthetic: it fits where my memory is missing. Trying to remember is an ongoing process that (like Keats, a favorite song) it never goes old. In place of remembering it feels like shuffling through the outside of one's own image repertoire. Writing "about" chronic pain invariably risks becoming a figure *for* chronic pain: "yet, to any monomaniac man, the veriest trifles capriciously carry meanings" (237). "Veriest trifles" practically undoes itself to the extent that their paltriness, following Melville's predilection for etymology, is bound up with the earlier sense of "trifle" (from the Middle English *trufle*) as "a false or idle tale."[6] If considering the etymological relation, however tenuous, between trifles and truffles further situates these truest falsities in the mushrooming subterranean of pain, their swindling depths are sounded only to buck capriciously (if not capsizingly) to the surface, given the origin, in turn, of capriciousness in the frisk of a goat—"here's the battering-ram, Capricornus, or the Goat; full tilt, he comes rushing, and headlong we are tossed" (433). All of which underscores the confectionary richness of the trifle's milk bowl striations.

These pages don't quite answer the questions that "about" implies. Etymologically, "about" is traced to the Old English *onbutan,* which by the thirteenth century had displaced *ymbutan,* which had meant "in the neighborhood of." Originally, however, it meant "on the outside of."[7] To say what a story is about presumes one grasps it, from the outside, beginning to end, that it can be paraphrased. When it comes to chronic pain, I can neither remember its beginning nor visualize its end, and what happens in between only sometimes dovetails with the interest of these pages. Like a difficult poem, pain resists the question of "about." It's the wrong question. Melville is a fiction writer who understands precisely this difference between genres, poem and story. *Moby-Dick* and *Pierre* produce continuities generically associated with the novel only so they can be abrogated. I write "chronic pain and phenomenology" rather than "phenomenology of chronic pain" because the pain is never simply the object of inquiry. If phenomenology describes a relation to an interior, the way the world feels on the inside, then the phenomenality of chronic pain lies further interior to that. Phenomenally speaking, inaccessible interiority is indistinguishable from a radical exterior; it equally falls short of purview. If it broke the surface a little more, it might be less difficult to describe if not what it is then what it's *about.*

Imagine: we begin with a surface. Parallel or perpendicular to a wall, a window, a whale (Old English *walu,* "ridge, bank" of earth or stone, later "ridge made on flesh by a lash")[8] is the interruption of a surface, its opening up, anticipated by the fin. "Even if not the slightest other part of the creature be visible, this isolated fin will, at times, be seen plainly projecting from the surface. When the sea is moderately calm, and slightly marked with spherical ripples, and this gnomon-like fin stands up and casts shadows upon the wrinkled surface, it may well be supposed that the watery circle surrounding it somewhat resembles a dial, with its style and wavy hour-lines graved on it. On that Ahaz-dial the shadow often goes back" (139). The fin, the syllable it gives to finitude, turns the gnomonically styled surface into a clock. Melville's writing—*Moby-Dick* and *Pierre,* but also "Bartleby" and others—illuminates this scene of phenomenological edge-work and shadow. Not where phenomenon meets logos, but where logos meets πόνος, the Greek word for pain. Phenomenology swerves in this beveled extremity, there being no more economical way through its impasse.

This chapter's exploration of the aesthetic vividness of chronic pain qua substance treats the iterative quality of chronicity as constitutive, since it's in pain's inexhaustible repetition that it becomes a thing. As Levi R. Bryant writes, "Qualities inhere in or belong to a substance, but do not *make* the substance what it is. Substance is therefore that which persists throughout time."[9] At its most general and ordinarily short-lived, pain interrupts the quotidian. In the case of chronic pain, however, pain *is* the quotidian. Along these lines, its temporality verges on the incessant, naturalizing engine of repetition described in Butler's account of performativity. Pain's iterative alchemy may well seem decreative rather than performative, presuming, that is, we install ourselves as the subject of its deterioration. At the same time, to the extent that its engine disabuses us of subjecthood's grammatical vantage, the pain allows us to see (in aforementioned sense of Peleg's speculative vision) that the interiority it performatively ratifies is its own. Parasite, periscope: the relentless discovery that this too is how it feels to be matter is a long humbling. This is where a phenomenology of chronic pain opens onto object-oriented ontology, registering the incongruity of this thing that both is and isn't one's flesh.

Chronic pain might feel most like an object rather than an apparatus, a syndrome, a condition, in the interminability of trying to figure it out: a series of concentrically maddening encounters (of varying medical, mundane, reflective, erotic persuasions) spiraling around and in this way augmenting the imperturbability of the thing, this stone thrown (for example) into the lake of the neck. Over time, its imperviousness to these efforts at intervention renders one's relation to it an interpretive dejection, the churned interface between one's self and self, less one hand resting on the other than an impingement.[10] The extent to which this unremittingness comes to feel like a textual object says less about its legibility than our desire for a literacy adequate to it. Graham Harman captures some aspect of these throes in his understanding of metaphor not as that which "turn[s] the withdrawn into the visible" but that which "make[s] the visible seem withdrawn: that is to say, *metaphor converts the qualities of objects into objects in their own right.*"[11] Metaphor's animating conversion of qualities into objects has as much to do with temporality as it does the sea-change of substance, since the object-form of a quality allows us to hallucinate the comprehension of what might be held were we less inaccessible to it. And so whiteness, for Ishmael, becomes as much an object of pursuit as the white whale itself, an "entic[ement]" "shed" from its "bright side" (548) in the manner of Lucretian figurae.[12] Figuration's especial disquiet is inseparable, for Ishmael, from an intractable duress experienced *as* chronic pain (often as *Contingent Figure* formulates chronic pain's relation to figuration the other way around), a whiteness that "keeps her ruins for ever new; admits not the cheerful greenness of complete decay; spreads over her broken ramparts the rigid pallor of an apoplexy that fixes its own distortions" (193). What's more, the unsightliness induced by this unwitnessable figure—"the strangest, saddest city thou can'st see"—grows further fearsome as the impasse of its tautology proves inarticulable from our experience of its narcissism as our own. After all, when Ishmael confesses that "the whiteness . . . above all thing appalled me" (188), it's not just that "the appalling," as Eyal Peretz observes, "contains within it an allusion to whiteness, or to paleness,"[13] but that it leaves us appalled in the face of its endless pallor, the figure of a figure.

Another word Harman associates with this process is "allure," which he describes as that which "invites us into a world that seemed inaccessible, a world in which the object must be even deeper than what we had regarded as its most intimate properties. Whereas black noise unfolds entirely within a single world, allure resembles a whirlpool or black hole sucking us into another."[14] And we are thus back to *Moby-Dick,* "floating on the margin of the ensuing scene, and in full sight of it, when the half-spent suction of the sunk ship reached me, I was then, but slowly, drawn towards the closing vortex" (573). Allure doesn't merely invite us into the inaccessible any more than a whirlpool merely obliterates. It's a process slow enough to respond, coral-like, to our powers of attention, dwelling in the discrepancy between "the attraction of something that has retreated into its own depths" and the depth itself. Consider in this regard the following 1930 description of *Pierre* by early Melville critic E. L. Grant Watson:

> There is a viscous and somewhat cloying quality about the style, which like the substance of the subconscious world, with which it deals, is at first repellent. Like some alien particle, unable to fuse or to accommodate itself to this deliberate artifice, the mind, which can not at once

> shake off the values of normal existence, rebels against the exaggerated virtuousness.[15]

In the startling rhetorical turn of Watson's second line, the mind discovers only after it has been named or recognized that it, not the Melvillean text, is the alien particle. If the mind is unable to fuse with *Pierre*'s artifice, it is also unable quite to refuse it, the difficulty of distinguishing between a mind unable to marry and a mind rebellingly repelled by the objects of its attention. Further flustering how we navigate the blur of these terms is the analogous compression of "deliberate artifice." The difficulty of thinking artifice apart from wilfulness invariably casts the example of *Pierre*'s exaggerations as more than deliberate at the same time that deliberate artifice's near-redundancy obversely expresses a symptomatic protest against an artifice that doesn't seem deliberate enough, lushly self-propagating with the indeliberate ease of a weed. Something is queerly awry, Watson suggests, in our navigation of this textual ambush whose viscous repellency has as much to do—"at first"—with our insufficient aversion to its cloying as it does the substance of the style's tack. Recalling from Thoreau's *Walden* that living deliberately has less etymologically to do with intention than with the balance of a scale, what we can't shake off in this encounter is the frisson of equalization between attention and the objects of our attention. If only from an outside however fictively immune to or free from this style's charms, the strained interval on which plays out this "half-spent suction" of attraction and repulsion comes to resemble the false stasis of equilibrium, the confusion of liaising industry with its opposite.

Melville's style reproduces this suctionlike movement as the membranous surface through which we read, that we travel through (rather than across, from A to B along a two-dimensional line).[16] Thinking about figuration as an evolving substance interrupts the convention by which description is treated as subordinate to the textual verisimilitude of characters and plot. A subsequent section will return to the suctioning quality of text in terms of the literal and figurative lubricity of moistness. On some other speculative register, I am also imagining these textual vicissitudes of lubrication in terms not only of sexual arousal but also of chronic pain's difficult movement of joints. *Cartilage acts as a shock absorber between vertebrae. Joint tissue is enclosed by a facet, lined with a thin material called the synovial membrane, which releases a slippery or sticky fluid called synovial fluid into the joint space.* In other words, if the secret around which *Pierre* is organized is too thinly drawn and emotionally ersatz for me to believe in, I'm nonetheless convinced—as by my own joints responding to weather—that the baroque of *Pierre* feels all the more adrift from itself because it's built on this series of secretions. "With kisses I will suck thy secret from thy cheek!"[17] threatens Lucy Tartan. And so Pierre "slid himself straight into the horrible interspace [of the Terror Stone]" (134) like pain in a synovial membrane.

"AN ORDINARY FELLOW": THE MANIFOLD

Figuration's disruption of textual verisimilitude speaks to some of the limitations of first-wave disability studies. The disruption, in turn, illuminates where theorists of chronic pain and disability alike might rethink the crossing at which the terms of engagement, however imagined, come to be. Citing foundational first-wave disability scholarship from the past twenty-five years, a 2014 essay on *Moby-Dick*, for instance, exemplifies the critical work my writing about chronic pain seeks to supplement. The essay notes that "Ahab is repeatedly represented as 'a product of his own physiological condition,' the victim of a physical injury that seems to situate him outside of the parameters of the 'traditionally able-bodied profession' of whaling."[18] None of this is untrue per se, but the vigor of its paraphrase scrubs the passage clean of what R. P. Blackmur calls Melville's "excessive sophistication of surfaces."[19] Readings such as this one depend on an assumed equivalence between Melville's characters and ourselves, as though there were an Ahab in Melville's text capable of being rehabilitated once extricated from the novel's effulgent figurative dynamo. But there is no Ahab if there is no dynamo. Readings of Ahab are unable to speak to, let alone inhabit, the novel's textual universe to the extent that they assume, in Susan Sontag's words, that "the most truthful way of regarding illness—and the healthiest way of being ill—is one most purified of, most resistant to, metaphoric thinking."[20]

It's in this spirit that Rosemarie Garland Thomson produces the following stupendous counterfactual:

> The plot or the work's rhetorical potential usually benefits from the disabled figure remaining other to the reader—identifiably human but resolutely different. How could Ahab operate effectively if the reader were allowed to see him as an ordinary fellow instead of as an icon of

> monomaniacal revenge—if his disability lost its transcendent meaning? . . . Thus the rhetorical function of the highly charged trait fixes relations between disabled figures and their readers. If disabled characters acted, as real people with disabilities often do, to counter their stigmatized status, the rhetorical potency of the stigma would be mitigated or lost.[21]

There is no universe in which we are "allowed" to see Ahab as an "ordinary fellow," because there is no universe in which he *is* one. Figuration isn't external to what Sharon L. Snyder and David T. Mitchell call "the variable experience of lived embodiment";[22] in Melville, it *is* lived embodiment. In its movement between phenomenology's *phenomena* and *logos,* figuration feels more palpable than the nonfigurative language for which "logos" stands. I imagine phenomenology as an axis rather than the merging of two disparate elements. If *phenomena* and *logos* are at opposite ends of a spectrum, the nonfigurative lives closer to *logos* whereas the figurative, as an event (in both time and substance), lives nearer the phenomenal. Figuration writes itself inching toward becoming an event (toward being). More importantly, however, figuration also describes what happens to pain, its infinitesimal movement between being felt constantly and constantly being thought. Character and plot work toward minimizing the force of figuration to the extent that it hypostasizes the energy of language in terms of a character's traits or a plot's surprising turn. Melville's writing is a lesson in relinquishing characterology and the forms of identification it seems to promise, disabusing us of the notion that a character's resemblance to persons is our only hold in the ethos of learning from each other.

It's the lure of characterology that cozens critics into suspending their disbelief that Ahab's humanness is coextensive with our own. To take a different example, Melville's playful soldering of radical queerness and domesticity impels readers to treat the scene of Ishmael in bed with Queequeg as a tableau of inclusiveness *avant la lettre.* What is most interesting about the scene, however, might well be its transposition of queer embodiment onto characters too thinly drawn to sustain it.[23] When Ishmael wakes with Queequeg's arm thrown over him, "tattooed all over with an interminable Cretan labyrinth of a figure" (25), it is a crash course in queerness beyond the guarantee of subjectivity. Without subjectivity, where does sexuality go, into what is it dispersed? In the genial absence of both, queerness appears autonomous from the bodies in and on which it ordinarily resides. Intimated by the "labyrinth of a figure," queerness disencumbered from bodies is queerness transfigured. But it is also queerness *interminable.* I understand this lesson as both an example of and model for my thinking about chronic pain as something that doesn't simply reside in the ontological structures it inherits. Rather, chronic pain alters the very shape of the ontological. No less radically, thinking about chronic pain becomes an occasion to rethink thinking ecologically.

Toward the end of *Pierre,* Melville writes, "Is Pierre a shepherd, or a bishop, or a cripple? No, but he has in effect, reduced himself to the miserable condition of the last. With the crook-ended cane, Pierre—unable to rise without sadly impairing his manifold intrenchments, and admitting the cold air into their innermost nooks,—Pierre, if in his solitude, he should chance to need any thing beyond the reach of his arm, then the crook-ended cane drags it to his immediate vicinity" (301). If the passage is alluring if not to some extent too convenient in its hypothesis of Pierre's explicitly (i.e., literally) "cripple[d]" state, it is arresting in its understanding of the latter not only as a "miserable condition" but in the pressing manner of "manifold intrenchments." However else we imagine its metabolism of materialism and figuration, *Moby-Dick* enjoins its readers to understand the fact of Ahab's injury in material terms: a whaling captain with a leg made from "the polished bone of the sperm whale's jaw" (124) dedicates his life to killing the whale that took the first one. Contra characterizations of "Ahab" as "the all-encompassing, all-responsible individual self"[24] who happens to have lost his leg, Ahab "is for ever Ahab" (561) not despite but because of his loss. Pierre, by contrast, is forever Pierre, not on account of any single injury or outcome, but because figuration riddles Pierre's body long before any "actual" tribulation occurs. To be sure, the narrative posits the consequences of Pierre's decision to flee Saddle Meadows as an extended period of unhappiness and bodily ailment. Narrative notwithstanding, however, Pierre's self (bodily and psychical alike) has already been rendered so thoroughly figurative that suffering, present and future, has no body to attach to. Textual elaborateness absorbs narrative and characterology (or at least our expectation of them) in its excrescent ooze, the figurative logic of *Pierre* calling back to the counterintuitive corporealization of *Moby-Dick*'s famous, decorporealizing squeeze of the hand:

> It had cooled and crystallized to such a degree, that when, with several others, I sat down before a large Constantine's bath of it, I found it strangely concreted into lumps, here and there rolling about in the liquid

> part. It was our business to squeeze these lumps back into fluid. A sweet and unctuous duty! No wonder that in old times this sperm was such a favorite cosmetic. Such a clearer! such a sweetener! such a softener! such a delicious mollifier! After having my hands in it for only a few minutes, my fingers felt like eels, and began, as it were, to serpentine and spiralize. (415)

Indeed, there is perhaps no better description of the acyrological purple of *Pierre*—what the novel's dedication winkingly calls "The Most Excellent Purple Majesty"—than the passage just following Melville's readily (and noncoincidentally) queerable account of the "abounding, affectionate, friendly, loving feeling" (416) that comes with squeezing the hands of fellow whalers while squeezing out the "gentle globules":

> First comes white-horse, so called, which is obtained from the tapering part of the fish, and also from the thicker portions of his flukes. It is tough with congealed tendons—a wad of muscle—but still contains some oil. After being severed from the whale, the white-horse is first cut into portable oblongs ere going to the mincer. They look much like blocks of Berkshire marble.
>
> Plum-pudding is the term bestowed upon certain fragmentary parts of the whale's flesh, here and there adhering to the blanket of blubber, and often participating to a considerable degree in its unctuousness. It is a most refreshing, convivial, beautiful object to behold. As its name imports, it is of an exceedingly rich, mottled tint, with a bestreaked snowy and golden ground, dotted with spots of the deepest crimson and purple. It is plums of rubies, in pictures of citron. Spite of reason, it is hard to keep yourself from eating it. I confess, that once I stole behind the foremast to try it. It tasted something as I should conceive a royal cutlet from the thigh of Louis le Gros might have tasted, supposing him to have been killed the first day after the venison season, and that particular venison season contemporary with an unusually fine vintage of the vineyards of Champagne.
>
> There is another substance, and a very singular one, which turns up in the course of this business, but which I feel it to be very puzzling adequately to describe. It is called slobgollion; an appellation original with the whalemen, and even so is the nature of the substance. It is an ineffably oozy, stringy affair, most frequently found in the tubs of sperm, after a prolonged squeezing, and subsequent decanting. I hold it to be the wondrously thin, ruptured membranes of the case, coalescing. (416–17)

Nominally addressing the knots of flesh from which the spermatic cure-all is separated, these extraordinary lines hyperbolically suggest that if Ahab is made of ivory, Pierre no less than the whales he follows is larded. Melville's jubilant taxonomy implies that the difference between literal blubber and figurative blubber is one of degree rather than kind.

Along these lines, that earlier passage's "manifold" anticipates a later chapter's "manifold wrappings," the multiply insufficient blankets with which Pierre girds himself against "the permanent chill of his room" (298). Some scenes later, however, Pierre's "manifold intrenchments" seem equally continuous with the abstraction of his "manifold and inter-enfolding mystic and transcendental persuasions" (353). Twice, we find him in the process of "setting all these [persuasions]" aside, in favor of what the narrator calls "plain, palpable facts" (i.e., concerning the supposed paternity of his "sister," Isabel). Facts might be "plain[er]" than the mystic persuasions he sets aside, but manifoldness is nothing if not a property of palpability, these persuasions he wears like a royal garment. It's not that these folds are either literal (wrappings, blanket) *or* figurative (intrenchments, persuasion). In the words of Deleuze's figuring of Leibniz, the "text also fashions a way of representing what Leibniz will always affirm: a correspondence and even a communication between the two levels, between the two labyrinths, between the pleats of matter and the folds in the soul. A fold between two folds? And the same image, that of veins in marble, is applied to the two under different conditions. Sometimes the veins are the pleats of matter that surround living beings held in the mass, such that the marble tile resembles a rippling lake that teems with fish. Sometimes the veins are innate ideas in the soul, like twisted figures . . . caught in the block of marble. Matter is marbled."[25]

Pierre and his implicitly diaphanous dermis experience the pleat of these two levels equally. When one's dermis is as literally and figuratively thin as Pierre's, every fold and inter-enfolding matters. Each morning, Pierre subjects himself to the "raspings of flesh-brushes, perverted to the filing and polishing of the merest ribs" (298). This painful ablution is *almost* literal—the bones of his emaciated body nearly as visible as the polished bone of Ahab's leg, or a "neck heavy with pendants of polished ivory" (70), with which the *Pequod* itself is compared. At the same time, to be sure, this emaciation bestows a figure for Pierre's susceptibility to the novel at large. To call the condition of his embodiment thin-skinned is to note, seeing through it, the extent to which he embodies (*such as that is*) a mode of italicized being: easy enough to imagine Pierre's "lean, philosophical nudity" (298) tilting into the italics of *Pierre.* The lean nudities to which Pierre and his fellow apostles are reduced further distill bodies to typography, as though the spines and spurs and stems of typeface prefigured their sodality of bones: "Oh, the rheumatical cracklings of rusted joints, in that defied air of December!" (298–99). This skeletonizing of character makes all the more sumptuous the textual largesse that washes over it: or creeps through it, effulgently, all those rusted rheumatisms.

MOIST EYE-FISH WITH WINGS

The introduction of Eve Kosofsky Sedgwick's foundational *Epistemology of the Closet* is composed of seven axioms that inform what Sedgwick calls "the otherwise implicit methodological, definitional, and axiomatic groundings of the book's project."[26] Ask any queer theorist for Axiom 1 and they'll tell you that "People are different from each other." Loved for both its salubrious obviousness and its incitement toward specifying texture, Axiom 1 has proved indispensable for literary critics in the field of disability studies and queer theory alike. No less essential, however, has been a similarly axiomatic supposition that for a literary text to resonate with or inform the vicissitudes of lived experience, it must be predicated on a verisimilitude drawn to the scale of our own waking world, a one-to-one ratio of persons and characters. *Pierre,* on the other hand, is at the heart of my chronic pain archive even as its nonequivalence to our own world (as I and others have elsewhere noted)[27] is nothing less than legendary. All the same, few texts come closer than it to illuminating my experience of chronic pain's perverse duress, and this has everything to do with what I've been describing as its aesthetics of figuration. For persons whose lives are absorbed with constant pain, there's a certain but incalculable sense that pain has depleted the very lineaments of which something like subjectivity is composed—their energy, stamina, libido, attention, and/or sense of agential capacity—and that what is left in this depletion's place is less than or at least substantively different from bare life as we've come to know it. Sometimes, of course, so drastic a depletion can be inhabited only as an endless proscenium unto itself. Inseparable from the acuity of constant pain but likewise not equivalent to it, diminishment's kabuki theater is something to which the person in pain acclimates. And each time the pain and its attendant depletions worsen, the person acclimates again, often, for the world they inhabit, in unremarkable ways.

How does a text depict this ongoing, unfolding eventlessness beyond its being dropped in the mouths of the sufferer, the narrator, the mouths of others? How does a text depict when the crux—the *rub*—of chronic pain is that no communication comes close to describing it: to describing, that is, how it feels for the person in it? How does a text envision this, the feel of it (as opposed to the mimesis of chronic pain's exhaustion of discursive speech), when the thing itself (such as that is), hardly seems to exist in the waking world at all? What's more, how does a novel depict it in a manner that enriches rather than merely repeats the frustration of chronic pain's intransigence? The task of living with let alone describing chronic pain from the vantage of its damage grows further difficult as it increasingly feels like the self lost in it. Trying to see past the pain can feel like trying to see the world when all one sees is a scratch in the glass. Not quite belonging to either the outside or to the apparatus of the interior, the glass—the pane, the lens—occupies what Henry James calls the middle distance. Chronic pain correspondingly feels neither literal nor abstract because our experience of it takes these two formerly discrete, bipolar categories and returns them as a constantly shifting sliding scale. What's more: unlike instantaneous injuries like burns or cuts and worse, chronic pain mostly lives near the interior. To this end (even before a text attempts to do it justice), it is less a part of the waking world than aligned with or caught in the mechanism by which that world is apprehended. We might think about chronic pain in terms of Emerson's understanding of life as "a train of moods like a string of beads, and, as we pass through them, they prove to be many-colored lenses which paint the world their own hue, and each shows only what lies in its focus. From the mountain you see the mountain."[28] Except that chronic pain is lived not only as the same bead after bead, but as the world being hued. Returning to the matter of pain dwelling in or near the interior (although how we visualize an interiority so particular as to justify the definite article can hardly go without saying), it's adjacent to what we conceive (and in doing so, spatialize) as thought, feeling, emotion. But unlike these categories, the pain doesn't belong to us, nor answer to us. Butler's parsing of Freudian melancholy offers a correlative for how pain takes over one's interior without feeling like it's one's own. Like melancholy, chronic pain tells however elliptically how the pearl of ontology cleaves itself from this alien, obstinate grit (save that pain, unlike the pearl, never stops being felt). And only over time: the making of a pearl is a myth of chronicity. But I digress.

It's not that the body free from pain (however such a thing can be remembered or imagined) doesn't traverse an optical field; after all, the clemency of an easeful body may be said to coincide with the mechanics of what it does or purports to do, vanishing into that coincidence. The style of invisibility that characterizes and confirms one's experience of self-accessibility is felt in terms of seamless space. By contrast, to the extent that an aggrieved or self-disappointed body can begin to make sense of its encumbrance, the withdrawal of pain comprises an invisibility twice removed. The first remove of pain is a function of how little it crosses one's path, optically speaking. A surgeon can view vertebrae with their own two eyes, inspect a patella or joint with the vigor of one able to take for granted the mere existence of objects pondered (the weight of attention shared between them and ponderative density), and yet the longer one lives with pain, the more one is confronted with less an object-in-retreat than an object long retreated. Maurice Merleau-Ponty asks of a related set of sensorial abruptions, "What if our eyes were made in such a way as to prevent our seeing any part of our body, or some diabolical contraption were to let us move our hands over things, while preventing us from touching our own body? . . . Such a body would not reflect itself; it would be an almost adamantine body, not really flesh, not really the body of a human being. There would be no humanity."[29] There is an especial cruelty for Merleau-Ponty in the idea of a sensorium so founded in grammar—the subjects and objects of attention—that the self's effort at studying itself could only short-circuit. Spurred by this prospective failure of adequation between reflected and unreflectible substance, the body long in pain tends toward an accretive rhythm of invisibility. One would think that the experience of not seeing one's self, of not being able to feel one's self, would turn the body into a ghost. Ever-present and unconfirmable, the body's bereavement nonetheless gives way, for Merleau-Ponty, to an experience of the self as stone. If pain leaves a body inaccessible to itself, the resulting almost-adamance amounts to an impossible substance, at once petrified and diaphanous. Not quite ossified, not quite unwavering, not quite Adamically nameable, this supernatural suspension introduces a chronological gradient more slippery and less graspable than the temporal idiom of perception's comparatively simplified grammatical apparatus. The flimsy petrifactions of this incessant self-deferral somewhat elucidate Melville's Pierre, named for stone and light as gauze.

> "Smell I the flowers, or thee?" cried Pierre.
>
> "See I lakes, or eyes," cried Lucy, her own gazing down into his soul, as two stars gaze down into a tarn.
>
> No Cornwall miner ever sunk so deep a shaft beneath the sea, as Love will sink beneath the floatings of the eyes. Love sees ten million fathoms down, till dazzled by the floor of pearls. The eye is Love's own magic glass, where all things that are not of earth, glide in supernatural light. There are not so many fishes in the sea, as there are sweet images in lovers' eyes. In those miraculous translucencies swim the strange eye-fish with wings, that sometimes leap out, instinct with joy; moist fish-wings wet the lover's cheek. (33)

My premise, in part, is that chronic pain wreaks a peculiar damage to what one calls a self that feels like the experience of disappearing into it. In this context, the task of articulating let alone understanding pain from the self's vantage grows all the more fraught, like trying to cultivate attention to the cracked lens through which one sees the world. A quiet attention to the scratches and abrasions of a lens is the very effect of Melville's "moist fish-wings." Held up close, I imagine them as wings of a fly, tessellations of stained glass. The passage suggests that the difficulty of looking *at* what we are accustomed to looking *through* touches on a specifically figurative strain, linked to the latter's divergence from the system of metaphorical tenor and vehicle to which Melville's Wordsworthian sea corresponds: "There, sometimes doth a leaping fish / Send through the tarn a lonely cheer."[30] I. A. Richards writes of "18th Century assumptions that figures are a mere embellishment or added beauty and that the plain meaning, the tenor, is what alone really matters and is something that, 'regardless of the figures,' might be gathered by the patient reader."[31] By contrast, notwithstanding the two-part structure of metaphor from which *Pierre*'s figuration pours, I'm not sure what the above passage, stripped bare of its "mere embellishment," would transmit. It's not clear if these "miraculous translucencies" are what the beloved amorously beholds in the lover's eye or if they are the reflection or amorous response (to what he sees in the eyes of the beloved) in his own. If these translucencies leap out "instinct with joy," is this the joy of the beloved or the joy of the fish, the translucencies, themselves, an affect to which we—let alone Pierre and Lucy—are hardly privy. These lachrymal fish wetting the wet paint of a two-dimensional character's besotted cheeks foresee Marianne Moore's famous conjuring of real toads in imaginary gardens. If Blackmur associated Moore with the likes of Melville and James on account of their shared attachment to aforementioned "excessive sophistication of surfaces and a passionate predilection for the genuine,"[32] it is just this sort of passage, I believe, that Blackmur has in mind.

Languishingly expiring in the air (i.e., *our* air) of the page, the ontological perplexity of Melville's tears anticipates the stagecraft of a rhinestone glued to a drag performer's cheek, an embellishment I've come to associate with Justin Vivian Bond's thaumaturgic channeling of Kiki. The alluring falsity of the rhinestone points in several meretricious directions at once, falling short (as far as conventions of affect go) of the sentimental truth of tears while replacing the latter's hydraulics of feeling with the complex precision—in Watson's terms, the "deliberate artifice"—of a single tear's decoupage. This substitution builds on and further complicates the premise of rhinestone as a poor woman's diamond (*almost adamant*), whose economical theorizing of emotional intensity, how it's recognized and valued, revises the more general aesthetic economy of luxury and imitation in which it's embedded. One may think one knows how to adjudicate between a rhinestone and a diamond, but how to speak adequately to a rhinestone's fungible relation to a tear? The insufficiency of our critical language for reproduction and realism becomes all the clearer when the stage light hits a glued-on tear just so. The question of whether or not such a tear is real misses the point, the dazzling Dido ardor it broadcasts to gallery and balcony alike. As Bersani reminds us, "there is no truth to tell, only, as James writes in the preface to *What Maisie Knew,* 'truth diffused, distributed and, as it were, atmospheric.'"[33]

The effect of Melville's "moist fish-wings" surfacing in a passage already inundated with lake and tarn and sea is "to retroactively place under suspicion the truth of that tear, that tear that may just be a drop, that tear that does not fall but sits thickly next to the eye without revealing its source or its embodied secret: whether it was secreted at all."[34] The observation, from Eugenie Brinkema's *The Forms of the Affects,* speaks to the queer discomfiture of the scene at hand, and to James's apposite interest in truth disarticulated from the contours of discrete persons, returned to the world as atmosphere; or, recalling Sedgwick's exquisite late work on Proust, as weather itself. Brinkema's subject isn't *Pierre* but the startlingly composed sequence concluding the shower scene of Hitchcock's *Psycho*. "Marion's tear," Brinkema observes, "is marked by *what it is not*. It is not expressive of the emotions of a subject, not an external production of an internal state; it does not speak to either its emissive past or to its judged emotional future, and it is ripped from, and sits only ever so gently on the surface of, the body."[35] The beauty of Hitchcock's composition and Brinkema's reading of it lies in their keen attention to affect's aesthetic animacy in the absence of those persons who'd be said otherwise to express it. Better yet, we may note that freed from Marion as its psychical or sentimental source, the aesthetic multiplicity of the tear not only unfolds independent of persons, but that its reservoir of feeling washes over the personate, reducing (or revealing) it in the process as an assemblage of parts. Obsolescingly arresting our language for interiority and ontic expression alike, its uncanny durance informs Melville's baroquely amorous Rube Goldberg as it kaleidoscopes and obviates the effect of the tears it yields. Both expression and expression's prismatically outlandish prosthesis, *Pierre*'s tears traffic equally in melodramatic inflation and deflation: what has inspired some critics to imagine *Pierre* as a sincere effort at a failed melodrama and others as an ironizing of melodrama.

Before leaving the convolutions of *Pierre*'s encomium to Love, let us consider the qualities of moistness (a variation on Watson's articulation of the novel's cloying tack) that characterize its wing-like tears. To paraphrase Bersani's remarks at the opening of "Is the Rectum a Grave?," most people—at least in our present late-capitalist macabre—do not like the word "moist." Sonically, our aversion responds in part to the interpellative coercion by which we are involved in its onomatopoeic production: the m-sound curling around its unctuous vowels like a pucker, the unpleasant sheen or hiss of its "s" implicating us in the small, secretious pool of its liquidity. Our implication in the word's erotism is challenged by the kitschy, Bidgood-like splendor of the passage's extravagance, in the face of which the text's relation to desire or arousal suggests at best the insufficiency of misguided paraphrase. After all, if the moistness of its "strange eye-fish with wings, that sometimes leap out, instinct with joy" seems ejaculatively or otherwise to punctuate the libidinal elations that precede it, it at the same time operates stochastically as a fish leaping—"sometimes"—

from the sea. Besides, that is, the extent to which the libidinally dubious vacancies of Pierre and Lucy practically empty the scene of erotic possibility, the moistness of Melville's figuration washes ashore as desultorily as jellyfish or some other seepage beholden to none of the persons at play. Designating less the exposure of any given character's or person's psychical interiority than the glimpse of a figurative world unto itself, the slippery interface transforms amorously mutual reflection into nothing so much as a glass-bottomed boat through which our voyeurism beholds a universe far stranger than even the most outlying proclivities. If the textual intensity metonymized by moistness seems less erotic or even somatic than aesthetic, its pang recalls Barthes's understanding of the *punctum* as a site of compositional susceptibility: "It is this element which rises from the scene, shoots out of it like an arrow, and pierces me. . . . A photograph's *punctum* is that accident which pricks me (but also bruises me . . .)."[36]

As it happens, some version of the passage's optical fantasia is borrowed not only from Wordsworth's tarn—a word that shimmers, in turn, between the bodies of water in whose textual depths Pierre and Lucy momentarily drown if not simply dissolve, and its oblique hinting at some lost participial form of tearing-as-torn (the text's own bruising puncture of itself)—but from Plato's *Phaedrus*. Describing for Phaedrus the physiology of falling in love, Socrates notes:

> At first a shudder runs through him, and again the old awe steals over him . . . then while he gazes on him there is a sort of reaction, and the shudder passes into an unusual heat and perspiration; for, as he receives the effluence of beauty through the eyes, the wing moistens.[37]

Like Melville's text, the disorientations of Plato's speculative account hover somewhere between the ridiculous and the ravishing. The derring-do of its bare balance is irresolvable, since the middle distance of its figurative field is formed in verisimilitude to nothing but itself. We bear its lavishness, the keen lightness of its depths, like a weight. By its own account, the name for this shuddering collapse is love, but by the time the fish-wings wash ashore, it's not clear to what love could refer, to what object or objects love could attach. Were we to consider the qualities of the thing being named rather than the diagnostic nomenclature itself, love might differently seem to participate in pain's effluent flummox. "During this process," Plato continues, "the whole soul is all in a state of ebullition and effervescence,—

which may be compared to the irritation and uneasiness in the gums at the time of cutting teeth,—bubbles up, and has a feeling of uneasiness and tickling; but when in like manner the soul is beginning to grow wings, the beauty of the beloved meets her eye and she receives the sensible warm motion of particles which flow towards her." (458). Strange materialism indeed, the soul's inflammations as angelic arthritis: how could characterological convention ever make itself known over and against such diluvial aberrancies?

As little as Plato's or Melville's passage manifestly has to do with chronic pain, it subjects descriptive surface itself to a series of bristling aesthetic maneuvers whose iterations are nothing if not potentially interminable, as though they could generate their nacreously figurative substance without end in sight. This titillated materiality grows all the more salient, juxtaposed with the text's counterattachment to a characterological method that leaves Pierre and his cohort at once discomfitingly vitiated and pneumatically fragile as soufflé. "In billowy style," (22) Pierre has driven forth his ancestral phaeton through the ancestral grounds of Saddle Meadows, accompanied by his fiancée, "Wondrous fair of face, blue-eyed, and golden-haired, the bright blonde, Lucy was arrayed in colors harmonious with the heavens" (33). As I have written elsewhere,[38] the narrator's generic descriptions of Lucy Tartan have the effect (regardless of intention) not of building up the specificity of her character but of depleting it, word by word. The more we learn of Lucy, the more epithets she is given, the more difficult it is for us to suspend the characterological disbelief she inspires. "Her cheeks were tinted with the most delicate white and red, the white predominating" (24).

Of *course* they are, the "most vivid transparency of her clear Welsh complexion, now fairly glow[ing] like rosy snow" (58). Even here, however, the gratuitous deliberateness of rosy cheeks is mostly banal at the level of paraphrase; taken on its own terms, the strangeness of its specificity reduces (perhaps *distills*) Lucy's cheeks to these two colors, white and red, one color dominating the other as though beyond Lucy's or even Melville's capacity operating as purely chromatic will. Slowing down what would otherwise be spontaneous in the cliché of Lucy's face, Melville's deconstruction of rosy cheeks turns color into an object of attention, which we experience differently from the overfamiliarity of the epithet. Somewhere within white-predominating-red, we watch as though something might happen, the incomplete beginning of a new narrative—narrative and figuration housing each other in turn like dolls.

Lucy's distinction as entity abides in her lack of particularity as character. This lack of particularity opens onto her inseparability from the world she might only loosely be said to inhabit. "Smell I the flowers or thee" (33)? The clover bloom of Saddle Meadows comes to Pierre from both sides of the hedges, but also from Lucy's "mouth and cheek . . . the fresh fragrance of her violet young being." Even as Pierre's prior question ("flowers, or thee?") seems nothing if not over-earnestly fey (the same holds for Lucy's reply), it also stages the jarring unison of Pierre's inflated musings with the science-fictional possibility that if Lucy and the landscape are continuous, he might be as well. In terms of affect and substance, that Pierre's question and Lucy's ("lakes, or eyes") are interchangeable as their respective referents is partly the point. The respective openness of each with the landscape implicitly attenuates the trace they leave as individual entities. Both individuality and the structures of subjectivity it makes possible are eclipsed by the fervor with which figurative description engulfs the novel's conventional elements. In the wake of description's own incessant velocity, *Pierre*'s plot is dead on arrival, like discovering the elements of undersea wreckage. Concomitantly, the novel's sense of character is both complexly substantial and dubious as the figures of a Francis Bacon painting. The aesthetic industry of *Pierre* conjures mimetic relation only so figuration's unbridled affect can throw it off. Pierre and Lucy inhabit figuration as an ongoing chronic condition.

As soon as this passage moves from Lucy's cry to her "own gazing down into his soul," she has for all intents and purposes disappeared for the duration into the depths her query conjures, in which her love for Pierre is silently transmuted into narrative attention. The hydraulic of figuration that characterizes both this passage and myriad others in *Pierre* is the flux of chronic pain. Interminable, impossible to slip, it takes the place of interiority (whether displacing some previous anteriority or simply supplying what hadn't existed), replacing the fiction of human depth with the even more astonishing fiction that we are dwarfed like stars by the figurative universe coexisting in our place. Chronic pain and Melvillean figuration alike aren't sufficiently describable because *they are description.* And they are autonomous: "I have a bad neck" meaning "my neck isn't mine; it doesn't belong to me." And on the other hand: "I have a neck too utterly." This feeling of besiege—neither mine nor its—is the consciousness we share.

THE IRON CROWN OF LOMBARDY

What's at stake in insisting that figuration is figuratively versus literally material? Even as there's no way for me to measure or prove it, I seem to experience Melville's indefatigable figurative engine as though it were real in ways that exceed how I think about abstraction, or how abstraction feels in the moment of its being thought. Like experience's nonequivalence to our textual approximations of it, the lapse between the event that figuration is and our account of it feels insufficient, even as it's untouchable, unseeable as a thought. I've grown attached to thinking about figuration in these terms, because they as nearly describe my twenty-year encounter with chronic pain. Early in *The Visible and the Invisible,* Merleau-Ponty writes that "in terms of its intrinsic meaning and structure . . . the sensible world is 'older' than the universe of thought, because the sensible world is visible and relatively continuous, and because the universe of thought . . . has its truth only on condition that it be supported on the canonical structures of the sensible world."[39] Stark as it is, Merleau-Ponty's distinction suggests that a phenomenology of chronic pain is unimaginable because it's done in the dark. If figuration so often is imagined as materially distinguishable from the illness or disability Sontag would say it obscures, how in the darkness of feeling chronic pain can one say where the phenomenon of it ends and our thinking of it begins? Like figuration, it occupies an outer edge of materiality that complicates our faith in the substance of its wake. Along similar lines, Nathan Brown invokes Descartes's experiment with wax and Hume's account of some never-before-perceived shade of blue. "Absent Blue Wax," Brown writes, "delivers the outside of rationalism to the outside of empiricism and lets them mingle in their mutual exteriority."[40]

I think about this wake between the outer edges at the outset of the *Moby-Dick* chapter "Sunset." "I leave a white and turbid wake," Melville writes, "pale waters, paler cheeks, where'er I sail. The envious billows sidelong swell to whelm my track; let them, but first I pass" (167). Although these lines are usually attributed to Ahab, the start of one of his soliloquies, the fervor of its iambs feels less like the outpouring of a character than of figuration itself pouring *in.* Its illusion of voice gradually seems to arise from or at least approximate Ahab's person. The voice is constituted by the words being spoken, or rather, what approximates speech, whipping itself like the wake of water into water into stiff peaks, less a voice than a hydraulic between "the diver sun—slow dived from noon" and Ahab's own soul, "mount[ing] up" as the sun sinks into the sea, "gold brow plumbs the blue" (167). What begins to take the shape of Ahab is the text's movement from sea to sun to soul to the Iron Crown of Lombardy. But our understanding that these words "are" Ahab's comes slow, as though to illuminate where figuration enters or becomes phenomenology, where it suffers its sea-change.

The Iron Crown of Lombardy marks the site not only where thinking about figuration and chronic pain overlap but where thought itself grapples with the feel of its materiality:

> Is, then, the crown too heavy that I wear? this Iron Crown of Lombardy. Yet is it bright with many a gem; I, the wearer, see not its far flashings; but darkly feel that I wear that, that dazzlingly confounds. 'Tis iron—that I know—not gold. 'Tis split, too—that I feel; the jagged edge galls me so, my brain seems to beat against the solid metal. (167)

In terms of its opening stage directions, *Ahab sitting alone, and gazing out* (167), the chapter enacts Ahab gazing out as his loneliness falls *in*. His and our attention are drawn equally to the sensations that the crown generates—its heaviness, the jagged edge where its inner seams abrade our temples, like the point of a compass inscribing the encounter's very circumference. And yet within the parameters of the scene, there's no way for Ahab to measure how it feels against the crown itself. That Ahab feels this darkly opens onto the baroque style of its phenomenological inquiry, an intuitive apprehension of the crown's dark matter. Knowing that one is wearing the crown ought be knowable as the back of one's hand; and yet in Ahab's case it cannot be verified. One almost gets the sense that Ahab, "*sitting alone, and gazing out,*" might be conducting an experiment. That the feeling seems real opens onto the equal possibilities that Ahab wears a crown on his head or that he contemplates one inside it: hence the astonishing supposition of brain beating against solid metal. Echoing this scene, Melville writes in *Clarel* of "gusts of lonely pain / beating upon the naked brain."[41] This reworking sharpens our sense of the loneliness of Ahab's enterprise. Said to contain a nail from the cross on which Jesus was crucified, the crown renders Ahab a king without a kingdom. If one were superstitious, one might worry wearing the crown would summon some of that earlier agony, quickening the pain it was forged in. And on the other side of the crown, as viewed through a periscope, do we readers see those distant far flashings across the long ocean of page upon page.

2. Queer Philology and Chronic Pain

Ce comme n'est pas un comme comme les autres.

—PAUL DE MAN, "ANTHROPOMORPHISM AND TROPE IN LYRIC"

Toward the end of *The Anti-Christ,* Nietzsche describes philology as "the art of reading well . . . *without* letting the desire to understand make you lose caution, patience, subtlety."[1] This very Jamesian proposition of desire sustained through patience and subtlety leads Nietzsche to the apothegm, "Philology as *ephexis* in interpretation."[2] *Ephexis,* which has been glossed variously as "scepticism" (H. L. Mencken), "undecisiveness" (Alan Schrift), and "constraint" (Richard Weisberg), comes from *epoche,* meaning "suspension."[3] Citing the same Greek root, Roland Barthes proposes "suspension (*épochè*) of orders, laws, summons, arrogances, terrorisms, putting on notice, the will-to-possess" as the first condition of "the desire for Neutral."[4] In Barthes's terms, ephexis is a koan about the possibility of recognizing desire in the absence of its terrorisms and will-to-possess. This chapter philologically considers the word *like* as it bears on the possibility of desiring neutrality without breaching its first condition, of being persuaded by a desire not despite but because of its depletion. *Liking* is a Venn diagram between wishing to feel desire less than one does and wishing to feel it more.

Like the Neutral, the affective, mimetic, and grammatical repertoire of *like* is queer in its capacity for incapacity, even as so compressed a turn of phrase only distorts what in *liking* seems mostly boring. Its semantic adjuvancy and affective insipidity are strongly felt (which is to say, at the same time, *not felt*) in the blistering opening sentence of Leo Bersani's 1987 essay "Is the Rectum a Grave?": "There is a big secret about sex: most people don't like it."[5] Such a sentence exemplifies the way in which the word *like* can get overlooked; for all the responses to Bersani's text, I'm struck by the paucity of any that take its turn to liking and not liking seriously. *Like*'s peculiar invisibility as the condition out of which its sometimes unexpected and disorienting density arises has led me to think about *liking* in terms of the inexorable everydayness of chronic pain.

My predisposition to think about *like* as a matter of pain and palpability has a lot to do with the fact that when I discovered Bersani's essay as an undergraduate, I "liked" sex as opposed to "loved" it more than I would care to admit. Liking it felt simultaneously like an affective downgrade and a euphemism for not liking it *more.* My desire to like it more than I did—which is to say, the extent to which I experienced *liking* as a metaphysical quandary—coincided with my first inklings of chronic pain. Holding up queer theory to myself to see what fit and didn't fit, the fantasy of voraciousness that overshadowed this mere liking of sex was predicated on the extensive, nervous labor of trying to bracket a rickety, brittle-feeling body long enough to experience the *jouissance* of that body being emptied out. And so despite Jean-Luc Nancy's supposition that "it is not impossible that in the end we will discover that 'the sexual relation' behaves like 'being' [*l'être*] (understood as verb and act) in relation to what will therefore be 'being' [*étant*] for it (that is, the entwined couple),"[6] my first "sexual relation[s]" never felt enough "like 'being'"; they felt like being *like.*

One of the strange things about the fatigue of chronic pain is that nerves are indefatigable. They treat each twinge with the same sensitivity as a first stimulus (whenever or whatever that would be). In trying to understand the experience of feeling constantly (a limb, a joint, an angle, a humidity) what other bodies disregard, learning to be attuned to *like*—the experience of this otherwise transparent, receding word as vivid and nondismissible—has become a way for me to think about the noninurable body's response to ongoing affliction. How can disability teach us about the experience of taking a word like *like* for granted? Conversely, how can *like* teach us about the experience of bodies flickering at varying speeds out of reliability, out of their own taken-for-grantedness? Philology, for me, names an affective circuit between this little word and a body whose relation to pain is like a sentence in which *like* suddenly doesn't disappear. What difference might it make to think about philology as the *like* (as opposed to love) of language? The philology I describe is a liking of words trained on the queer vibrations of *like* as it pulses in and out of legibility. As such, it suggests a way of thinking about the phenomenology of a word inhabiting itself as an analogy for thinking about how pain inhabits and is inhabited by a body—a body whose relations beyond itself are like a syntax where that little word *pain,* like *like,* only sometimes sinks below synapses.

"LIKE ME": DESIRE, AVERSION, APPROXIMATION

"There is a big secret about sex: most people don't like it." As far as pickup lines go, this one does something splashier and more deceptively vicious with the word *like* than one would think possible. Imagining a "kind of lightning thing about first sentences," Bersani recalls this opening to "Is the Rectum a Grave?" as the kernel for that essay's account of the "terror[s] of gay sex": It's "all connected," he notes, "to that aversion."[7] Even as this founding aversion resonates with Freud's "original aggression of the conscience," it's no less striking for the way it fails to observe the opening gambit's provocative blandness. Slightly differently put, and contra Facebook's recalibration of experience as a barrage of *likes,* Bersani's sentence illuminates the degree to which "most people"—a group that may or may not include *you or me*—might be less averse to sex than to the notion of *liking.* Even as we queer stalwarts flinch from what in *liking* feels over-safe, the rhetorical irresolvability of Bersani's proposition is an abrupt lesson in what he will eventually call the "dangers attached to the pastoralizing of any form of sexual relation."[8] This is to say that it's less clear at the outset if we are being asked to agree or disagree than that our doing so—all the more keenly in the context of the *October* AIDS issue in which the essay first appeared—might be a matter of life or death. Almost thirty years after the essay's first appearance, it seems easier to articulate a position on the government's handling of the AIDS crisis than on how one feels about liking or not liking the sex at that debate's rhetorical epicenter.[9]

For the rest of the first paragraph, Bersani teases the commutability of *like* and sex, the former's representational fugacity seeping from and through the latter like an object's shadow. "I don't have any statistics to back this up, and I doubt (although since Kinsey there has been no shortage of polls on sexual behavior) that any poll has ever been taken in which those polled were simply asked, 'Do you like sex?'" (3). The conversion of "most people don't like it" to "Do you like sex?" yields a question as overdetermined as the essay's title. The winking salaciousness with which Bersani channels Kinsey suggests with unquantifiably equivocal irony that his unwitting hypothetical test group is being asked a question equivalent in intrusiveness or implication to something taboo or (to apply one euphemism to another) questionable. "Nor am I suggesting," Bersani continues, "the need for any such poll, since people would probably answer the question as if they were being asked, 'Do you often feel the need to have sex?' and one of my aims will be to suggest why these are two wholly different questions" (3). The repetition of need from a matter of polls to one of sex rhetorically flags the oddness of anyone's supposing these wholly different questions commensurate. Liking sex, for instance, opens onto questions of *why* in ways not thinkable in the context of necessity. Bersani further complicates our hermeneutic handle on *liking* in repeating his hypothetical population's symptomatic translation of one set of terms into another. "In saying that most people don't like sex, I'm not arguing (nor, obviously, am I denying) that the most rigidly moralistic dicta about sex hide smoldering volcanoes of repressed sexual desire. When you make this argument, you divide people into two camps, and at the same time you let it be known to which camp you belong. . . . Rather, I'm interested in something else . . . which may be a certain *aversion*" (4). The underappreciated perversity of this opening paragraph's torques all the more foretells the inadequacy of our parsing of the essay's competing forms of aggressive and sacrificial subjectivities, so long as it treats *liking* as external or ancillary to it. This is no less true as we continue tracing the patterns of relation shared between one's more customary erotic economies and chronic pain. Bersani's turn to the rhetoric of necessity suggests as much, since asking about the feeling of necessity when it comes to sex invariably entails an ambient sense of necessity's temporal logic, the oftenness that liking (and not liking) sex impels.

The abjection that *like* is capable of inspiring when it *doesn't* disappear is evident in our collective introjection of Sally Field's 1985 Oscar speech. "This means so much more to me this time," Field mewls. "I don't know why, I think the first time I hardly felt it because it was all so new." Converting her acceptance of the award into a belated primal scene, Field's *Nachträglichkeit* notoriously continues, "The first time I didn't feel it, but this time I feel it, and I can't deny the fact that you *like* me, right now, you *like* me."[10] That we misremember that line as *you like me, you really like me* signals the profound extent to which we find Field's *liking* unbelievable. Field's last *like,* tearing in her throat like a banshee, figures the depths of affect to which we aversely respond. Her interpellation's drastic present tense collapses the futural space of illocutionary command into flat declaration of fact. It restages our, the audience's, captivity as sexual avarice: even as "we" had nothing to do with Field's win, we are the ones scripted as having taken (not once but twice) some version of Gidget's virginity. This is the bidirectional work, perforce, of *I cannot deny the fact.* Part of our uneasiness with Field has to do with the fact that her plea for being liked is asymmetrical to how we might respond. Even if we do or did like her, our liking just can't match her *like*'s ferocious melodrama. If Field's *liking* seems less fact than somewhat hysterical fiction, we might imagine it in terms of Bersani's earlier account of what he calls the Jamesian lie, a prevaricating unmoored from truth in its brazen wish for what it declares less to *be* than to *become* so. Our *like* aversion has less to do with being coerced into or misrepresented as liking than with the fear that we are latently capable of some analogous eruption. More lurid, that is, than liking Field is our wondering if our own hysterical fantasy of lack sounds or feels like hers.

To return to Bersani: the nonequivalence of "most people don't like [sex]" and sexual aversion invites us to take seriously the seemingly insipid, mercurial affective categories of liking and not liking alongside the lightning demonstrativeness of desire. Whatever difficulty we might have thinking about liking and not liking sex is compounded by *like*'s shrinking, self-vitiating withdrawal. After all, except when *liking* (in the manner of Sally Field) strikes us as embarrassingly tenacious, it more often registers weakly as insufficient response: to paraphrase one of our earliest lessons in the comedy of affection-as-analogic-system, *liking* is a Goldilocks that seldom lands on *just right.* Philology, following Roman Jakobson citing Nietzsche, slows our experience of *liking* down, like a Bill Viola photograph of emotion. It returns the word to us when it flits away too fast. Like the *like* of simile or the quotative (*Bersani was like, people don't like it*), some *likes* leave no fingerprints. Exemplarily, in a sentence such as *I was, like, happy,* investing in *like* is complicated by its near half-litotic divesting gesture. *Like,* here, might be loosely translated as "I was *something like happy,*" or to note how one Valley Girl idiom sluices into another, *I was happy, or whatever.*

Like unscrews the doorjambs of the objects it modifies. On the other side of Goldilocks, when *we* flit too quickly past *it*—when, in the manner of Bersani, *like* seems mostly ironic or euphemistic, or in the manner of Field, we squirm because it doesn't seem ironic *enough*—philology teaches us more patiently to sit with the squirm. The second clause of Bersani's salvo ventriloquizes the bourgeois reading public of which his essay is a critique, whose demurral of sex (*no thank you, I just had some,* as if sex were a serving of quinoa) is equally coextensive and at odds with the opening clause's Gothic shudder, "there is a big secret." In terms of the caricature Bersani asks us to imagine, the *pudeur* of "most people don't like it" suggests some outer valence of *politesse* predicated, as Foucault might say, on "a fragile treasure."[11] Bersani turns the repressive hypothesis out like a glove, his disdain (itself a refraction of "their" disdain) accruing in the word *like,* where we can almost hear his impersonation of the drive's disingenuously suburbanized disavowal. *Like,* that is, doesn't seem to be Bersani's word at all—hence the alacrity with which he converts it to "aversion." Or is it vice versa? What if the big secret of sex weren't its capacity to harbor aversion so much as our capacity for nondevastating erotic investment? Along these lines, we approach this *like* with the further ambivalence of not liking to think of ourselves as belonging to the bourgeois group that *like* inscribes any more than we know how to take Bersani's *like* nonironically. Frances Ferguson observes that "philology demanded that texts carry their identity papers on them."[12] Here, philologically speaking, *like* is the word with a feverish forehead, its papers least in order.

Is it possible to have a nonironic understanding of Bersani's *like*? Or is its euphemistic ring inexorable? On the one hand, *like* serves as a placeholder for the rage that's enlisted in the simultaneous maintenance and jeopardization of our fragile selves. On the other hand, there is the story of the twelve-year-old who doesn't like champagne: He may not like it now, but just you wait. *Not liking,* in that context, is the prerogative of persons who don't yet recognize *like* and *dislike* as ultimately untenable erotic categories. It is this very erotic implausibility of *like* that makes it so queerly promising. At its most emphatic, *liking* treats as endlessly stalled what usually is imagined as incremental—hence the filmic convention of liking (or disliking) someone as a step toward loving them. The perversity of liking involves inhabiting the transitional as though it were *hexis,* Aristotle's word for disposition, even as transition and disposition seem as superficially incompatible as Barthes's Neutral and desire. If sex were only unlikable, it wouldn't inspire the rage of the vicar who in Bersani's example threatened to kill his son if he were gay. And if it were only, merely, likable, a son thus threatened by his father might not risk gay sex at all. When the son notes that sometimes it seems his father would like to kill him regardless of his being or not being gay, the joke of *would like to kill him* recasts the vicar's rage as quotidian melodrama (5–6). The vicar's homophobic aversion is something the boy presumably encounters so often that it gets expressed not as a rupture of the everyday (which is how the vicar might construe his son's hypothetical coming out) but as the everyday itself. Something that is likable is take it or leave it. What if, beyond our aversion to sex, there brooded the possibility of desire as something we could take or leave? What if this low-grade attraction were somehow eloquent enough to circumnavigate the blasé feeling that often accompanies our regard for objects that we don't fear losing, to which we are capable of growing at least somewhat inured?

The somewhat-ness of *liking* is important. In the case of Bersani or Field, *like* doesn't quite meet our criteria for real feeling, even as it's unclear what it would mean to imagine it as hallucinatory. *Liking*'s challenge as insufficient delusion informs the tragicomedy of Stuart Smalley's daily affirmation, *I'm good enough, I'm smart enough, and doggone it, people like me.* Against the singularity of desire, the affirmation of *liking* (and, likewise, the affirmation that *liking* is) structurally inspires and perhaps even depends on this dailiness. That it could seem simultaneously dismissible and imperative illuminates the little word's sneaky, funny relation to desire. Take it or leave it: *liking* gives a different toehold in the lemming-edge of what Lauren Berlant calls cruel optimism: "What's cruel about these attachments, and not merely inconvenient or tragic, is that the subjects who have *x* in their lives might not well endure the loss of their object/scene of desire, even though its presence threatens their well-being, because whatever the *content* of the attachment is, the continuity of its form provides something of the continuity of the subject's sense of what it means to keep on living on and to look forward to being in the world."[13] *Liking,* as neither quite attaching nor disavowing, sidesteps this cruelty; its style of occupying the impasse between the poetics of attachment and disavowal corresponds to what Berlant elsewhere calls "a desire to sense nearness more than nextness."[14]

Like Anne-Lise François's theory of the open secret, *liking* is most vivid in its inconsequentiality, presenting "the formal problem of how to evaluate, recognize, and name a dramatic action so inconsequential it yields no *peripeteia* and seems to evade the Aristotelian definition of plot."[15] If *liking* at one end of its spectrum describes the inconsequential consequence of attending to what defies dramatic legibility, it suggests on the other a practice of holding free from a theory of object relations predicated on the opposed operations of clutching and letting go. In his essay "Experience," Emerson writes, "I take this evanescence and lubricity of all objects, which lets them slip through our fingers then when we clutch hardest, to be the most unhandsome part of our condition. Nature does not like to be observed, and likes that we should be her fools and playmates."[16] Alongside and against what nature likes and doesn't like, *liking* extends an Emersonian mode of clutching less hard, what Barthes ephectically invokes as the suspension of the will-to-possess.[17] Following Berlant, our response to Sally Field highlights the jangly misfit between *liking* and melodrama, between handling and clutching. It shouldn't be possible to want *liking* as much as Field proclaims. In a sense, Field's conjuring of a bottomless pit of shallow affect recalls the difficulty of imagining Barthes's desire for the Neutral. To ask if *liking* is really possible is to ask what *liking* in this psychical middle distance feels like. Philology in this Nietszchean mode is a discipline that teaches us what *liking* is like. Like other forms of queer phenomenology, it tests the inner edges and folds of a range of feelings we don't entirely know what to do with.

I've taken to italicizing *liking* as a way of marking the difference between the word and itself. That we hardly notice *like* when it's used as an adverb or conjunction makes it all the more likely we'll overlook it when it's used as a verb or noun. All the more so when *like,* as verb or noun, already and perhaps preemptively strikes us as an affective watering down. *Like*'s nugatory ubiquity stymies concordances and other digital humanities versions of word-sleuthing. For instance, entering *like* on the Ralph Waldo Emerson database is a no go, just as performing an MLA search for *like* yields so many workmanlike instantiations of the word that *like-as-subject,* like a needle, gets lost in the haystack. This is to say that despite the largely correct sense that digital humanities expands and equalizes philological accessibility, the parameters of digital engines likewise rearticulate little words like *like* as pebbles in philology's shoe, flies in its ointment. Our propensity for taking *like* for granted says something about its inclination toward the chronic. One encounters this chronicity in Eve Kosofsky Sedgwick's claim in *Tendencies* that "I 'love' the work that lets me like the world."[18] Liking the world, in this case, entails feeling just enough affection to survive our repeated encounters with it. Sedgwick's point salubriously reverses *like*'s usual temporality: liking, here, is the goal rather than precondition of love. What does it mean, when *liking* so often gets inscribed as affectively developmental, to imagine *liking* as constitutively self-sufficient?

I situate *like* in the context of accessibility and chronicity because philology, like chronic pain, wakes us from what in utility we normally take for granted. Not related, *likely* posits a belief in the continuity or cohesiveness of events, an epistemological comfort that pain and other contingencies interrupt—but only to a certain extent, since the rounded edges of *likely* swaddle it from disappointment in ways unavailable to more frangibly uncompromising prospective positions. I'm not yet sure of the difference between thinking about *like* in terms of disability versus thinking about *like* in terms of disability theory. Intuitively, I'm inclined to situate philology and *like* alike in the mirror that draws one to the other. Philology, conventionally understood, is a reconstructive project. It dreams, if not of an impossible textual origin, then of reparatively approximating textual completeness; to this end, it resembles our fantasy of bodies restored in the likeness of some delusively reliable anterior. Hence the aptness, in the context of the therapeutic and therapy-resistant energies of disability studies, of Jonathan Culler's remarks on philology: "There is in philology, then, a tension between the reconstructive project . . . and the valuable attention to what undermines the aesthetic and ideological assumptions about the meaning of texts on which reconstructive projects depend."[19] Or, in the words of Berlant: "This means that a poetics of attachment always involves some splitting off of the *story* I can tell about wanting to be near *x* . . . from the *activity* of the emotional habitus I have constructed. . . . To understand cruel optimism . . . one must embark on an analysis of indirection, which provides a way to think about the strange temporalities of projection into an enabling object that is also disabling."[20]

Ascertaining what is disabling about an enabling object entails approaching the story about the object that we tell ourselves as though it were a story we were reading rather than living. To recognize, that is, what is disabling about the object requires that the story itself be disabled for the sake of the lineaments of its storyness coming to the fore as aesthetic rather than what François might call the consequential elements of inhabited plot. The disabling suspension of the story—our "release from the ethical imperative to *act* upon knowledge"[21]—corresponds to what Culler calls philological attention. Ironically, the tension between attention and reconstruction most saliently arises in Culler's essay at the very moment that the notion of reconstruction is first introduced. "A second example might come from what has been a particularly impotant [*sic*] philological activity, the reconstruction of texts, the proposing of emendations, when texts seem as though they might be corrupt."[22] As a disability theorist, I like this ostensible typographical error, *impotance,* whose Derridean affinity with *différance* simultaneously signals what is both most impotent in and important to reconstruction's impossible fantasy.

In "Shame in the Cybernetic Fold," Sedgwick's collaborative essay with Adam Frank, Sedgwick quotes a long passage from Silvan Tomkins's *Affect Imagery Consciousness* whose "rhythms," Sedgwick notes, "remind one of Gertrude Stein's": "If you like to be looked at and I like to look at you, we may achieve an enjoyable interpersonal relationship. If you like to talk and I like to listen to you talk, this can be mutually rewarding. . . . If you like to be kissed and I like to kiss you, we may enjoy each other. . . . If you wish to be like me and I wish to have you imitate me, we can enjoy each other."[23] *Liking* is like enjoyment and is sometimes, it would seem, interchangeable with if not equivalent to it. The pleasure that Tomkins's lines seem to take in themselves furthermore suggests that liking not only inspires or comes to fruition as reciprocity (*you like to be kissed and I like to kiss you*) but that it's tacitly but happily responsive to the structures of affection invoked in the proliferation of *liking* as a lexical object. There's something so molecular in *liking*'s facilitation of other positive affects that it's not implausible to imagine its atomism participating in negative affects as well.

"Like writing," Lee Edelman writes, "homographesis would name a double operation."[24] *Like writing and homographesis, liking likewise names a double operation.* "By exposing the non-coincidence of what appears to be the same," *liking,* like homographesis, like writing, "confounds the security of the distinction between sameness and difference."[25] More often than not, however, *like* is neither affective nor mimetic so much as constructively transparent. The routinized industry of *likely* and *like* challenges our capacity to discern texture or interest in forms to which we are ever increasingly habituated. In the manner of what John Ashbery, discussing Stein's *Stanzas in Meditation,* calls that poem's colorless connecting words,[26] *like* is especially vivid in Stein's stanzas when it is *least* connective: "It is a difference in which I send alike / In which instance which. / I wish to say this. / That here now it is like / Exactly like this. / I know how exactly like this."[27] Stein's *Stanzas* refuse syntactical hierarchies, and in doing so stage lexical interaction between words such as *like* (and *which, often,* etc.) as though they were approaching each other on the moon. It's not just that *Stanzas* is almost entirely composed of pronouns and conjunctions, but that Stein gives these units equal standing as their grippier, more colorful grammatical counterparts. *Stanzas* treats its words as though their outer electron valences bore identical ionic charges. To return to Bersani, it's not, for instance, that aggression doesn't exist in *Stanzas,* but that it has no more attractively aggressing pull than anything else. As Stein writes, "It is not often that they are always right / It is not often that they are always right / But which aggression or a guess / Or please addition or please a question. / Or please or please or please."[28]

Stein's equalizing poetics of liking suggests the challenges of philologically slow reading. Indeed, Werner Hamacher's "95 Theses on Philology," like Tomkins, sounds most Steinian when it woos us into thinking of philology as the like, rather than love, of language: "Philology can only like and like itself, because it is *not* philology itself that likes and that it likes. It is each time another that likes, each time another that is liked. Thus it will even like its dislike and its being disliked."[29] Philology, like sex, redistributes active and passive implication only to find the differences between them unsustainable. Or, as Stein writes, "I have been and have been amounted to it. / When they come in and come in and out. / Naturally it is not. / Or however not a difference between like and liked."[30]

"AS IF HE WERE AIR": LIKENESS AS HORIZON

Stein's and Hamacher's echo chamber articulations of *like* help me appreciate what happens to the word when it's returned, as it were, to the wild. *Like,* as good enough grammatical mother or transitional object, brings a simile's vehicle into contact with tenors it could hardly otherwise imagine, which usually results in *like*'s attenuation to the point where the contours of its usefulness nearly disappear in the figurative allongé it helps to choreograph. More than any other author I can think of, Herman Melville treats the word *like,* even when it behaves grammatically as it should, as a word resistant to disappearing into its function. Along these lines, Melville constructs analogies with the Byzantine fastidiousness of someone setting traps. The extravagance with which persons and things in Melville's texts are like and unlike other things recalls in its overdetermined relation to irony the perversity of Bersani's "most people don't like it." Melville's particular brand of this irony highlights the difference between reading a story as though it were the plot one inhabits and reading as a practice of aesthetic attention. The implications of Melville's deployment of *like* reach an apotheosis in "Bartleby," whose theorization of *like* is coextensive with its eponymous character's coming across as consequentially inconsequential in a way that suggests that the embodiment of *liking* and what Barthes calls desire for Neutral and what in the context of Culler I call *impotance* are sometimes one and the same.

Before turning to "Bartleby," let's consider the masterly involutions of *like* and *unlike* in a passage from "Benito Cereno" in which its hazardously naive American sea captain first espies a Spanish ship recently undone by slave revolt: "With no small interest, Captain Delano continued to watch her—a proceeding not much facilitated by the vapors partly mantling the hull, through which the far matin light from her cabin streamed equivocally enough; much like the sun—by this time hemisphered on the rim of the horizon, and apparently, in company with the strange ship, entering the harbor—which, wimpled by the same low, creeping clouds, showed not unlike a Lima intriguante's one sinister eye peering across the Plaza from the Indian loop-hole of her dusk *saya-y-manta.*"[31] That Delano as a character is entirely incapable of this hair-raisingly extravagant comparison is of a piece with the text's meditation on hermeneutic inaccessibility. The passage is notable for its proliferation of details without discriminating between what in the accretion of specificity Delano overlooks that might shed light on the plot's unfolding and what, "equivocally enough," indicates on the part of the narrator less perspicuity than ingeniousness. The elaboration of how the matin light streams, at least as relates to questions of plot (in terms of both the story Melville has written and the script produced in the wake of the revolt to which the story's titular character is beholden), is less illuminating than it might initially seem. It is not enough to distinguish Delano's inability to see the loophole from our corresponding ability to do so, since these details, less informative than descriptive, less speak to the analogy's vehicle than are self-illuminating. The stakes of this passage acquire clarity in our noting that the answer to *what is going on here?* lies somewhere between *I don't know* and *nothing,* which aptly enough describes Bartleby's perplexing range of inactivity.

Throughout the text's first half, it is in Delano's fumbling relation to *like* that the semblance of plot, eluding his grasp, swerves into narrative description. That *like* lies beyond Delano's field of vision is borne out in his final conversation with Benito Cereno, whose unappeasability following the revolt is as incomprehensible to Delano as the revolt itself:

> "But the past is passed; why moralize upon it? Forget it. See, yon bright sun has forgotten it all, and the blue sea, and the blue sky; these have turned over new leaves."
>
> "Because they have no memory," he dejectedly replied; "because they are not human."
>
> "But these mild trades that now fan your cheek, do they not come with a human-like healing to you? Warm friends, steadfast friends are the trades." (116)

Delano's near equivocation between persons and personification—"mild[ly] trade[d]" back and forth—hinges on *like*'s alchemizing of the sea wind's salubriousness as human-like and, less directly, a person's corresponding commensuration with the "steadfast[ness]" of winds in the sails. If he could inhabit the world with as much anthropomorphic ingenuity as the world itself, so Delano muses, Don Benito might remember less tenaciously the scene he's just barely escaped. The combinatory work of likeness to which the pirate horizon pays homage exhorts, for Delano, the value of turning "over new leaves," as though the blue sea were discovering the blueness of sky for the first time. And yet it's Don Benito, haunted and stalled, who appears sky-like at this exchange's close, "unconsciously gathering his mantle about him" like the sky gathering its "grey surtout" of clouds (46), or the *intriguante* whose *saya-y-manta,* our narrator avers, is dusk itself.

Melville wrestles with *like*'s fever dream throughout his career, as though sensing the word shining a light on his work without quite reaching the force of illumination. For instance, just moments before Billy Budd fatefully strikes Claggart, the latter's eyes, "those lights of human intelligence, losing human expression, were gelidly protruding like the alien eyes of certain uncatalogued creatures of the deep."[32] In this interval between the actual and imaginary, *like* marks the shifting of free indirect discourse, the sentence's turn to simile betrays in advance of Billy's pugilist hand the hand of a narrator capable of brandishing this astonishing science-fictional comparison. As a semaphore for perception's migration from one consciousness into another, the pivot of *like* is instrumental to the novella's more general theorization of indirection. "But for the adequate comprehending of Claggart by a normal nature," Melville writes, "these hints are insufficient. To pass from a normal nature to him one must cross 'the deadly space between.' And this is best done by indirection" (74). As in "Benito Cereno," the eschewal in *Billy Budd* of what Barbara Johnson in the context of this last passage calls "referential validity"[33] attests to Melville's sustained fascination with ontologies of *being like.* We find in the latter an anachronistic origin story for the volatile enunciating frames that pepper Valley Girl dialect. After all, if free indirect discourse deprives utterance of its enunciating frame, and if as Lynn Huffer suggests it is neither as direct as "She said, 'I love you'" nor explicitly indirect as "She said she loved her," *she was like, I love you* seems surprisingly adequate.[34] We'll return to Valley Girl shortly.

A few lines following Claggart's gelid alien eyes, we fall into the narrator's description of Billy's tortured face "like that of a condemned vestal priestess in the moment of being buried alive, and in the first struggle against suffocation" (99). Comparison, here, is fatal. There's something not right about the air we breathe: either there's not enough of what we'd taken for granted or it's been replaced with something else, as when we are told that Billy, hygienically apprehensive of apprehension, is "like a young horse fresh from the pasture suddenly inhaling a vile whiff from some chemical factory, and by repeated snortings trying to get it out of his nostrils and lungs" (84). *Like* is like air that only sometimes distinguishes itself from itself. In this sense, and with a feel for philology's resonance with chronic pain, Dickinson's "After great pain a formal feeling comes" provides an exemplary instance of *like*'s queer capacity to resemble itself. I'm thinking of the line "A Quartz contentment, like a stone."[35] In the manner of chemical equations, "quartz" and "stone" nearly balance each other out, leaving us with the inner geode of "contentment like." How is contentment like a redundant analogy (quartz's likeness to a stone foreclosed by its already being one)? What can the pivoting, contentless content of "like" teach us about pain and the formal feeling?

We've been thinking about *liking* in the context of Billy Budd, who is liked by everyone ("like hornets to treacle") except the one whose dislike belies a case of liking too much. Billy's stutter, as many have noted, is anticipated by Bartleby's tic. No less than the stutter, however, "I would prefer not to" anticipates the penchant of *Billy Budd*'s narrator for flagging his orchestrative presence with like-comparisons: as he says of the stutter, "one way or another he is sure to slip in his little card" (53). Like that narrator's *like,* "I would prefer not to" marks the text's deciduous retreat if not from itself than from us. And just as *Billy Budd* seems to map the consequences of like-as-analogic-system onto the narrator's simiIetic acumen, the meditation on analogic affection in "Bartleby" is inextricable from *that* narrator's correspondingly maladroit capacity for comparisons.

I would prefer not to most saliently bears a relation to liking in the former's resistance to being translated into the latter. "Now what sort of business," the lawyer asks, "would you like to engage in? . . . Would you like a clerkship in a dry-goods store? . . . Would you like to travel through the country collecting bills for the merchants?" (41). Bartleby does not like any of these things. He is, as he tells the nonplussed lawyer, *not particular.* His lack of preference is a crop circle ingrained on the field of feeling, and it's only in the context of Bartleby's disinclination—something akin to one's fatigued perception in Stein's *Stanzas* of sedulous nonaggression—that the lawyer's *like* acquires a legible heft of which *like* itself usually falls short. Along these lines, the asymptotic crystallization of Bartleby's colorless words—the extent to which Melville's story serves as the archive of an otherwise unintelligible utterance—inversely corresponds to Bartleby's own sublimatingly airlike self-dispersal. "I might enter my office in a great hurry," the lawyer notes, "and pretending not to see Bartleby at all, walk straight against him as if he were air" (35). Each successive iteration of "I would prefer not to" falls between lawyer and Bartleby like a "dead brick wall" (28) or "dim window" (32). To complete the simile in this way, however—the wall, the window—falsifyingly gives Bartleby more shape than he actually has. It would be more accurate to say that each successive iteration of "I would prefer not to" (again, despite *not* being equivalent to *liking*) falls like *like*, like a simile whose vehicle and tenor have been snuffed out.

Attempts to complete the simile repeat the lawyer's miscarried collations of Bartleby and the objects to which he is metonymically but not metaphorically propinquitous. The lawyer's comparisons say less about the character they seek to illuminate than they do his own epistemological fluster. In this respect, they inversely correspond to the ways that the comparisons of *Billy Budd* say less about Claggart and Billy than they do that narrator's seductive charisma. "Dead letters!" exclaims the narrator of "Bartleby": "does it not sound like dead men?" (45). Although this syllogism is slightly less ridiculous than that of Bartleby and the ginger-nuts, we should note all the same that a text hinging on the impossible translation of preference into likes ends with the impossible translation of one likeness into another. The lawyer's trafficking in *like,* as simultaneously affective and analogous, is not coincidental. His question—*does it not sound like dead men?*—returns us to Edelman's homographs, which sound alike without being so. And to the extent that the lawyer's acoustic attention (to words that sound alike rather than concepts that resemble each other) signals a specifically etymological fantasy, we might well imagine "Bartleby" as a text about the vicissitudes of philology. Hamacher writes that "where ontology stalls, philology moves."[36] Along such lines, a philological project surely circulates around the stalled ontology that is the scrivener. The relation between stalled ontology and philology defined as the stalling or ephexis of interpretation returns us, perhaps unsurprisingly, to the neutrality of liking. This stalling of ontology reminds me of Barthes's suggestion, via Blanchot, that "the exigency of the neutral tends to suspend the attributive structure of language: < 'it's this, that'>."[37] *Like* is the ghost in the machine that ephectically converts "it's this" into "it's like this" (or in the manner of Valley Girl, *it's, like, this*), the metaphorical instantaneousness of being becoming the similetic indefiniteness of analogy incapable of closing the distance of approximation, no matter how hard we try.

DROWNING IMAGE: DEGENERACY AND DETACHMENT

The lawyer's unsuccessful attempt at forcing Bartleby's preferences into the deeper (less *neutral*) shade of liking has everything to do with the lawyer's wish to restoratively fix language (Bartleby's and his own) along an axis of utility: which words *do* something versus which ones degeneratively take up space, parodically pantomiming lexical function? Whether in Stein's *Stanzas* or Dickinson's quartz contentment, the insubordinate affirmation of *like* erodes our prejudicial understanding of function itself. If degeneration is the trope by which linguists have historically figured the deleterious effects on language of the word *like*—treating the latter as expression of Whitman's reprobative loafer's temperament, "Suchlike I love"[38]—the rhetorical industry of *like*'s studied indolence reaches an apogee in the extravagant vacuity of Valley Girl, whose perseverative *like* strains toward inertia, deceptively industrious as the word's syncopated repetitions prove. Take, for instance, Moon Unit Zappa's 1982 song "Valley Girl," which lampoons the Valley Girl's like-as-tic as a compulsive symptom. On account of permission issues, I can only refer to the song's lyrics (the prospective citation of which the Zappa Family Trust has met with exasperating pertinacity). Zappa's lyrics are ready-made clichés of lexical malaise and labor, or in Michael Fried's terms, absorption and theatricality. If in the case of Claggart's sea-monster eyes, *like* marks a switch point between observation and abstraction, the Valley Girl's *like,* as performed by Zappa, is a switch point between talking to others and talking to one's self. Whereas a lyric poem, generically speaking, is encountered by its reader as though it were being overheard, Valley Girl utterance invites us via *like* to listen. I was at first inclined to describe *like* as an eavesdropper's glass held up to a door, but this is wrong. We don't need to eavesdrop on a Valley Girl, because not only does she seem to want us to hear, she seems to want us (however rudimentarily) to *understand. Like* is the gratuitous form of clarification without its content, an explicating lagniappe analogous to the Frenchman's macaronic *how you say.* As Barbara Johnson writes of D. A. Miller's account of Barthes, "It is emphatic about an expression that may not be exact. . . . Barthes, the elusive object, has to be pursued in the vicinity of bad translation."[39] *How you say,* that is, like *like,* is a "convention adopted by English speakers to put an expression in quotation marks."[40]

For its first two verses, the song's eponymous speaker—she tells us her name is Ondrya Wolfson—conforms to our received sense of both a Valley Girl's range of "interests" and the disaffection with which she riffles through them. We ought perhaps to say, however, that our expectations for a Valley Girl's affective/aesthetic repertoire conform to *it,* given the song's missionary hand in spreading the allure of this persona's listlessness across the country via Zappa's performance of it on *Solid Gold*. Like Warhol's silkscreens, the cartoonishness of Zappa's channeling of Wolfson makes subsequent impersonations easy if not inevitable. While the lyrics' mention of miniskirts and the Galleria suggest that these are her nominal interests, Wolfson's tone never quite rises to the level of interest per se. If Wolfson is a creature of late capitalism, it's as though the energy expended in her routinized flatline of acquisition is just about all she can muster. When Wolfson relates to us the time some guy asked her if she was into S&M, her response, moving from curtailment ("yeah right") back to the sartorial (incredulously daring us to picture her in a leather teddy), registers blasé less as libidinal blockage than erotic disposition in its own right. Her bored scoffing at this guy's perversity turns in the third verse to analogously derisive gossip about the perversity, as chance would have it, of her English teacher, to whom she refers as "Mr. Bu-fu" and "Lord God King Bu-fu." In the simultaneously theatrical and quasi-somnambulist unspooling of her soft attention, Wolfson recounts how this English teacher does nothing but flirt with the male students in his class. Recalling Bartleby's absorbing suspension of industry, Mr. Bu-fu's sleeping or not sleeping with men matters less, in Wolfson's account, than the seeming torpor of—how you say—his sleeping on the job.

Mr. Bu-fu, who calls to mind the "too pretty" Monsieur O. at the anal-erotic center of Sedgwick's "A Poem Is Being Written," is sustained by and dissolved in *like*'s mechanical reproducibility (his flirting, as told by Wolfson, consists of, "like, play[ing]" with his rings, a dandy's version of twiddling thumbs). Like the throbbing give-and-take of enjambment through which Sedgwick's identification with Monsieur O. is felt, Wolfson's *likes* generate the rhythm through which her interest in pedagogical flirtation pulses between grossed out and engrossed. But again, even her capacity for aversion is overstated, the verse's concluding "gag me with a spoon" implying disgust so vitiated that even it has to be initiated by something else. In the context of her own terminal acedia,[41] we might imagine Wolfson's interest in Mr. Bu-fu in terms of the confusability of intellectual work itself, the difficulty and as often impossibility of demarcating when or where doing nothing, lucubratively speaking, yields some new flint of substance. Here, Zappa's song anticipates the already obsolescent joke of professors spending their time liking things on Facebook. What does it mean to waste time liking? How has this formulation even become possible? Even more suggestive in terms of an earlier moment's erstwhile dallying with Facebook competitors, what did it mean that I felt the pang of not being able to like something on Ello (itself, of course, already obsolescent, a ready-made relic of the virtual age), like liking were the feeling of a phantom limb?

In an essay on Andy Warhol's practice of collecting, Jonathan Flatley cites a moment from an interview in which Warhol brings together his interest in like-as-resemblance and like-as-affection. "Everybody looks alike and acts alike," Warhol says. "I think everybody should like everybody. . . . [Pop Art] is [about] liking things."[42] Flatley notes that in "play[ing] with the multiple meanings of 'like,' 'alike,' and 'liking' . . . Warhol appears to be suggesting that the apprehension of similarity . . . is the condition of possibility for affective affiliation" (73). While Flatley goes on to note Warhol's collections of cookie jars, ray-gun toys, and Twomblies, it bears repeating that one of the things that Warhol most lavishly collects in this passage is the word *like* itself. If, following Flatley's reading of Warhol alongside Benjamin, "the basic move for the collector . . . is detaching the object from its original functional relations" (80), then part of the pleasure in Warhol's fussing with the word *like* arises from its capacity to install itself within the collection it syntactically curates while retreating to the security of arranging function.[43] Unlike love, which conventionally depends on exclusion and singularity, *like* is amenable to aggrandizing and becomes more itself, not less, in its multiplying. This is to say that *like,* unlike love, follows a principle of number rather than intensity. Across Warhol's terrain of *likes,* it's less possible to glean whether one thing is liked more or less than others than that liking is inspired not to like more deeply so much as qualitatively *more.* If Sally Field's Oscar speech is partly risible, then, it is because she seems to treat *like* as though it *were* singular—to return to her troping of virginity and first times, as though being liked were special in ways the word can't always promise.

Flatley quotes Rupert Smith's observation that "the pleasure of collecting [is] the act of acquisition" (82), but I think that the pleasure of collecting has as much to do with our reexperience of otherwise useful objects removed from utility. Collectible objects, that is, aren't used; they're appreciated. Warhol not only treats the word *like* like a thing but as a collectible. He shares this predilection with Stein, Melville, and Hamacher. Again, what makes Hamacher most sound like Stein in a line like "Philology can only like and like itself, because it is *not* philology itself that likes and that it likes"[44] involves the sentence's curation of *like* as collectibly alluring. The pleasure of experiencing words as they're catechized out of utility into aesthetic appreciation speaks to my recent thinking about philology. As earlier suggested, this catechism is crucial to my understanding of disability and chronic pain.

Walter Benjamin's 1931 essay "Unpacking My Library" vouches for the mutual interlineation of disability—in particular, disability's relation to time—and the avidity of a collector amid their objects. "For what else is this collection but a disorder to which habit has accommodated itself to such an extent that it can appear as order? You have all heard of people whom the loss of their books has turned into invalids."[45] If the accretive principle of collecting is made possible through the simultaneous operation and vanishment of *like*, this chapter has retroactively found itself drawn to the chiastic appearance of *like* in those moments at which disability, however peripherally or abstrusely, most resembles collecting. Benjamin's words for disorder and order, *Unordnung* and *Ordnung*, urge us to imagine the labor of habit (itself fading into a reflexive instantaneity taught through time)—that is, the work of chronicity—as that which allows not only illness to pass as health or aesthetic entropy to pass as system, but that which allows the ordeal of ungovernable distress to pass as one's only perceptible dictum. At the same time, how we reconcile disorder and order's respective and overlapping saturations no less depends on the passage's curious tacitness when it comes to the undecided matter of appearing for *whom*, since how a collector views their collection can't in advance be made equivalent to how the collection might be viewed by the world at large.

The body in pain collects itself, as pain collects in the body's infrastructure. That a collector in the absence of his books risks becoming an invalid hints at an affinity such as that shared between a person and their dog. The compositional practice of collecting having removed its specimens from circulation, the collector's experience of (or, perhaps, startling inexperience with) books out of order or beyond reach displacingly removes the collector from themselves—no longer where they might be found (recollected), no longer ready-at-hand. As briefly discussed in an earlier section of *Contingent Figure*, my appreciation of this aesthetic scene of disability is indebted to Maurice Blanchot's rewriting of Heidegger's tool.[46] I remember feeling the same surprising recognition upon encountering Blanchot's pages as I felt, fumbling toward and through a language for queerness other than the long, unspeakable childhood of dread and shame, first reading *Epistemology of the Closet:* here was a text that described chronic pain in a language adequate to its vivid and confounding rigor and, concomitantly, here was the reorienting readerly gratitude of likeness where one had least expected it. As it happens, Blanchot's account of the utensil itself arises from a meditation on the sorts of resemblances at the heart of *liking:*

> Each man, in the rare moments when he shows a similarity to himself, seems to be only more distant, close to a dangerous neutral region, *astray* in *himself,* and in some sense his own ghost. . . .
>
> By analogy, we can also recall that a utensil, once it has been damaged, becomes its own *image* (and sometimes an esthetic object: "those outmoded, fragmented, unusable, almost incomprehensible, perverse objects" that André Breton loved). In this case, the utensil, no longer disappearing in its use, *appears.* The appearance of the object is that of resemblance and reflection: one might say it is its double. The category of art is linked to this possibility objects have of "appearing," that is, of abandoning themselves to pure and simple resemblance behind which there is nothing—except being. Only what has surrendered itself to the image appears, and everything that appears is, in this sense, imaginary.[47]

Blanchot's account of the "dangerous neutral region" of resemblance anticipates Paul de Man's claim that "the mind 'is' to the extent that it 'is like' its other in its inability to be."[48] Stranded by and within the likeness of analogy between image, object, and (sometimes) esthetic object, man's "similarity to himself," for Blanchot, occurs in "rare moments" into which chronic pain indefinitely (incomprehensibly, perversely) settles. At the same time, when it comes to the putative ephemerality of man's self-haunting, the passage's opening insistence on short-livedness—that such episodes occur as moments, and rare ones at that—rests so curiously beside the implicit temporal prolonging of "astray" that we might say man's experience of being "perfectly like himself" (421) is known through, as, the keen discrepancy between the two.

It befalls the unsteady, like-making alchemy of analogy to stitch a person's straying to the ensuing passage's account of damage, the irreversibility of which would seem to last without end if not beyond time itself (at least what time had been). Recalling a different line from "After great pain a formal feeling comes," the spectrality of time surrendering and surrendered—the self *as* phantom pain—echoes the questioning stupefaction of "Yesterday, or Centuries Before?" But I would be remiss in my ongoing attachment to the resemblance between queer disability aesthetics and nineteenth-century American literature not to point out the debt of Blanchot's "dangerous neutral region," the difference it splits between the imaginary and more conventionally robust forms of material being, to Hawthorne's remarks on Romance toward the end of "The Custom House":

> Nothing is too small or too trifling to undergo this change, and acquire dignity thereby. A child's shoe; the doll, seated in her little wicker carriage; the hobby-horse;—whatever, in a word, has been used or played with, during the day, is now invested with a quality of strangeness and remoteness, though still almost as vividly present as by daylight. Thus, therefore, the floor of our familiar room has become a neutral territory, somewhere between the real world and fairy-land, where the Actual and the Imaginary may meet, and each imbue itself with the nature of the other. Ghosts might enter here, without affrighting us.[49]

This chapter began with an account of liking as a form of aesthetic affection somewhere between Kantian interest and Adornian detachment. To be dissolved in this aesthetic affection is to become aesthetic. This becoming informs the reciprocity of Tomkins's *I like this and you like this* or Hamacher's and Stein's interest in liking and being liked, and, conversely, the nonreciprocity of Sally Field's acceptance speech. *Liking* as ghost-making refraction suggests what sometimes is at stake, vis-à-vis Bersani, in the aesthetics of liking sex. This is what I thought I was writing about, but chronic pain, like a broken tool, doesn't displace a painless body with a friable one—the two are coterminous.[50] The pulsation of philology involves an analogous doubling of two versions of what only reductively could be called the same word, and it's in this spirit that this chapter sometimes feels like it's diaphanously trailing itself. Differently put, there are at least two *likes* in these pages. Whether in its queer capacity for affection or similarity, the first one is so absorbed by the grammatical system it brings into being that we are almost startled when this otherwise indistinguishable second *like* absorbs the words around *it;* or perhaps these words, dissolving into themselves, leave us face-to-face with an indissolubility withdrawn from the capacities with which it's ordinarily charged. Almost startled rather than startled, since like the narrator of "Bartleby" we are unaccustomed to so arresting a banality. This *like* is patient, as Dickinson writes, like a pain. Its aesthetic intractability brings me nearer the Dickinson line already quoted, which I've been contemplating for some time: "After great pain a formal feeling comes." It's not that the pain is replaced with a formal feeling. In the wake of pain, the formal feeling of aesthetic being appears, which only wishfully is equivalent to the pain having gone away.

3. "The Vision – pondered long"

Chronic Pain and the Materiality of Figuration

> Thus, in the case of a consciousness of reading which is accompanied by an ocular pain . . . it is only beneath the gaze of reflection that it can appear as such and henceforth be known and named as a "pain of the eyes." Nevertheless, of itself such a pain is not different from the consciousness of reading; it is its very Being, the "translucent matter of consciousness."
>
> —MICHEL HENRY, *THE ESSENCE OF MANIFESTATION*

> Perhaps there is only ever a phenomenology of figures: readings not theory, readings that respond to the force of such figures in action.
>
> —IAN BALFOUR, "FIGURES IN EXCESS AND THE MATTER OF INVERSION IN THE DISCOURSE OF THE SUBLIME"

I'd like to propose a variation in our customary thinking about the relation between the notion of Dickinsonian pain and the epistemologically deceptive undertow of vantage as it shapes those elements of inquiry it professes only to stage. For instance: when it comes to those poems that seem most keenly moored in pain, to what extent is our impression of their difficulty informed by some inkling of an ulterior distance—in Sharon Cameron's words, the "outlandishness of their extremity"[1]—from which the affliction at hand seems to operate? To what extent, that is, does our appraisal of these textuary scenes of hurt presuppose an understanding of inscrutability's distancing retreat from the ordinary?[2] In contrast to the terrain of estrangement these questions imply, this chapter is premised on a belief in the peculiar responsiveness of Dickinsonian pain, however biographically or otherwise understood, to being thought *with,* alongside, even as the work of this chapter's articulation of disability theory will be in part to query just these physical and figurative parameters of poetic constraint.[3]

Frequently as critics have interpreted Dickinson's elliptically harrowing texts along the lines of grief, distress, and loss, fewer have been drawn in a sustained way to the affinity between the specifically figurative dimensions of this psychical archive and those aspects of suffering associated with, if not summarily reduced to, autobiography's physical object-world. It's in the face of this disparity that I've come to understand Dickinson's intimacy with chronic pain—its fitful hydraulic between the wakefulness of poetic aperture and an unreliable body's arresting attention—as that which catechizes her feel for the rich, unremitting breakage by which her poetry's figurative universe is drawn.[4] Lest one assume more broadly that pain's conversance with this lexical ecology is an effect merely of its poetic inscription, allow me to clarify my sense that a figurative idiom as vividly mercurial as Dickinson's might be uniquely suited to articulating chronic pain's phenomenal field to the extent that her experience of the latter is shot through with a figurative capacity in its own right; they learn from, or at least live with, each other. Like a single repeating bead in Emerson's "train of moods," a glitch or broken record, pain's perpetual mood may thus be said to "paint the world [its] own hue." Inscribed above pain's Sisyphean gate might be this next line from Emerson, in a particularly Dickinsonian vein: *from the mountain you see the mountain.*[5]

From the shadows of foreboding to an aftermath never quite distinct enough from the event itself, the murkiness of this interval is stitched into Dickinson's life as a poet, an unsettled sharpening of awareness that spurs no less than interrupts her most moving work. And yet critical disinterest in this crisis is such that explorations of Dickinson's remarkable industry across this period usually depict it—more glancingly, as it were, than not—as "eye trouble," and leave it at that. As Thomas H. Johnson writes in his 1955 biography, "In the autumn of 1863 began the trouble with her eyes, which bothered her to such an extent that by late April 1864 she was compelled to spend some weeks under a physician's care, in Boston. . . . The condition of her eyes made imperative her return to Boston for a similar period of time in the following year."[6] Both Johnson and subsequent critics rely on what scant textual evidence may be found, but there is less material than one might hope, not least because the strain on her eyes increasingly leaves Dickinson unable to read or write with her accustomed fervor. In an oft-cited June 1864 letter to T. W. Higginson, Dickinson writes, "I was ill since September, and since April, in Boston, for a Physician's care—He does not let me go, yet I work in my Prison, and make Guests for myself." She ends the letter asking if Higginson "can . . . render [her] Pencil," as "the Physician has taken away my Pen."[7] The anguish running through her Boston correspondence embellishes and refracts the nonplussment inherent to the ailment itself. In the spiral of poetic industry giving way to a malady experienced as writing trouble, the uncanny doubling of writerly distress and ongoing affliction pressures us to reassess as constitutive what would otherwise seem merely coincident.

Contra Johnson, Dickinson's time away from Amherst appears to have lasted not weeks but months, from April 1864 to the end of November, and then from April 1865 to sometime in October. For the duration, her treatment was supervised by Dr. Henry Willard Williams, first ophthalmic surgeon at Boston City Hospital and eventually chair of Harvard's newly formed Department of Ophthalmology. As Donald L. Blanchard notes in an article for the American Medical Association, "no record survives of any diagnosis of her condition during her lifetime."[8] However Dickinson's ailment is imagined let alone named, her Boston correspondence proves a stark measure of its debilitating effects, an eloquence all the more ironically striking in the record's paucity. "I have been sick so long," Dickinson writes, "I do not know the Sun" (L296). It's practically impossible to know whether or not surgery was performed on Dickinson's eyes,[9] just as it's impossible to rule out for however many years complications may have followed. One is left wondering for how long her physician ordered Dickinson to wear blindfolds in bright light when, spending so much time in the dim indoors, she writes to Susan in June 1864, "I knew it was 'November,' but then there is a June" (L292). And one can only guess for how long Dickinson needed to be led by the arm when she writes in another letter that, "the Doctor says I must tell you that I 'cannot yet walk alone'" (L295). When it comes to these and similar inquiries, to say that the correspondence won't tell is an understatement. After all, one acclimates to chronic pain, however ambivalently; in the idiom of contemporary medicine's corporatized rhetoric, one supposedly learns *to manage it.* Whether therapeutic hook or crook avails any form of relief, one unwittingly ceases to remark upon what no longer seems remarkable. Notwithstanding the lesser portion of her Boston correspondence, the quotidian of Dickinson's epistolary practice occupies her days regardless of questions of travel. The relative volume of this archive is critical to understanding the scale of the challenge of distinguishing how little Dickinson's letters reference pain on account of its invariant intensity from how little it's referenced because of its remission.[10]

I raise this point as a way of forestalling the assumption that when Dickinson returns from her second trip to Boston in October 1865, her subsequent epistolary quiet on the matter necessarily means her eyes are cured. In the absence of further evidence, it's unclear as to whether she felt "healed," then or ever, or able to return to the industry of poetic insight without enduring it—simultaneously, anxiously—as a pang. After such excruciating, extended worry over the possibility of losing sight altogether, after how long is one able to see again without needing to stifle the former, habitual apprehension that one is going blind, that the blindness so often worried about would permanently return? While the absence of a diagnosis isn't equivalent to there having been none, it's reasonable to surmise that for at least some span of time, Dickinson's debility eluded both her doctor's interpretive efforts and her own. Without a sense of either its internal principle or the chance of its eventual subsiding, how could Dickinson not experience the crisis of her ailment as an unremittingly hermeneutic no less than corporal conundrum? In this sense, her life writ large comes to resemble a puzzle in the grain of her poem's major idiom. I mean in particular to suggest a kindred element shared between the lived deliberations of chronic illness and the figurative brilliance that unfurls, wavelike, from her effort to cozen into further being—resolving, calibrating, if not stopping (in the manner of a photographic bath)—the event with which her lyric experiments are obliquely continuous. To wit: if the figurative mettle of her poetry's sternest (from the Old English *starian,* "to look or gaze upon") inquiries seems most to matter in its navigation between some former realism's exhaustion and the rarefying fiddlement in its wake, it's no less unthinkable when it comes to chronic pain's strain on the physical itself—bearing down, as Allen Tate might suggest, on the body's own broken machinery[11]—that some commensurable interfulgence subsists in what is left behind. From where "formula had failed" to this latter "formal feeling," figuration halts somewhat between pain's own dispositional means and our exasperating effort to better, less painfully, habit it.

Taken together, the above claims point to a simple but defining aspect of Dickinson's experience of this wearing event: her eye trouble renders vision and pain coincident. Whether in relation to the atrocities of the Civil War or our own present era, it might seem to go without saying that bearing witness can feel like an agony. The strain of seeing that follows Dickinson to Boston and back calls into clarity, however, a more peculiar duress inherent to optics itself. That wakeful attention (irrespective of interlinked economies of empathy or sentiment) could be pain-inducing independent of the object in view conjures a grim corollary to Emerson's account of a transparent eyeball's elating sense of empowerment. "There," Emerson's 1836 *Nature* euphorically reports, "I feel that nothing can befall me in life,—no disgrace, no calamity, (leaving me my eyes,) which nature cannot repair."[12] Whereas the frisson of Emerson's fantasy of becoming a "transparent eyeball" is predicated on the vanishment of the body and its attendant, obtruding egotism, Dickinson's ocular impingements intimate an erethism toward the body's vulnerability to the world the eye lets in,[13] unless so indurating a pain simply leaves the body merely, ancillarily, dumb. The latter scenario complicates the titular premise of Elaine Scarry's *body in pain*—that is, that pain resides in the body or, at least, that the body is where it's felt to occur—by positing the "body" as the un-vibrant matter of whatever pain happens *not* to touch.[14] The longer one experiences ordinary vision as this vibratory, collateral damage, the more likely the eye will come to be conceived as a frangible opacity, disrupting the effortless lubrications by which ordinary vision all but vanishes into sight. So exasperating an encounter proliferates epithets, tributes of infelicitous grappling (willful, recalcitrant, unreliable) that render vision a threshold for epistemology's reinscription as a wrinkle or tear in embodiment: to paraphrase Jean-Luc Marion, as the flesh of the eye impinging on the eye's experience of the world, the pink blur of an immovable, uncomic thumb at the edge of every photograph.[15]

INTERVAL: PHENOMENON AS FIGURATIVE SURPLUS

In addition to the normatively physical aspects of her optical condition, the subject-object of Dickinson's chronic pain thus signifies pain's own expression of and propensity toward a specifically figurative capacity consubstantial with (rather than predicated on) that of her poetry. So semiotically complex a duress calls for a phenomenological conception of pain's specifically figurative moorings that neither Dickinson criticism nor disability theory has yet quite to articulate. When it comes to theories of pain more generally, the timeliness of this undertaking may be all the more felt in terms of the continued influence of Scarry's alignment of chronic pain with narrative theory and tropes of narration. If the figurative gestures of Dickinson's chronic pain have been biding in her poems all this time with the ongoing urgency of lyric triage, the makings of a criticism adequate to them is nevertheless perceptible at the edges of our present criticism. Like a premonition in the wings, a critical account of chronicity's figurative logic beats into perceptibility, for example, from the purlieus of Cameron's foundational readings in *Lyric Time.* "As most critics agree," Cameron writes, "there is no development in the canon of poems. The experiences recorded by these poems are insular ones, subject to endless repetition. Indeed it sometimes seems as if the same poem of pain or loss keeps writing itself over and over."[16] Shifting quietly between substance (the haecceity of what is recorded) and form (sharpened into being as later poems repeat what has been recorded in the latter's idiom), Cameron's account of poetic inertia suggests that experience is not only reported by the poems but also made to fit inside them. Chronic pain interrupts this aesthetic ratio, in that its temporality might be represented by a single poem but not "recorded," per se. To "fit" a single poem, the essential persistence of duress would have to be shrunk in a fashion at odds with the fidelity we've come to expect of Dickinson's uncompromising attention not to a world outside the poems (including, reductively speaking, her extrapoetic weathering of the optical ordeal) so much as an absolute presence of mind to the coincidence of world and poem named by the meteoric scene of writing.

This effortful conformation of single poems to single experiences is complicated by the further puzzlement of distinguishing the substance of a poetic self's experiences, "over and over," from the lyrical matter it becomes; an analogous complication informs Cameron's association of the canon's apparent lack of development with the hectic industry sounded in the compulsive auxiliary verb *keeps* (writing itself over and over). In an endnote following the text's invoking of "endless repetition," Cameron cites David Porter's claim that "perhaps the principal reason for [Dickinson's] early success is that she addressed herself again and again to a single theme."[17] "Over and over," "again and again," in the seeming equivocation between Porter's account of iterative "theme[s]" and Cameron's revision of the latter as "insular" experiences "subject to endless repetition," both critics express a lingering presentiment over experience's rapport with poetic substance in the crosshairs of an ongoingness ever susceptible to the sphere of figurative activity by which Porter's notion of the thematic is comprised. Notwithstanding Cameron's and Porter's consignment of poetic substance to the unporous privacy of what Cameron calls the "insular[ity]" of a lone poem's autonomy, the refrains of "over and over" and "again and again" symptomatically gesture toward an experience of chronicity exceeding an individual poem's means. The textual scenes toward which these descriptions of iterance correspond draw us toward an appreciation of the chronic as an injury to just this autonomy. Whether taken as "experience" or "theme," chronic pain's subject-under-duress demands a shift in the poetic machinery: an impoverishment of the single poem's phenomenal unity, redistributed across the accumulative breadth of the larger poetic assemblage's pulsations. Where before had been suggested the same poem repeated indefinitely, we find the reverberating fractal of a pain-frequency irreducible to synchronic or diachronic substance alone. Beyond the glimmer of sequence and amplification teased in the curated shapes of Dickinson's fascicles, a bewitchment occurs in the temporal grain of a poem's absorbing participation in some larger textual constellation, cooperatively invested in the borealis of pain-across-time. Such a system and the affective openness it generates anticipates the queer aesthetic of artists such as Félix González-Torres: endless silver stacks of a single image rebuilt as the real-time ruinousness of a column, a bird in flight, the rippling surface of sun on sea. Much as one such sliver seemingly invites our experience of it as a discrete object, each likewise belongs to a temporal environment in imbruing excess of any one phenomenal field. Gonzáles-Torres's investigations of multiplicity backward-illuminate the challenges posed by the figurative repeats of Dickinson's poems, the radical self-absorptiveness of the work of art in an earlier age of reproduction.

"Again and again," Cameron writes, Dickinson "tells us that pain is atemporal."[18] This may sometimes be true, but the poems no less frequently communicate that the medium of pain is time itself, even or especially stretched past recognition. "'Twas like a Maelstrom, with a notch," for example, narrates an oneirically indeterminate account of torture in which the glitchlike sharpness of a partially recollected gauntlet belies the speaker's founding exposure to the horror of time itself:

'Twas like a Maelstrom, with a notch,
That nearer, every Day,
Kept narrowing it's boiling Wheel
Until the Agony

Toyed coolly with the final inch
Of your delirious Hem –
And you dropt, lost,
When something broke –
And let you from a Dream –

As if a Goblin with a Guage –
Kept measuring the Hours –
Until you felt your Second
Weigh, helpless, in his Paws –

And not a Sinew – stirred – could help,
And Sense was setting numb –
When God – remembered – and the Fiend
Let go, then, Overcome –

As if your Sentence stood – pronounced –
And you were frozen led
From Dungeon's luxury of Doubt
To Gibbets, and the Dead –

And when the Film had stitched your eyes
A Creature gasped "Reprieve"!
Which Anguish was the utterest – then –
To perish, or to live?[19]

This uncharacteristically long poem (by Dickinson's standards) posits a series of macabre metaphors, each of which amplifyingly substantiates the opening figure of the maelstrom and its notch, a "synecdochic distortion [whose] isolat[ion] and magnifi[cation] is frightening," Cameron writes, "precisely because it lacks a context."[20] In its sharply carved interruption of the maelstrom's spiraling circuit, however, Dickinson's notch allows for the chronicization of otherwise undifferentiated space. That time proves markable (and in its persistence, remarkable) while making its own unremitting impression subtends the lyric apparatus by which a world of limitless feeling can be delineated at all, calibrating nothing less than the speaker's experience of herself at the shifting edges of a universe felt otherwise as blindness. The speaker of the poem comes into being as an effect of a pain that (the poem all but imagines) precedes her, into whose vortex she is roughly asserted. Just enough climbing out of her pain to be interpellated as its residue, the queer resolve of the speaker's utterance lies somewhere between Hawthorne's *I am a citizen of somewhere else*[21] and Melville's epigraph to the epilogue of *Moby-Dick, And I only am escaped alone.*[22]

A value collects in the poem's figurative aggregation beyond any correlative diegetic import, a thickness that isn't impenetrable so much as beyond translation. As with "I felt a Funeral, in my Brain" (F340), "Maelstrom" exploits stanzaic length less for the sake of developing a narrative over time than for populating the chronicity signaled in the poem's multiple aspectual gerund forms—"Kept narrowing," "Kept measuring,"—and temporally inflected conjunctions: "And you dropt," "and let you from a Dream," "And not a Sinew – stirred," "And Sense was setting numb." The sheer accretiveness of the poem's articulation of pain-in-time counters Cameron's suggestion that "the impulse to tell and retell the same story has a quality of hysteria to it,"[23] or the like-minded insinuation of a Freudian compulsion-to-repeat in Helen Vendler's sense that "the insufficien[ce]" of the first simile's "two-stanza span" prompts the further clarifying efforts of the second simile and, in turn, the third.[24] Like the "Goblin with a Guage – / Kept measuring the Hours," the poem exactingly conserves this series of displacements as they occur, a waxing phenomenological density that inversely tallies what is "lost" when "you dropt . . . / When something broke." The poem's recitation of preterite analogies doesn't belong to a speaker per se so much as a style of vocal effects. The self that precedes the event being relived while being pieced together is at best holographed through the machine of a poem it can't without doubt be said to survive: hence the speaker's self-ventriloquized "you" where we might expect an "I." Somewhat differently put, the breakage that the poem haltingly depicts collectively analogizes the breakage of a lyric self incompletely memorialized in the text's friable parts. To imagine otherwise prematurely assumes that the fission of which the "you" is remaindered is reversible, that a lyric self thus strewn across time could be salvaged without consequence from its lagan. Just past the industrious parallax of pain's scriptorium, the self hovers as an impression of stillness.

Sinking into itself—digging in its heels as though to reckon a ground for counteracting the queasy weightlessness of the last stanza's questioning, gasping air—the generative heft of "Maelstrom" insists on figuration as quasi-entelechial force, self no more winnowable from world than tenor from vehicle, form from power. It's along these lines that the substance of chronic pain may be understood not only as liminal but indivisible, speculatively adumbrating and exceeding the gentrified force of metaphor and simile's component parts. Even as its accounts of metaphorical coupling depend on the centripetal break around which a subject's stabs at cohesion dehiscingly collect, *Lyric Time* invokes a conception of figurative difficulty's unified stuff consonant with my sense of chronic pain as aesthetic medium. For example, Cameron hypothesizes that the rehabilitative value of similes lies in their crystallization of space between oneself and those things that seem most to resist one's pains to hail or otherwise bring them within one's ken. "Similes," she writes, "are both the acknowledgment of this space and, since it cannot be overcome, the effort to make connections within it." Cameron's suggestion that "such connections are painful, for they remind us that each of us is neither identical to nor opposite of any other," echoes her earlier claim that "metaphor. . . . is a response to pain in that it closes the gap between feeling and one's identification of it."[25] In the first statement, connection's consciousness of itself—like an eye made conscious of its seeing—is felt as the painfulness of a simile, as though in its awareness of imperfect alchemy a self were being carved from what didn't hurt just long enough to feel the hurt return: hence simile's mnemonic structure, both awakening painful recollection and analogizing pain's own self-recursive matter. In the second statement, by contrast, pain isn't a response to figuration (momentarily following *Lyric Time*'s lead in allowing the term to mean either metaphorical or similetic rapport); figuration is itself a response to pain. Taken together, these claims conjure pain and figuration as so nearly at each other's heels as to comprise a single entity. Pain emanates from the hollows and rifts between self and the affective weather to which it is exposed, even as it names the bone-chilling, alien affect by which a self is "frozen led," as though reduced to the lead of a pencil (her pens taken away) that could render pain's inscriptive force pronounced, if not processed or understood. In both cases, the matter of figuration serves as a proxy expedient, epoxy for filling the cavity of pain it has itself hollowed. As these attempts to represent figuration's relation to pain bend in on themselves—simile's figuration-as-distress grown indistinguishable from the substance that metaphor's capacity for connectivity would seem to allay—we're left with a chiastic sense of figuration not only on both sides of a divide but washing over it, nimble submergence.

The simultaneously pernicious and seductive ease of figuration's uncannily looming internal resemblance informs the following late text, "We send the wave to find the wave." It's not a poem about pain per se; pain isn't named in its lines. And yet the manner in which its notionally governing self disperses in the poem's atmosphere couldn't be more germane to how we understand the naming function obsolesced at the persistent, bruising heart of "Maelstrom." In its place we find an attention to conspicuity all but submerged in the haptic—call it sea, call it pain—loosely shaped around the latter's only apparently discrete principle of attraction:

> We send the wave to find the wave,
> An errand so divine
> The messenger enamored too
> Forgetting to return,
> We make the sage decision still
> Soever made in vain,
> The only time to dam the sea
> Is when the sea is gone. (F1643)

Figuration is to pain as wave is to wave. Whereas *Lyric Time* evokes such transactions from the perspective of a self in pain, "We send the wave" vitally dramatizes the work of figuration from the vantage of figuration itself, the difference between viewing a ship from land and straining to see the land from sea. If figuration's adequation to the unfolding event of chronic pain requires, for some, an article of faith, I admit that my own intuitions are harbored in and sharpened by a familiarity with the "livid Surprise" (F584) of a dogged, degenerative hurt whose contours and qualities have for a long time felt no more nor less than figurative. Living with chronic pain, that is, has come to feel like a partial education in feeling's figurative content, in figuration's capacity to be felt.

While the idea of queer affinity's divining orientation of reader to text isn't a new one, bringing this self-permitting apparatus to bear on speculative philosophy's attention to the matter of thingness orients us to the phenomenal *terra nullius* of chronic pain in a way that allows the latter's distinct pressure on a self's relation to nonself to be imagined beyond the externalizing rhetoric of impairment and debility, alone. Figuration inhabits them insofar as it inhabits us, the grit in the system. I find myself in this spirit returning to a supposition made by Scarry in the opening pages of *The Body in Pain* regarding the impossibility of knowing the pain of others:

> Vaguely alarming yet unreal, laden with consequence yet evaporating before // the mind because not available to sensory confirmation, unseeable classes of // objects such as subterranean plates, Seyfert galaxies, and the pains occurring in // other people's bodies flicker before the mind, then disappear.[26]

The *sfumato* of the first line's accretion of participial epithets at once confuses and delays our sense of relation between the subjects and objects prospectively at play. If between the third and fourth lines we come to recognize the pains of others as one element of this long single sentence's compound subject, our grammatical understanding is upended by the last line's penultimate phrase, "before the mind." Even as the mind—less the one cited then one's own—strains to make sense of the scalar turbulence of moving from tectonic plates to galaxies plummeting back down to "the pains . . . in other people's bodies," even as it strains to summon the pain that this miniature, quasi-Whitmanian catalog proffers as it is simultaneously proscribed (since the brain processes objects described as unseeable more vividly than it does the word "unseeable," itself), the pain nonetheless does seem to form before the mind's eye. For just a moment, pain appears as a subject "before the mind" reclaims as its own intellectual property the notional autonomy of both other bodies and the pains within them—even as the ephemerality of "flicker," like "evaporating" before it, means such property is retainable in name alone.

The text coaxes us all the while into metonymically aligning its hypothetical demonstration of cogitation with the person (rendered further abstract by "the mind['s]" definite article) from whose perspective the previous claims have come into being, or no less formatively, haven't. This mechanism of identification tacitly impels us to imagine ourselves in this person's (the "the['s]") exemplary shoes, insinuating that we readers experience the sentence's thought experiment from more or less the same position with little room for variation beyond disidentification's unspoken margin. If one feels delivered to the latter in one's inability to see one's self in Scarry's account, it's also from this periphery that the statement's most conspicuous assumption comes into focus: namely, that this hypothetical person who experiences another person's suffering as "vaguely alarming yet unreal" *presumably does not live with any commensurable pain of their own, for whom suffering on this perceptual order has yet to become ontologically inescapable if not verifiable.* In this fashion, the sentence's tableau confers subjectivity in the moment of epistemological failure, phenomenological blockage. Lured by the passage's first line break—and most editions of *The Body in Pain* are faithful to this original formatting—my eye failed on first read to notice that the penultimate phrase, "before the mind," has in fact already elsewhere occurred, buried if not broken between the end of the first line and the beginning of the second, "yet evaporating before / the mind because not available."[27] Whether or not determined by contingencies of layout and design subsequent the scene of writing itself, both the splitting of the phrase and the optical tricks it induces generate something like an incidental anacoluthon. This first time around, before the eye loops from the end of one line to the next, "before / the mind" potentially seems to indicate that we treat "before" as an adverb: that pain evaporates at a time or rate anterior to something else. And once we connect this first "before" to "the mind" that is *its* complement, we may yet adverbially understand the syntax in terms of "[pain] evaporating before the mind" is able to crystallize, codify, or otherwise accomplish something else. But as the syntax itself flickers in and out of clarity, we come to realize that the prepositional phrase preceding Scarry's list of "unseeable classes" is the same as the one that follows. The repetition and variation of "before / the mind" turns this short paragraph into a poem whose redoubled "before" introduces into an account of how the mind's interaction with pain is unthinkable apart from the unspoken medium of narrative time a sense of the difficulty by which the painlessness of perspective is secured.

There has always been just enough space in Scarry's brilliant work for "the body in pain" to be recuperated as a subject position, almost a subject, and just enough possibility in pain itself, textual and otherwise, to sustain aforementioned affinity with a queer form of literacy. This pleasing shiver of premonitively catching the glimpse of some shared ort or sliver of sympathy allows for imagination where it once only "flicker[ed]," to take hold. To say the least, *The Body in Pain* is a powerful testament to the pathos of imagination's constraints. Its repeated scenes of epistemological discomfiture and frustration can be traced not only to what the book frequently articulates as pain's "activ[e] destr[uction]" of "language"[28] but also to its allegiance, when it comes to considering literary representations of pain, to narrative.[29] Much as Judith Butler and others have wondered how psychoanalysis may have differed from itself had Freud's center of gravity been Antigone rather than Oedipus,[30] I find myself wondering what difference it would make had *The Body in Pain*—three decades old and counting—somewhat differently imagined lived experience according to the ethos and phenomenological resourcefulness of what Allen Grossman designates the difficult poem,[31] the generative, inhabitable impasse that has drawn me again and again to Dickinson's figuration of pain not as a break in the quotidian but the quotidian itself.

"THE AXIS ALONE": SUBTRACTION AND CONSPICUOUS EXPERIENCE

"A Pang is more conspicuous in Spring" (F1545B), another late text invested in dissolving the dream of visualizable feeling in the divagating entropy of felt intensity, presents a phenomenal field only fortuitously shared with its notional speaker:

> A Pang is more
> conspicuous in Spring
> In contrast with the
> things that sing
> Not Birds entirely – but
> Minds –

And Winds – Minute Effulgen-
-cies
When what they sung
for is undone
Who cares about
a Blue Bird's Tune –
Why, Resurrection
had to wait
Till they had moved
a Stone –[32]

Contra Dickinson criticism that takes for granted that a poem's communication of pain is given from the position of a lyric self for whom that pain is centrally constitutive, this poem's rhizomatic turns through itself somewhat differently imagine pain's unsettling motion. If its speaker is able to reconceive her hurt at all, it's only from the latter's nebulous periphery, at once too close and too far away. As often is the case in Dickinson's poems, "A Pang is more conspicuous" begins with a claim about sharpened perception quickly enough overtaken or undermined by the subsequent lines' real-time, muddling enactment of pain's affective impingement. Like that of "Further in Summer than the Birds" (F895), this opening statement treats as self-sufficient a phrase that seems to signal incompletely just half of an argument. Further than the birds from, more conspicuous than, what? Even were "in contrast with" treated as a synonym for "than" (i.e., "A Pang is more / conspicuous in Spring / [*than*] . . . the / things that sing"), the prepositional phrase's circumlocution gives the sense of syncope in the connective tissue just long enough to place the comparison's complementary term out of reach. In the fragment's elongation of ligature into substantive entity—that "In contrast with the" occupies its own line all the more induces one's eye, for example, to pause in the material fold of *its* quasi-Steinian abstraction—the purposiveness of the first line's plosive "Pang" gets caught somehow in the mesh of comparison, almost wriggling from the haptic to the visible of conspicuity to the audibility of birdsong, mimicked, to a certain extent, in the jingle of the "ng" digraph perseverated across "Pang," "Spring," "things," "sing." More precisely, though, these opening lines and the "things" they ponder converge on neither song per se nor bird that sings it, rendering instead the apparent strain of the latter's particularity upon a register of "things" so generalized as to further unmoor what it would otherwise winnow. An echo of the equivocal contention found in "'Hope' is the thing with feathers" (F314), this turn to sweeping abstraction over and against the flesh of pang's smarting extends the poem's census of hypothetical singers not only to poems and poets but nearly anything capable of expression—"Winds – Minute Effulgen- / -cies"—including bodies and the pangs they may be said to house.

The poem's opening lines thus dilate and contract (*springlike*, in the manner of coils) from the sharpness of a pang and the conceptual spaciousness of a season to the further wavering of things to birds/not birds to the ultimate, involutive magic (a rabbit vanishing into the hat) of "Not Birds entirely – but / Minds –." In the surprising, qualifying pause of "entirely," the song in the mind of a bird—how a bird hears itself singing, how a writer imagines her writing in advance of or apart from its ultimate expression—is made continuous with the song in our own, trying to hear as readers what the poem hears. Like so many elements of Dickinson's lexicon, "Entirely" radiates in several directions at once. Compared to the sharp legibility of conspicuousness, "Not entirely" suggests a rounder mode of speculation, as though in the inability of the poem's speaker to identify the source of what she hears beyond the fluster of "things," the song could belong to anything and nothing at all. At the same time, the text is equally careful not to supply (to itself as much as us) the word "song." That we infer song from "things that sing"— as we infer birds from song—articulates the obscure pastoral against which the poem's "pang" appears (or, more precisely, can only be *said* to appear). In other words, "Not Birds entirely" not only speaks to the inability to establish *which* bird (and, etiologically or at least more generally, which *cause*) but registers the deceptively simple extent to which birdsong and "Birds entirely" can only coercively be made to coincide. In its attention to experiential tenderness, the poem stages the perceptual difficulty of tracing expression to its source as a pang in its own right. We hear the pathos of this sundering in the further intimations of "Entirely," whose etymological nearness to "integer" qualifies its adverbial wholeness or completion as that which is unbroken or untouched (*in* – "not" + *tangere* – "to touch"), even from or by itself.

This detachment of expression (pang, song) from the nominally closed environment it at once escapes and comes differently to fill is at the heart of the poem's saltatory aims, not least in its difference from the indivisibility by which the hurt of conspicuousness holds fast to itself. As presented in the 1844 *Webster,* the double definition associated with the etymology of "conspicuous"—"[L. *conspicu-us,* visible, striking]"—reminds us that the unremittingness of Dickinsonian chronic pain is coincident with attention's optical quotidian. Returning once more to the embedded litotes of "Not . . . entirely," the poem's fragmented efforts at articulating its enterprise of conspicuousness suggest—this time via false etymology, like attributing a song to the wrong bird—not only the pang of perception but its endlessness, the wear and tear of it. Imagining the prefix of "entirely," that is, in terms of enshrouding interiority rather than negation, the business of parsing expression from origin, as volleyed between pangs and songs, proves exhausting. Not only tiring, but *entiring;* wrapped in tiredness, as though fatigue were in, or simply *were,* the air of our encounter.

Following conspicuity's calibrative shifts between vision and hurt, the pulsing quality of chronicity's encompassment of looping sequence and faltering repetition recalls the affective landscape at the start of Emerson's "Experience," where "sleep lingers all our lifetime about our eyes, as night hovers all day in the boughs of the fir-tree."[33] Sleep and night are never absent per se so much as loom—deepening, darkening, in the language of Emerson's "Beauty," at the edges of experience, "a pungency . . . in the frame of things."[34] It's along these lines that a pang—and as much to the point, the punctual stab of conspicuity itself—might seem more conspicuous in spring than birds or birdsong (albeit such a paraphrase in the face of so idiosyncratically compressed a poem must be taken gingerly), given the difficulty of perceiving the latter in a season so replete with chirps as to seem thoroughly interladen with them and, thus, less an object of attention than the atmospheric background against which other phenomena appear. Under such conditions, a pang all the more keenly commands our attention because, unlike birds in spring, it is never out of place. Its acuity is specific to where it is felt, unlike the ambient ubiquity of birdsong, which one hears as though everywhere and nowhere at all; hence the poem's insistence less on birds themselves than "things that sing," as though our own difficulty moving through the poem generated an experience akin to hearing a voice in the woods without being able to pinpoint the voice's source. Whereas the pang lives nowhere (as Scarry and others might attest) beyond the body to which it is pledged, a song hardly exists *until* it has left its corresponding body behind. We revisit this contrast in comparably demotic form in the poem preceding "A Pang is more conspicuous" in both

Franklin and Miller editions. Dickinson includes this text, "An Antiquated Tree," in a letter to her lifelong friend Elizabeth Holland from early spring of 1881. The letter begins (they refer to each other sororally), "Dear Sister, Spring, and not a Blue Bird, but I have seen a Crow – 'in his own Body on the Tree,' almost as prima facie –" (L689).

The prospect of birdsong isolated from the body that yields it grows all the more pressing in light of the threat posed to eyes so photosensitive as Dickinson's by springtime's brighter, longer days. Transfixed with music, one might close one's own eyes and imagine, "almost . . . prima facie," the body's diaphanous disappearance into the acoustic. That song could give its listener the impression of the singer's deciduous body being shed presents a sublimating model for the poet's dream of escaping pain, were the latter's expression extortable from the body's inexorable mechanism. Dickinson's otherwise overstating insistence on spotting the crow "in his own Body" hammers this conflicting vision home, as though the crow could be anywhere else. To the contrary, the text's allusion to the Gospel of Peter—"Who his own self bare our sins in his own body on the tree"[35]—doesn't glorify the crow so much as reduce divinity to the latter's cawingly unpoetical/untransformable nature, an ornithological banality, and turn the reliquary limbs of the cross, in turn, into any tree's unremarkable branches.

The ocular anxiety pervading this tableau is underscored by Holland's own intimacy with chronic optical distress, severe enough at some earlier point as to justify the surgical removal of one of her eyes.[36] Indeed, the penultimate paragraph of the same letter begins, "I hope the Little Sister's Eyes have refrained from sighing." Notwithstanding the charm of its solicitude, the passage's synesthetic compaction almost luridly transforms the eye into a mouth, while calibrating the latter as a distinctly chronic mechanism. The politesse of Dickinson's "refrained" takes the pathos of a single sigh's exacerbated breath and multiplies it to the point of distress. In Dickinson and Holland's adopted sentimental idiom, a sigh's ordinary perceptibility in response to some other restricted event (physiological, narrative, etc.) becomes in its implied chronicity an event in its own right. In a different context, to be asked to refrain from sighing is funny to the extent that the phrasing's careful etiquette conjures someone outside the circle of pain for whom one's troubled breathing has become a nuisance; or perhaps it is the optically aggrieved who hears the eye's sighing as evidence of its own theatricalized passive aggression. For Dickinson and maybe Holland, the chronicity of pain wears down the differences between malingering (a back-formation under the possible influence of lingering's temporal dilation) and chronic pain, in contrast to those ailments more straightforwardly confirmable by medicine; pain's bondage to the body it borrows may seem absolute, but in its felt detachment from explanatory apparatus, its persistence is also experienced by those who feel it as pure message without referent or, rather, message as referent. How could a semiotics of symptomatology learn to know what to do with illness thus fashioned?

And so, the eye's sighs transfigure pain as a strain of birdsong all the more incrementally driven to cut itself short (*refraindre,* to repeat, break off), the longer it lasts. Affectively ponderous as it is vexingly, lexically vacuous, the refrain of sighs names in shorthand the remainder of chronic pain's propulsive, self-aggrandizing efforts at nothing so much as its own subtraction. *From the mountain you see the mountain.* All of the above, to be sure, is adjusted to Dickinson's microscope of feeling—even the most disconcerting sigh isn't quite audible in the grand scheme of things. Nevertheless, the formulation's wire-crossing of optical and oral signals has an uncanny effect: what is barely perceptible in relation to a mouth grows surreally remarkable—one might even say *conspicuous*—moved to the eye, jarring in the manner of noticing the rise and fall of breath from an object—a book, a Buddha, a snowglobe—that isn't supposed to breathe. Both more and less than sight, sight's graphic echo (resisting in sound the latter's alveolar closure), a sigh's ability to render visible the ordinarily subliminal constancy of breath casts the labored vision of both Dickinson and Holland as the heightened legibility of sight's own ordinarily imperceptible operation: as though in the wake of vision's throbbing hurt, the eye itself were heaving (so it felt), the rising and falling of a sighing chest. One finds possible correlatives to this uncanny pulse even deeper in the poem's tissue, the visual similarity of "Minds" and "Winds" cleaving against their phonic differences. That two eyes might look the same on paper belies the potential difference of their expression, as the force of each word's "i" responds to the pressure of its surrounding consonants. Even the curves of Dickinson's penmanship seem to voice a corollary to this breathlike shift in intensity from hard to soft vowelling, as the bird-in-flight shape of the "r" in "Birds" flutters into the shape of the "n" in "Minds" and "Wind" (linking back in turn to the second consonant of "Pang"), avian Muybridge stills on the wing. The season of spring against which the pang's nominal conspicuousness is first achieved returns us to the springlike mechanism of expansion and contraction that characterizes the poem's recursively unarriving motion. In this way, the "ng" digraph not only recalls an audible note or chord resung but also echoes the spring of a pang's own elastically coiling phenomenal shape. If the poem's figurative growth falls short of a description (per se) of the Pang that occasions it, it elaborates instead the halting rhythm, at once associatively dispersed and radially concentrated, by which a "Pang"—so the opening line states with deceptive composure—"is more," the enjambing break between the latter and "conspicuous" anticipating, a symptom within a symptom, the quasi-fibrous spool and tear intrinsic to the poem's texture.

I mean to call attention to the perceptual heft of the poem's catalyzing subject—not only its odd conspicuousness per se but our vision of its felt presence—in comparison to the trailing hypothetical fragments of landscape it calls into being. Just what is or isn't conspicuous seems to break down in the text's equivocation between feeling and seeing sharply, between the terms of optical availability as from the internal vantage of the poem's speaker and the terms of intelligibility from our vantage as readers. Interestingly, the only other instance in Dickinson's poetic oeuvre of the word *conspicuous* likewise subjects this very notion of optical access to a specifically figurative scrutiny:

The Outer – from the Inner
Derives it's Magnitude –
'Tis Duke, or Dwarf, according
As is the central mood –

The fine – unvarying Axis
That regulates the Wheel –
Though Spokes – spin – more conspicuous
And fling a dust – the while.

The Inner – paints the Outer –
The Brush without the Hand –
It's Picture publishes – precise –
As is the inner Brand –

On fine – Arterial Canvas –
A Cheek – perchance a Brow –
The Star's whole secret – in the Lake –
Eyes were not meant to know. (F450)

Like "Patience – has a quiet – Outer –" (F842A) and "Pain – expands the Time –" (F833A), the poem's opening asserts as gradient a set of relational values we might otherwise take as fixed. Indeed, the quiet radicalism of these lines suggests that our attention to the interdependence of outside and inside potentially undermines the conceptual discreteness that their respective names provisionally reify. The exact meanings of Outer and Inner remain importantly unclear, as though these terms themselves belonged to a field of external signification at equal remove from any original referent. At the same time, whether one takes "Inner" to correspond to originality, abstraction, or psychical life is as moot as whether one understands "Outer" in terms of physical body, natural outer-universe, or textual field. As Maurice Merleau-Ponty writes in his working notes to *The Visible and the Invisible,* "movements, rests, distances, apparent sizes, etc., are only different indexes of refraction of the transparent medium that separates me from the *things themselves,* different expressions of that coherent distention across which Being shows itself and conceals itself."[37] More than the wilderness or cultivation on either side of it, it is this approximate landscape to which the poem is drawn, the variously reflective, porous, clear, or glaucous surfaces by which refraction and other modes of contact take on the appearance of a sea-change. Merleau-Ponty's suggestive naming of distention reverberates with what in the same notes he calls a "'lake of non-being,' a certain nothingness sunken into a local and temporal *openness.*"[38] Looking ahead to the poem's last stanza, the lake's punning play on Merleau-Ponty's exploration of phenomenological lacunae (from *lacus,* lake, hollow, opening) sharpens our sense of Dickinson's lake and eye not only as manifestations of Outer and Inner but as miscible homologues (the eye, in turn, grown indistinguishable from its own lacunar blind spot, swallowing itself up like a star's reflection sunk to hypolimnion). Although, as Maurice S. Lee notes, "Mood, axis, and painting are all main tropes in Emerson's essay 'Experience,'"[39] Dickinson may well have recalled from Emerson's 1836 *Nature* his oracular conviction that "the axis of vision is not coincident with the axis of things, and so they appear not transparent but opake. The reason why the world lacks unity, and lies broken and in heaps, is, because man is disunited with himself."[40] If the "fine – unvarying" aspect of Dickinson's axis gives the impression of a regulating mechanism, its invariance also marks the system's constraint, able only to see from one given axis of vision a world that constantly shifts. In Emerson's words from "Poetry and the Imagination," an 1872 essay largely composed of earlier lectures, Nature gives us innuendoes that "the creation is on wheels, in transit, always passing into something else, streaming into something higher; that matter is not what it appears. . . . Faraday, the most exact of natural philosophers, taught that when we should arrive at the monads, or primordial elements (the supposed little cubes or prisms of which all matter was built up), we should not find cubes, or prisms, or atoms, at all, but spherules of force."[41]

This speculative continuity between Outer and Inner ought be distinguished from "romantic oneness"[42]—the achievement of some absolute whole against which Lee characterizes Dickinson's waning interest in romantic subjectivity as it "give[s] way to a more empirical outlook."[43] The Dickinson poems we've been considering are drawn less to the matter of essence than to the lyric (or in Hawthornian terms, Romantic) ecology of contact between theory and event, an uncanny crystallization of what Merleau-Ponty postulates as "the difference between the identicals,"[44] the notch in the maelstrom. Merleau-Ponty names this site of self-undoing (of everything and nothing) the chiasm, in part to mark the affinity between this speculative material and the optic chiasm, where the optic nerve fibers of each retina cross at the base of the brain.[45] For Merleau-Ponty, as for Emerson and Dickinson, the quiet enthrallment of this scene appears on, if not as, an axis—or as Dickinson puns, "as is": the central mood, the inner Brand:

> The axis alone given— —the end of the finger of the glove is nothingness—but a nothingness one can turn over, and where then one sees *things*— —The only "place" where the negative would really be is the fold, the application of the inside and the outside to one another, the turning point— —
>
> Chiasm I—the world
> I—the other—[46]

This juxtaposition of "The Outer – from the Inner" with Merleau-Ponty's meditation on the same ideally draws out the peculiar surface area of Dickinson's pang, allowing us a little longer to "lean . . . opon the Awe –" (F440) where chronic pain illuminates the middle distance within or along the spectrum of physical embodiment and imaginative abstraction. In this regard, Eve Kosofsky Sedgwick's *Epistemology of the Closet* has been a vital intertext to *Contingent Figure*'s enterprise. Sedgwick's description of the homo/hetero divide along universalizing rather than minoritizing lines powerfully models the revisionary work of positing hitherto ineluctable systems as potentially fungible, even as the queer closet's epistemologically radioactive proscenium suggests the violent, life-shifting distributions that occur in the threshold where Outer and Inner are said to meet, where their incommensurability is most reinforced. Nonetheless bound up with even the most vigorous assumptions of their ingrained contrariety, so Sedgwick and Dickinson imply, is a potentially tenderizing strain of accord. Thinking less guardedly about the affective sympathy between exteriority and interiority rescues some of Dickinson's more seemingly withdrawn texts from the flatness of those coarser optics impressed into the work of policing the distinctions between the two.

An attachment to the performatively self-evident incongruousness of Outer and Inner partly spurs the polemic of *Dickinson's Misery: A Theory of Lyric Reading,* Virginia Jackson's 2005 analysis of the distance between Dickinson's writing ("as it was written," as Gertrude Stein might say)[47] and a myth of lyric poetry that the past century's editorial and critical practices have revealed that writing however falsifyingly to be. Thus Theo Davis observes that "for Jackson the objects around us are indisputably just there. . . . Go back to the paper, the scrap, the desiccated bug skeleton: objects are obvious, without the doubts that our thinking minds produce."[48] If, indeed, Jackson's "animus against [lyric] poetry is fueled by a commitment to the material object, and this commitment is grounded in a view that flowers, like pieces of paper, escape the tangles of our minds,"[49] *Dickinson's Misery* demonstrates many times over that its vehement suspicion regarding the mind's capacity to ensnare what it thinks about amounts to an "aversion"[50] not only to "the mind alone with itself"[51] but to the errant aesthetics of figuration that troubles the border between the inviolable historical particularity of Dickinson's archive and the vertiginous range of inner experience that sustains it on either end. In Jackson's words, "If 'Life is over there—' when it becomes a metaphor, where is it if it does not? Is there any alternative to the privative fatality of figuration?"[52] For Jackson, that is, figuration isn't merely something that occurs in poems, but something that happens *to* material things, to which material substance is queerly susceptible. Opening onto the temporal field of chronic pain that charges my own investigation, figuration by this account becomes all the more potent a threat to the thingness of historicity with the passage of time. Ultimately, *Dickinson's Misery* seems to admonish that the nearly viral stultification of our solipsistic tendencies trades in lyric figurativeness as the alibi by which we seduce ourselves into erasing the relational grain of historical poetic culture. The ensuing blur of real dogs in figurative pursuit of their imaginary tails generates along these lines the dementia by which, ironically, we lose contact with Dickinson in the name of some newly bracing hold on her purported psychical exposures.

Jackson locates in Dickinson's writing a clairvoyant critique of this will-toward-ambush, no less present in the critical misogynies of her own day than our own. Just as frequently, however, poems such as "The Outer – from the Inner" and "A Pang is more conspicuous" seem less litigious toward than empirically engrossed by objects at the verge or in the throes of this figurative alchemy. D. W. Winnicott shares this abiding interest in the fibers by which things communicate their relational attention to and potential danger for each other, describing these interactions, these "pangs," in terms of impingement. "Let us examine," Winnicott writes,

> the concept of a central or true self. The central self could be said to be the inherited potential which is experiencing a continuity of being, and acquiring in its own way and at its own speed a personal psychic reality and a personal body scheme. It seems necessary to allow for the concept of the isolation of this central self as a characteristic of health. Any threat to this isolation of the true self constitutes a major anxiety at this early stage, and defences of earliest infancy appear in relation to failures on the part of the mother (or in maternal care) to ward off impingements which might disturb this isolation.[53]

Winnicott, here, takes impingement to refer to an infant's experience of the world pressing in. In this period before speech or weaning, however, before the infant's oneness with its mother untangles into hazarding its first vague experience of autonomy on the one hand and object relations on the other, it seems reasonable to consider Inner and Outer as equally inchoate on the infant's psychical horizon. Indeed, as Winnicott notes in an earlier paper's theorization of the origins of masochism, in certain cases "the 'individual' then develops as an extension of the shell rather than of the core, and as an extension of the impinging environment. What there is left of a core is hidden away and is difficult to find even in the most far-reaching analysis. The individual then *exists by not being found*."[54]

Winnicott's investment in the word *impingement* is a relatively recent discovery for me. My eye surely happens to pick it out because it's a word I've been living with for some time. That I have the neck of an eighty-year-old is something doctors began telling me in my twenties, twelve or so years after the condition worsened into a distracting concern. What the doctors meant is the extent of degeneration in my cervical spine, bone spurs crowding the spinal cord and nerve roots, a shrinking of the bone tunnel through which the spinal cord runs. The nerve roots are impinged by the discs, and by the facets between them that otherwise allow for movement between vertebrae. If the degeneration of these ossified bits suggests time sped up, their aberrant velocity lives inside the differently deviant temporality of chronic pain itself: less accelerated than an endless repetition of the scratch in a record further wearing into the gash across the groove (*same old same*). One is made to feel aware of these depletions and by extension believe in them because the point of these bones and joints and leaking, collagenous sacs is to not be felt at all, to vanish into the ease of motion they're supposed to facilitate. That a certain intransigence of feeling comes to be felt as an expression of the body's harboring of degeneracy repeats the somatic syntax of degeneracy's early-nineteenth-century linkage with queerness, whose newly taxonomized perversity supposedly betrayed a tendency toward regressing devolution. But I digress.

As Emerson observes in *Nature* (1836), "Every word which is used to express a moral or intellectual fact, if traced to its root, is found to be borrowed from some material appearance."[55] In this manner, the early lexical history of impingement includes Robert Burton's 1621 reflection from *The Anatomy of Melancholy,* that those who "offer violence to their own persons, or in some desperate fit to others, which sometimes they do by stabbing, slashing, &c . . . know not what they do, deprived of reason," as a "ship that is void of a pilot, must needs impinge upon the next rock, or sands, and suffer shipwrack."[56] With time, degeneracy would seem to sublimate toward abstraction. For instance, Cecila Sjöholm notes that, like that of Merleau-Ponty, Hannah Arendt's understanding of aesthetic reflection posits a "vision of the world . . . shaped in and through the impingement of the view of others."[57] And yet Sjöholm's notion of impingement as a specifically visual phenomenon is telling in the context of Dickinson. That the view of others impinges on us or, rather, our vision of the world (however we and it are to be distinguished) is a way of describing not how our given optical field is amplified, obtruded, or otherwise altered by what others see but rather how vision would feel if we had tactual access to what *it* feels. The lexical trajectory of "impinge" is thus more slippery than "merely" degenerating from more to less concrete, effervescing into the figurative ether. Sir Isaac Newton expounds on impingement's spectacular activation of visibility's impressible threshold, its participation in a veritable Brueghel of activity along an otherwise imperceptible membrane:

> Thus may rays be refracted by some superficies, and reflected by others, be the medium they tend into denser or rarer. But it remains further to be explained, how rays alike incident on the same superficies (suppose of crystal, glass, or water) may be, at the same time, some refracted, others reflected; and for explaining this, I suppose that the rays when they impinge on the rigid resisting aethereal superficies, as they are acted upon by it, so they react upon it, and cause vibrations in it, as stones thrown into water do in its surface. . . . The shock of every single ray may generate many thousand vibrations, and by sending them all over the body, move all the parts, and that perhaps with more motion than it could move one single part by an immediate stroke; for the vibrations, by shaking each particle backward and forward, may every time increase its motion, as a ringer does a bell by often pulling it.[58]

That an eye potentially experiences sunlight like a thousand bells cascading across a valley suggests just how noninnocuous the sheer fact of visibility might seem to eyes awakened to the mechanics of their ordinary industry if only in that industry's abrading interruption. As Christopher Smith Fenner observes in *Vision: Its Optical Defects and the Adaptation of Spectacles* (1875), "waves [of ether] having shorter periods of duration, falling on the skin scarcely produce any sensible heat, but entering the eye and impinging on the retina, cause a sensation of light. It is to the luminous sensation caused by waves of elastic ether falling upon the retina that has been given the name of *light*. It is evident," Fenner remarkably concludes, "that light does not exist in nature; it is simply a sensation produced by mechanical irritation of nerves of special sensation."[59] Fenner's remarks hinge on a shifting grammar by which the site-specificity of impingement amplifies ether's effectual register beyond the imperceptibility of its otherwise "imponderable substance."[60] The difference between "falling on the skin" and "impinging on the retina" has less to do with any change in either original substance or that substance's movement through space than in the surface textures of its destination. There's something uncanny about trying to envision this trajectory of ether when it is the trajectory itself that comes to explain the possibility of vision at all. That light makes visible the world around us, this vestigial model hypothesizes, erroneously persuades us that it is a cause rather than an effect. More than this, our conceptual attachment to light depends on our ability to suppress the mechanical irritation as which vision comes into being before, that is, it appears. I imagine Dickinson finding consolation in this model's terms, their reframing of the pain of her optical encounters less as disorder than some elemental history internal to seeing itself.

The archaism of Burton's example similarly depends on impingement's entanglement with optical hyperbole and distortion, extending its tableau of shipwreck as lurid supplement to melancholy's imperceptible throes. The violence of the former's "suffer[ing]" doesn't lend its legibility to the outward crisis of melancholy's attack (whose desperate fits when witnessed are all too indelibly registered) so much as asks that we imagine a ship's pilotless calamity internal to melancholy, where something like the helmage of agential mechanism had been. Although Burton's analogy is galvanized by the resemblance between "stabbing, slashing" and impingement's splintering effects, its force all the more bears, like Fenner's example, on discrepancies between competing forms of animacy and matter. Impingement may name a catastrophe of substance at risk of narrative distortion (like the misprision of mechanical irritation as light), but from this present vantage at least I'm struck by the way narrative impulse more generally reduces the overdetermined folds of the scene's multiplied surface contact. If a person caught in melancholy is like a ship caught between abandonment and disaster, we may no less envision such a person as the "rock, or sands" on which melancholy wracks itself. Impingement works in fractals, the magnification of contingence that it realizes intensifying our perceptual powers in the manner traced by Dickinson's "Crumbling is not an instant's Act" (F1010). And yet we are at the same time unmoored by the aphoristic scenelessness of Burton's analogy, an optical prosthesis in which "everything," as Blanchot writes, "has already disappeared."[61] That we are both too close and too far isn't correctable: impingement's sharp alteration of figurative surface area as the experience on which we are being trained to strain our eyes.

In the spirit of such interrupting fragmentation, "The Outer – from the Inner" and "A Pang is more conspicuous" express (as though for our own empirical regard) something intrinsic to the experience of pain they describe. Dickinson's description isn't abstruse; there is no more accessible version of the pang than what is presented. To a certain extent, this reading can't help but dovetail with Jackson's delineation of "sentimental poetry's stress on an unrepresentable embodiment, on a historicity threatened by the elevating aims of figuration."[62] But whereas Jackson laments the "rhetorical difficulty of pointing to an experience . . . before it becomes a metaphor,"[63] I'm drawn to where figuration seems not to threaten historicity—specifically, the historical textures of chronic pain—so much as indicate it. Whether or not any given experience can be rescued from the metaphor into which our deictic apperception converts it, there is no version of Dickinson's ocular duress that isn't figurative (rather than metaphorical), if only because something so ontologically forged in duration has no single originary counterpart. Somewhere between entropy and ecology, the figurative commotion of these lines doesn't "elevate" some truer, less ideational experience of pain: it comes as close to pain as Dickinson, or we, can get. Our shared experience of the pang—experience *as* pang—is one of lived impediment, sedimented in or sutured to the poem's experience of time. These moments of suspension impress upon us the pause of temporally being in or as the absence of an understanding that would propel us through it.

CANDESCENCE, ORNAMENTAL INCESSANCY

"A Pang is more" makes a brief cameo in *Dickinson's Misery,* introduced as the lyric poem it is deemed by Mabel Loomis Todd and Millicent Todd Bingham's 1945 edition, *Bolts of Melody*—alongside an approximately coterminous one, "When what they sung for is undone"; the first lines of the latter comprise in part the second stanza of "A Pang is more." Although the substance of neither document can scarcely be said to behave more or less like a lyric poem than the other, the shared DNA between them makes for a cautionary retelling of *The Prince and the Pauper,* since "When what they sung for" has been characterized by Dickinson's twentieth-century editors, notes Jackson, as anything *but* a poem: "a worksheet, a variant, a fragment . . . , an unfinished poem."[64] This is to say that while Jackson rightly suggests the case could be made for describing either of these texts as lyrics, history has made the case for only one. The brevity of her own account as to how one might recognize if not justify the burden of lyric inherited by "A Pang is more" amounts to a refusal to recapitulate any aspect of a critical archive whose promulgation of Dickinson's writing as lyric canon has left that writing fatally intelligible at the expense, Jackson argues, of the historical world in which it once participated and of which it survives as trace. Accordingly, she notes that the lines beginning "A Pang is more," are "beautiful, and so may give the impression that they were added to the lines that begin 'When what they sung for' as a more developed and finished composition."[65] This curt assertion of beauty is jarring less for the faintness of its praise than for its exposure of Dickinson's text, or at least the lyric it has become, to the vulgarism of a fire sale. That its meretriciously Keatsian charge implicitly (if disingenuously) posits beauty as its own chiastic self-evidence substitutes for a reading—what Jackson more pointedly would term lyric reading—what we might imagine as the tautological end point of the latter's self-confirming ministrations. The hermeneutic violence of this "Auction of the mind" (F788) treats as purgatively therapeutic the notion that critical—which is to say, lyric—appraisal might be enough emptied of literary value per se to correct a previous generation's will toward lyric inflation. Better, apparently, for some analyses to be thrown out with the bathwater than to give the false comfort that some more rigorous or thoughtful form of lyric reading could be less distortive or foreclosing than those that are the object of her critique.

That Jackson makes "A Pang is more" representative of the marmoreal entrapments of a lyric poem while allowing "When what they sung for" to stand (if only in the temporariness of analysis) for itself, apart from lyric's warping pressure, anticipates Jackson's later consideration of Paul de Man's "Anthropomorphism and Trope in Lyric," its examination of the relationship, "structured like a symbol," between two Baudelaire sonnets, "Correspondances" and "Obsession." De Man reads the former as a "negation" of the latter's "figural stability" even while reading the latter "as a negation" of the "positivity of an outside reality" coextensive with the former's terms.[66] The mutually abrograting *hysteron proteron* of negation preceding what it negates gestures toward the strangeness of the time of reading spun, suggests de Man, between these two texts. If not the opposite then perhaps an inversion of belated comprehension, the *Nachträglichkeit* of this spectral and specular temporality exceeds, unless it withdraws from, the reach of historical trajectory hinted in the external granularity that the interiorizing act of reading[67]—less invited by "Obsession" than enacted—cannibalizes. If lyric names a movement or style of relation rather than a thing, it is nonetheless a constricting movement *toward* this hypostasizing legibility of thingness. It's along these lines, I think, that de Man opines that "no lyric can be read lyrically nor can the object of a lyrical reading be itself a lyric,"[68] since once a text has been hypostasized *as* lyric, it can hardly become more so; the diminishing returns of flogging a dead horse leave only the flogger further exhausted. That the stabilizing premise of lyric recalls the homeostatic tendency of Freud's pleasure principle illuminates within de Man's analysis a corresponding sympathy between the resistance of "Correspondance" to the explicative congealments of lyric and the psychoanalytic drive: less the reversal of "Truth is beauty" than an unraveling thread pulled in a way that leaves disrupted the fixity that the trope of chiasmus comes to name.

Jackson appreciates de Man's articulation of this undoing force, internal to lyric and which no lyric transfiguration can entirely exorcise. At the same time, however, de Man's work loses sight for her of what he finally conjures as the "non-anthropomorphic, non-elegiac, non-celebratory, non-lyrical, non-poetic, that is to say, prosaic, or, better, *historical* modes of language power,"[69] on account of its ironically unconscious, elegiac investment in the vulnerability of lyric to the very deformations that his essay lays bare: to paraphrase Poe's "Philosophy of Composition," as though the only subject more effecting than a beautiful poem were one's mordant sense of a beautiful poem's decomposition. Much as "Anthropomorphosis and Trope in Lyric" delineates the nonlyrical disposition of "Correspondances" in terms of its ability to check precisely this melancholy's backsliding allure, that it has the oppositely enabling effect is symptomatically predicted, argues Jackson, in de Man's insistence that "in the paraphernalia of literary terminology, there is no term available to tell us what 'Correspondances' might be. All we know is that it is, emphatically, *not* a lyric."[70] This unnameability confers to nonlyrical motion an abstractive quality made possible only in the repudiation of its nominally historical commitments. In response, the recuperative project of *Dickinson's Misery* is all the more happy to supply a name for the genre indicated by this undoing force, the one championed by Jackson, Yopie Prins, and others under the aegis of historical poetics: "According to de Man's own (Nietzschean) logic, 'language power' should read as an oxymoron, since the 'unintelligible' force of extreme materiality is what the language closely read as lyric, in its 'defensive' or purely aesthetic aspect, cannot admit. That is as far as de Man got, and it is a long way. But when de Man wrote, elegiacally, that lyric pathos cannot allow for '*historical* modes of language power,' . . . he was not allowing that before modern lyric reading became a form of critical power, poetry itself may have been such a mode."[71]

Jackson's sense of de Man's seduction by lyric abstraction sets in relief her own argument that "what may come closest to defining" Dickinson's "'genius' . . . is the way in which 'a Life' remains in her writing in excess of the figures of that writing, the way in which her practice contained without becoming the lyric stuff of which she made it and out of which it was to be made."[72] I wonder about chronic pain's relation to "a Life," especially as it consumes the perhaps more historically legible stuff of which a life less beholden to pain is composed. No matter how long it is suffered, how much it comes to feel like an actual, thinglike object, chronic pain remains diaphanous, equivalent to neither external cause (if there ever were one) nor the tissue, bone, or tendon it befalls. What beyond tautology are its intrinsic qualities, when one's experience of its sharpness, aching, or throbbing conveys nothing properly its own so much as one's relation to it? Unlike a leaf or cloud, pain is ontologically intermediate. When we call it physical, we refer more frequently than not to its location, not its constitution. Whereas it's understood that "water lily" does not designate a lily made of water, when it comes to physical pain we allow a certain metonymic slip. Its emotional or intellectual qualities seem analogously confidential, unconfirmable: under the right pressure, an old knot in one's back might release a torrent of grief, a lashing across the body, as though this were where the sadness lived. We may note, however, that the eruption of this archive feels confusingly less or differently emotional than sadness encountered in relation to some specific object or loss of object within the purportedly nonsupernatural, causal purview of real time. In what terms can so elusive a substance be made visible to history? Ironically, chronic pain may be most commensurable with history not as a historical object or event embedded within it but as an analogous, temporal structure, insofar as one of the few things we may know for certain about it is that it *lasts.*

Another is that no matter its felt intensity or duration, its phenomenological vividness withdraws from the visual field. How to arrive at or refine an idiom for something incapable of being perceived (like things of the world) or internally envisioned (like things of the mind)? How to accomplish this when, as in Dickinson's case, pain's phenomenal radius so neatly adumbrates that of the organ of vision it eludes, as though pain were in the arduous process of translating sight into another system entirely? If figuration is unable to say what chronic pain is, it nonetheless comes close to describing how it proceeds, the low-grade vertigo of its indigestible difference from the workaday, no less resisting the amalgamating protocol of metaphor. Its selfishness and speed catch in the ordonnance, troubling the givenness of reliable efficiency weighed against its own antinomian dynamism. If figuration, like chronic pain, occupies a body (the world) one can neither be nor have, to what third option (*tertium organum*) might one yet aspire in the hyperbolizing interval between its *noli mi tangere* and *flagrante delicto*? Figuration's excrescent pivots comprise the expressive stuff of this next, late Dickinson text. The left-side version of the poem follows the editorial convention of Johnson, Franklin, and Miller; the right side approximates the narrower gulley of Dickinson's original pencil draft, which all the more graphically draws out the influence of the Latin root *pluere*—to make to flow, a flowing outward—on the "Plush" of its exploratory syncopations:

Opon a Lilac Sea
To toss incessantly
His Plush Alarm
Who fleeing from the Spring
The Spring avenging fling
To Dooms of Balm – (F1368)

Opon a Lilac
Sea
To toss
incessantly
His Plush
Alarm
Who fleeing
from the
Spring
The Spring
avenging
fling
To Dooms
of Balm –[73]

These strange little lines appear at the start of Davis's recent study of Dickinson's radical ornamental aesthetics. Complicating the commonplace of ornamentality as ancillary—a triviality implied, for instance, in Elisa New's wish to rescue the substance of Dickinson's brilliance from the "merely decorative"[74]—Davis understands the ornamental in terms of "how one object rests upon and in relation to another."[75] I appreciate that word "rests," its conjuring of an objectual scene that is at once intimate and affectively unspecified. One may rest one's head on the shoulder of the beloved when the restlessness of desire has been however temporarily stayed. At the same time, we may hear in the rest of ornamental objects an expression of entiring fatigue, "whence Blanchot's (weary!) cry," writes Barthes, "'I don't ask that weariness be done away with. I ask to be led back to a region where it might be possible to be weary' . . . Weariness = exhausting claim of the individual body that demands the right to social repose (that sociality in me rest a moment = topical theme of the Neutral). In fact, weariness = an intensity: society doesn't recognize intensities."[76] It's possible to hear in Davis's conception of ornamental rest an invalidism experienced as the intensity of one's own ornamental being, opening onto a sharpened need for rethinking usefulness against the competing weight of lassitude, the need for rest. The tacit correspondence of ornament and disability is suggested in an epithet given to the former by William Wordsworth. "It is not, then, to be supposed," Wordsworth opines in the *Lyrical Ballads* preface, "that any one, who holds that sublime notion of Poetry which I have attempted to convey, will break in upon the sanctity and truth of his pictures by transitory and accidental ornaments."[77] Wordsworth's understanding of ornamental accident is echoed, in turn, in Walter Pater's assertion that "what applies to figure or flower must be understood of all other accidental or removable ornaments of writing."[78] Even as these accounts depend on an earlier sense of the accidental as inessential, to follow Davis's elaboration of ornament as nonperipheral substance in its own right is to learn potentially an aesthetic idiom for when contingency's interruption of the life one desires becomes, without warning, the life one is dealt.

I don't mean to personify ornament's positioning of objects so much as to emphasize the noninstrumentality of ornamentality as a range of aesthetic object-feeling. For Davis, "Opon a Lilac Sea" demonstrates this perhaps counterintuitive animacy in the exhilarating instability of its opening preposition, "opon," whose idiosyncratic spelling suggests for her a hybrid of "upon" and "open."[79] For Davis, the pulsating quality of Dickinson's "opon" speaks to ornament's vivifying buoyancy, the unsteady attention with which a bee, for example, seems momentarily placed upon a spray of lilac. One of the consequences of thinking about the temporality of ornamental rest is that placement comes to seem somewhat more or less effortless than it might otherwise be. The perceived buoyancy of a bee's hovering depends on a recognition within flight of an instance of flotation, even as the blur of a bee's wings (like those of a hummingbird) more closely corresponds to the busyness of treading water. Ornament doesn't obscure this labor so much as illuminates the near perceptibility of its maintenance. "Opon a Lilac Sea" registers the strain of composition's capacity for absorbing the labor that realizes it in the word "incessantly." After all, under ordinary circumstances that which rests upon and in relation to another doesn't do so incessantly, and yet this is what Dickinson's text seems to claim. This surprising industry of rest, its quiet labor of equilibrium, recalls Kant's reflection on the mechanism if not affective shading of the agreeable: "Everyone strives after it, and the idea of [the] uninterrupted comfort of life is called happiness.—Every discomfort or pain requires us to leave our present condition, and this is its definition. But comfort is the sensation that moves us always to prolong the condition we are in. Enjoyment: every moment we seek it and are driven to leave the condition we are in: hence it seems that we have pain incessantly."[80]

The ironic discomfiture of rest informs a subsequent example Davis cites of Dickinson's animatingly ornamental "opon": "Surprise is like a thrilling – pungent – / Opon a tasteless meat" (F1324). As Davis ingeniously writes, "The logic of this displaced simile is that surprise tastes like an unexpectedly intense condiment, as if one were eating something 'tasteless' that turns spicy. But it is also, somewhat differently, that being surprised is like having a pungent placed upon oneself."[81] Although that which is pungent gives taste to the tasteless, the root shared between pungency and puncture suggests that what rests on another object may do so agonizingly, as though Dickinson's lexical juxtapositions might burn a hole through the paper on which they're written. R. P. Blackmur's word for this dermal burning is "candescence." Of the poem "Renunciation – is a piercing Virtue –" (F782), Blackmur observes that "only one word, *piercing,* is directly physical; something that if it happens cannot be ignored but always shocks us into reaction. . . . Some function of the word *pierce* precipitates a living intrinsic relation between renunciation and virtue; it is what makes the phrase incandesce. . . . The piercing quality of renunciation is precisely, but not altogether, that it is a continuing process, takes time, it may be infinite time, before the renounced presence transpires in expectation in the 'Not now.'"[82]

And so Dickinson's ornamental principle bestows a buoyancy not wholly removed from the world of pain, even when the latter's intensity obscures its relation to a body proper, seeping through it: hence the hyperbaton of "Dooms / of Balm," where balms of doom at least would achieve the superficial closure brought with doom's slant rhyme with the earlier line's "Who" (not least since Dickinson's lineation renders the poem in a sonnet's fourteen lines). Who indeed: to borrow from Melville's *Pierre,* the poem is disorienting in part because it presents the motion of its subject "but not its form."[83] Davis's adroit exposition of the poem's subject as a bee all the more returns us to the text's comparable density, on which the clarity of analysis, perhaps ornamentally, rests. Beyond the seventh line's interrogative pronoun—itself fleeing, trying to flee, the scene before the appearance of its predicate—the closest we get to the bee per se is the plushness of its alarm, calling back as plushness does to an earlier text such as "Like Trains of Cars on Tracks of Plush / I hear the level Bee" (F1213). The short, staccato breaks of the text not only dramatize the distance (or, in terms of the poem's stringent verticality, depth) between the lilac sea and the object tossed upon it; they invert it, since what would toss above the sea on its surface only comes into focus (such as that is) as what has sunk below. The poem's hyperbatic begining and end reflect the "exacting excess" of figuration dictated, so Ian Balfour observes, "just by attending to" hyperbaton's "dizzying dynamics of inversion."[84] Balfour quotes the following passage from Longinus whose attention to being "blown this way and that" uncannily duplicates the concentrated pastoral turbulence of Dickinson's "Lilac / Sea":

> Hyperbaton . . . is an arrangement of words or thoughts which differs from the normal sequence. It is a very real mark of urgent emotion. People who in real life feel anger, fear, or indignation, or are distracted by jealousy or some other emotion (it is impossible to say how many emotions there are; they are without number) often put one thing forward and then rush off to another, irrationally inserting some remark, and then hark back again to their first point. They seem to be blown this

> way and that by their excitement, as if by a veering wind. They inflict innumerable variations on the expression, the thought, and the natural sequence. Thus hyperbaton is a means by which, in the best authors, imitation approaches the effect of nature [ἡ μίμησις ἐπὶ τὰ τῆς φύσεως ἔργα φέρεται]. Art is perfect when it looks like nature, nature is felicitous when it embraces concealed art.[85]

"Opon a Lilac Sea" presents a textually occluded saturation felt along the lines of Longinus's innumerable figurative "inflict[ions]." Where the bee would be, the incessance of "His Plush / Alarm," as though the velvet nap of the bee's pile were extendible to the apprehensively impressible surface of its quickening affect: the panic not only of being out of one's native element but of one's beholdenness, one moment to the next, to contingency with no end in the abreacted sight lines of the poem's topsy-turvy.[86]

Dooms of balm, balms of doom. Davis's theory of ornament importantly articulates this affective agitation as aesthetic phenomenon. The bee bobbingly ornaments the sea, as plush ornaments alarm, as alarm perhaps plushly surrounds the bee, a second skin. Like a pungency so strong one hardly tastes the meat it spreads, the "Plush / Alarm" all but eclipses the body to which it belongs. The poem's closing lines are disorienting in part because the body that balm would appease is so hard to salvage from this lyric dizziness. In a way, the ornamental extravagance of the text pulses in and out of itself like the Cheshire cat's aforementioned smile afloat in the absence of the body that begot it.[87] If, as Davis suggests (along the lines of Wordsworth and Pater), the accident of ornament is as removable as it is affixable, the text's vivid figures acquire a sensorial liveliness, for better or worse, independent of the substances to which they would otherwise adhere. Peeling off from their predicates, Dickinson's figures once again return us to the curious behavior of Lucretian *figurae,* "structures that peel off things like membranes and float round in the air."[88]

The queer salience of "Opon a Lilac Sea" plays out between outer and inner, material and abstraction, a figurative indetermination less solipsistic than shared between world and self as that which neither can completely metabolize nor jettison. In the context of a related set of Dickinson poems, Gillian Osborne notes that "the mechanism of the poem . . . has led the collapsed subject here to suffer the pain of misplaced and presumptuous identification."[89] Osborne's account of pain in the ligatures between collapsed subject and poetic mechanism articulates at a wider optic a kind of intrigue that the figurative iridescence of "Opon a Lilac Sea" at most implies. The latter's impactions neither metaphorize nor bear witness from any single, guarded vantage, and in this respect their peculiar disorientation resembles the antinarrative subversion of perspective found in late Assyrian palace reliefs.[90] They pulse minutely between something like pain as though viewed from a poetic perimeter and a poem that is *pained,* as Bartleby's lawyer might say, perceived from (and simultaneously *as*) pain's own core. In their asymptotic resistance to the poetic repertoire of symbolic/representative/personified, the optical rhythms of "Opon a Lilac Sea" evince a textual passion that "never quite arrive[s]"[91] where we await them. However we understand the grammatical subject of these lines—whether bee, or Being, or what Osborne, discussing "The nearest Dream recedes—unrealized," calls "the bee in the brain"—it is always already submerged in the poem's nebulous medium.[92] So dissolvingly enveloped is this textually brilliant scene that it's difficult to see within it anything but the "Sea" itself.

We may glean in the unfamiliar literacy of this textual liquefaction several things. First, its impersonal infinitive, "to toss," refers alike to both textual solution and the subject of its apparent obscuration. The verb form takes the lurching movement of the sea and pauses it at the same time that it indefinitely projects it beyond itself, the temporal singularity of a wave at once disrupting and coalescing in the sea's endlessly oscillating surface. Deleuze helps us conceptualize this simultaneously frozen and recursive impact: "When a body combines some of its own distinctive points with those of a wave, it espouses the principle of a repetition which is no longer that of the Same, but involves the Other—involves difference, from one wave and one gesture to another, and carries that difference through the repetitive space thereby constituted."[93] The vibrant, claustral space that the poem enacts likewise gives to our experience of reading the sensation of being held too close to see what it is we are seeing. Deleuze continues:

> We are right to speak of repetition when we find ourselves confronted by identical elements with exactly the same concept. However, we must distinguish between these discrete elements, these repeated objects, and a secret subject, the real subject of repetition, which repeats itself through them. . . . As a result, rather than the repeated and the repeater, the object and the subject, we must distinguish two forms of repetition.[94]

Deleuze's distinction between the repetition of "discrete elements" and the "subject of repetition . . . which repeats itself through them" clarifies within the apparatus of Dickinson's work the difference between the repetitiveness of nominally discrete poems and the current that pours through them. If "pour" too indulgently translates the mechanical care by which Deleuze characterizes the subject of repetition "repeat[ing] itself," I'm nonetheless struck by the spatial richness of his preposition, "through," repeating figures as though animated by a repetition that doesn't resemble them in concept so much as holds them together "As Staples – driven through –" (F292) or like the "iron wire" on which Emerson strings the beads of our passing moods.[95] Gesturing toward a spatial fluency as much as a representative logic, the almost interiorizing work of "through" transforms repetition into its own serially puncturing stitchwork. The narrative grammar—"repeated and . . . repeater, the object and the subject"—gives way to the energetics of a thoroughness that sharpens our attention, in turn, to the surprising specificity of Dickinson's *incessantly*. Even graphically, the allure of this word within the above poem is marked by its syllabic length, occupying as much metrical space as the first two lines combined. Although an uncommon word in her corpus (it appears in just one other late poem), "incessantly" names a temporal milieu found throughout Dickinson's oeuvre. A far more frequent word, corresponding to a nearly equivalent experience of time, is "perpetual." Consider this second stanza of a late fragment beginning "A not admitting / of the wound":

> A closing of the
> simple (Gate) lid that
> opened to the sun
> Until the (unsuspecting Carpenters) (sovereign) tender
> Carpenter
> Perpetual nail
> it down –[96]

Bearing in mind Allen Tate's account of the absorption of Dickinson's poetry's less in Calvinism than the latter's desuetude illuminates a perpetuity pried from its religious aspect, leaving in its place a sense of pain's ongoingness as an afterlife stripped bare of redemption.[97] Dickinson's captivation with the possibility of sensorial consistency on both sides of the afterlife not only posits immortality as the tenor that figuration vehiculates but can't quite reach, but subjects it to the more finely searching analysis of a metaphorical vehicle in its own right, the "remnant" reliquary material of time without interruption by which one might come to fathom pain's enigmatic chronicity. If, as with "Opon a Lilac Sea," the speaker's experience of visual obstruction reverberates as our own, the stanza's last lines reorient this ocular relation as haptic vulnerability, the carpenter's "tender[ness]" distributed through the poem as that which belongs to neither wound nor wounded self so much as the fiber of the poem writ large. As the lid is secured and we too are left in darkness, the bruising delicacy of the carpenter's calling converges with the tenderness of the "simple lid," a transmutation of the first stanza's hurt into a vision of the lid's own experience of impingement, one nail at a time. Up until this point, the predominant temporal mood of the poem had moved between the gerunds at the start of each stanza (a not admitting, a closing) and the deep bass note marking the pluperfect submergence of the speaker's Life—"the wound / . . . gr[own] so / wide / . . . my / Life had entered it"—into pain's wake. In this light, the present tense of the poem's last lines, "Perpetual nail / it down," grows all the more jarring: the urgency of a command, no matter the difficulty of saying to whom it is directed or by whom it is spoken. If only in the figurative florescence of the text, the speaker's excruciation gives way to the horror of an abstract, "perpetual" crucifixion. The haecceity of a single nail driven into the poem's tender surface proliferates into as many times a single nail is struck by an absent hammer, further kaleidoscoping into however many nails are needed to secure such a lid against the sun to which in some dream of a prior life it had opened: exponentially multiplying unto perpetuity, sharp waves of pain vanishing into the sea's horizon, far as Dickinson's figurative eye—its own tender lid always on the verge—can see.

4. Inveterate Pagoda

Late James, Ongoingness, and the Figure of Hurt

Imagine poetry. You are ill-equipped to talk about it. But I'm not asking you to talk about it, I'm asking you to imagine it.

—JEAN-LUC NANCY, *THE BIRTH TO PRESENCE*

Such obscure hurt—*is it real or not?*—defines, I think, Henry James at his hardest.

—JEFF NUNOKAWA, "THE HARDSHIP OF HENRY JAMES"

In May 1899, from the Hotel d'Europe in Rome, Henry James writes a letter of solicitude to Howard Sturgis, a close friend whose life in certain crucial respects parallels James's own. Sturgis, too, was a novelist (of invariably lesser degree) who lived openly with his life partner, William Haynes-Smith, "known simply," Edmund White writes, as "the Babe."[1] Sturgis, like James, was descended from a Boston Brahmin family but lived in England; he was the cousin of George Santayana, William James's Harvard colleague,[2] and distant relation of Caroline Tappan Sturgis, who enjoyed close friendships with Margaret Fuller, Ralph Waldo Emerson, and Henry James's own father, Henry James *père*. Literary criticism owes a debt of thanks to whatever injury on Sturgis's end occasions James's affectionate apprehension, as the letter in question proves an invaluable testament to James's own intimate experience with chronic pain:

> It's a great pleasure to hear from you in this far country—though I greatly wish it weren't from the bed of anguish—or at any rate of delicacy: if delicacy may be connected, that is, with anything so indelicate as a bed! But I'm very glad to gather that it's the couch of convalescence. Only, if you have a Back, for heaven's sake take care of it. When I was about your age—in 1862!—I did a bad damage (by a strain subsequently—through crazy juvenility—neglected) to mine; the consequence of which is that, in spite of retarded attention, and years, really, of recumbency, later, I've been saddled with it for life, and that even now, my dear Howard, I verily write you *with* it.[3]

In 1862, James was eighteen; in 1899, Sturgis is forty-four. We may forgive the passage's fuzzy math, so pressing seems James's need to tease through the mediumship of Sturgis some renewed correspondence with his own younger self. James lavishingly returns to this venture in the *New York Edition* prefaces (1907–9) and his triptych of dense autobiographical texts: *A Small Boy and Others* (1913); *Notes of a Son and Brother* (1914); and *The Middle Years* (unfinished at the time of James's death). The second of these is the principal concern of this chapter, which presents less a unified argument about the queerness of James's chronic pain—what *Notes of a Son and Brother* denominates "a horrid even if an obscure hurt"[4]—than an exhortation to take seriously the latter's textual strangeness as a formal concern. The overdetermination of this conceptual field animates the innuendo of James's "bed of anguish," site of suffering shading into a delicacy that answers to the fragility of James's and Sturgis's constitutions while opening onto the competing politesse of indelicacy's scene of sex acts better left unsaid. At once mutually depredatory and titillating, these filaments of recovery and communicability traverse James's oeuvre. Whether or not misery acquaints a man with strange bedfellows, its bed becomes a palimpsest on which desire and illness write and revise each other, were their respective energies ever separable in the first place.

The following pages are shaped by a belief in the critical appeal of James's "obscure hurt" independent of any external, historical referent on which said hurt might otherwise be said to be predicated. My commitment to thinking pain however provisionally apart from the compulsions of historical or cultural substance is born in turn of an investment in the commensuration of pain's phenomenal existence with a textual obscurity that doesn't ask to be solved so much as lived with. Loosely assembled from

Notes of a Son and Brother and James's late fiction, this chapter's constellation of close readings seeks to clear a space within our understanding of James's queerly lucubrative difficulty for chronic pain's acutely attendant temporal rhythms. Its guiding wish is to do justice to the above passage's penultimate preposition, the plangency of "writ[ing] you *with*" a pain that outlasts and consequently exceeds its cause, acceding past mimesis to the figurative complexity of an event in its own right.

This attention to chronic pain's impaction on James's writing is all the more remediatingly needful, given the short shrift biographers and critics have accorded the subject in this century since James's death. Sheldon Novick's biographical study of young James suggests, for example, that "Harry . . . carr[ied] on as well as he could, and the injury to his back again became a part of his private existence."[5] For all intents and purposes, this wistful dispatch is Novick's final word on the matter, an unsteady briskness belying a discomfiture not uncommon among the interlocutors of the "obscure hurt." At once gesturing toward the injury's place in James's psychical life and consigning that life to a privacy beyond Novick's scope, the trope of reclusive enterprise beneath the business of outwardly carrying on intimates a morphology shared between James's experience of chronic pain and the imagined obscurations of James's queerness, more narrowly understood. But where James's indelicate bed teases an opening between duress and desire, the vanishing point of privacy serves for Novick as placeholder for if not simply terminus of further inquiry.[6] Admittedly, Novick's express concern with the early life of James (hence the puzzling title of his biography, *The Young Master*)[7] confines his analysis to an apparatus that can only so much look ahead to its subject's eventual prolificacy. At the same time, however, the *sfumato* by which a swath of James's life is made to fade into the background too quickly resolves a tension between private and public spheres that the sheer publicity of James's eventual oeuvre unsettles, and which chronic pain's transverse element only further troubles. Eve Kosofsky Sedgwick's foundational analysis of Jamesian queerness illuminates by analogy chronic pain's permeating knack for seeping into the texture of James's writing. Sedgwick's intervention in how we think about the interwoven epistemologies and ontologies of the closet guides my own present caution against hypostasizing the peculiar fluency of the "obscure hurt" as anything so discretely internal as an element of privacy per se. Writing of John Marcher, the protagonist of James's "The Beast in the Jungle" (1903), Sedgwick hypothesizes that "the presence or possibility of a homosexual meaning attached to the inner, the future, secret has exactly the reifying, totalizing, and blinding effect we described earlier in regard to the phenomenon of the Unspeakable."[8] Along these lines, it's vital that we not reduce the semantic challenge of James's "obscure hurt" to an epistemological zero-sum, nor assume in advance the textual contours of chronic pain much less what the latter "means." In the case of both queerness and chronic pain,[9] identifying the shifting rhythms of *éclairecissement*[10] depends ultimately on how and where the vicissitudes of inaccessibility are permitted expression, and for whom the literacy of such experiences, eidetic and otherwise, are imagined possible. We must then salvage Jamesian duress from the assumption of its withdrawal. Like Poe's purloined letter, the obscure hurt for some time has been hiding in plain sight.

April 1861. The James family has just returned to the States following two stints in Europe. Like many former expatriates, they settle in Newport, Rhode Island, "its opera-glass turned for ever across the sea" (245). The Civil War hangs in the air like ominous impending weather, and James's younger brothers, Wilkie and Bob, have already joined the Union army. It's in the midst of this disquiet, *Notes of a Son and Brother* tells us, that eighteen-year-old James injures himself while helping put out a nearby fire. And it's this accident—along with the years of pain, bafflement, and concern that follow—to which the "obscure hurt," half a century after the fact, will come to refer. Effectively answering the question of his prospective relation to the war, the injury leaves James bedridden just as his brothers and peers begin the work of reimagining themselves as soldiers. As biographers and critics have remarked, both James's injury and subsequent experience as a patient come to inform the aesthetic economy of passivity, its tactical fascination with remediated patience and potentially generative hamstrung being, to which James's late work so frequently attends. "Newport" no less than the "obscure hurt" comes to signify this formative experience of the vulnerated self as a violent contingency's vulnerable object: the germ of a career-long investigation of patience whose principled and complex quiet anticipates Blanchot's understanding of the neutral: "the contradiction between the need for communication that must affirm itself from the basis of affliction and through the '*ardent patience*' of the man who suffers, and the need for communication that is affirmed on the basis of fire and through the knowing, impatient, ecstatic and glorious seizing of the man who conquers."[11]

My commitment to the "obscure hurt," as opposed to obscure hurt, marks a fidelity to Jamesian textuality as an object of experience. In this sense, my insistence on quotation marks evinces less a preference for formalism over paraphrase so much as a belief in the "obscure hurt" as lived form. Admittedly there's an irony in the cognizance that while the words "obscure hurt" are James's, both the quotation marks and aphoristic economy of the quotation itself exist beyond the scope of the autobiography's textual consciousness. At the same time, quotation marks nonetheless register something elemental to the experience *of* the "obscure hurt," both the life of those words as sensation and the sensation of them as figurative substance. Deborah Esch beautifully observes these twined phenomena at work in "The Jolly Corner" (1908), a text whose spectrally doubled and disfigured protagonist no doubt bears the impression of James's injury, refractingly suspended between selves across time:

> In other words, Brydon cannot read the word "figure," though he uses it repeatedly, because he cannot tell (or admit) the difference between its literal and figurative senses. He has forgotten, if he ever knew, that the figure of his *alter ego* is a figure by virtue of the linguistic process of figuration. Moreover, he is unable to read the quotation marks that are of his own inscription, unable to tell (or admit) the difference between walked and "walked." His claim to knowing "what he meant and what he wanted" becomes a self-deception based on a refusal *not to* literalize his own figures of speech.[12]

Esch adjures James's readers against "repeating the characters' error in taking a figurative likeness for an identity."[13] In the case of the "obscure hurt," however, framing the episode in terms of whether James is able to "tell (or admit) the difference between" chronic pain's "literal and figurative senses" distorts the differently vexing dilemma of a phenomenon experienced as literally figurative, even as it's no less true to say that James's pain, contra the litotes of Brydon's "refusal *not* to literalize his own figures of speech," at once fails and exceeds the criteria for literal and figurative substance alike. If to believe in the veracity of the "obscure hurt" is to reckon with the disarticulation of the literal from the real, it is also to experience physical infidelity—the beleaguerment of a body's disappointment—as aesthetic duress, in the manner of a word that isn't literally in quotation marks yet at the same time is never quite able to escape the attritive weight of its own unconfirmable and miscarried citational being.

Without exception, then, my preference throughout will be to place "obscure hurt" in quotation marks for the sake of forestalling the false ease with which the formulation gives, in their absence, the impression of a corresponding injury too quickly ascertained as actual, external, empirical, physical, and so forth. After all, whatever there was of an original external injury was never, as depicted in the autobiography, external enough: though the hurt's illegibility according to medical expertise is nothing, as we will see, compared to the inscrutability it poses for James himself. At the same time, quotation marks reflect the hurt's paradoxical externality (deeply, internally withdrawn though it simultaneously is) to both James and James's writing, the frustration of not being able to cozen it any closer to articulateness. At once too near and too far, the spatial pathos of quoted substance dovetails with a correspondingly peculiar temporal suspense. Again, Blanchot's meditation on the incessancy particular to what he calls the "passion of the outside" illuminates chronic pain's unmooring temporal aesthetic. "In impossibility," Blanchot writes, "time changes direction, no longer offering itself out of the future as what gathers by going beyond; time, here, is rather the dispersion of a present that, even while being only passage does not pass, never fixes itself in a present, refers to no past and goes toward no future: *the incessant*."[14]

When it comes to whether the "obscure hurt" belongs to 1861 or 1914, *Notes of a Son and Brother* ultimately insists on both and neither, even as belonging (notwithstanding its etymological suggestion of durational *longueur*) simplifies the quality of encounter with an injury by which however perversely one feels possessed. Novick's aforementioned paraphrase aside, it's impossible to say whether James experiences the injury in 1861 as "obscure"—whether this is how the hurt *felt* at the time, in all its epistemological recalcitrance—or whether the future James of 1914 plants this formulation in the landscape that gives rise to it, all those decades after. In this way, the irresolvable equivocation that the "obscure hurt" maintains expresses in miniature the autobiography's larger, experimental preoccupation. The formulation operates as a temporal contraction by which the sensorium of James's younger self is shown, hydraulically and nonidentically, to coexist with the sensorium that strives to preside over the later scene of writing, to withstand the fatigue and interrupting distance posed by pain-in-writing, writing-in-pain. If the perverse aliment of the "obscure hurt" umbilicates adolescent James to his elder self, we might more precisely say that the formal interest of the "obscure hurt," like *Notes of a Son and Brother* writ large, lies in the exhilarating discovery that relating autobiographically to a prior self proves inseparable from—is nothing without—one's profoundly unsettled, ligamentous involvement in a field of experience only accessible through, as, writing. The "obscure hurt" names one such node of textual self-impingement. Were it not quite so affected, some further punctuative refinement might specify a single quotation mark instead of two—the *"obscure hurt*—indicating, in the manner of an open parenthetical, the Pygmalion-like site at which written and nonwritten selves suffer the sea-change of one into the other, the indefinite article of "a horrid even if an obscure hurt" on the verge of becoming the definite article that will come to characterize "the 'obscure hurt,'" its redoubtable singularity, for both James and his readers.

POETICS OF OBSCURITY (CONTINGENCY)

Over and against the distortive ease by which criticism has treated the "obscure hurt" as biographical or historical aphorism, the following pages seek to repair that which in the "obscure hurt" feels most irresolvably vivid. My sense of repair, here, is informed by Sedgwick's articulation of a reparative mode spry enough to complicate the comparative inflexibility of paranoid reading. Indeed, Sedgwick's gloss of the latter in terms of "a distinctively rigid relation to temporality . . . averse above all to surprise,"[15] illuminates the reparatively bristling fervor of James's own mercurially autobiographical enterprise. In Lauren Berlant's words, "the impasse not yet or perhaps never caught up in the drama of repair is neither life existentially nor life posttraumatically but existence, revealed in the stunned encounter: with the contingencies of structuring fantasy; in what one loves in one's own incoherence; and in the bruise of significant contact."[16] As we will see, *Notes of a Son and Brother* mobilizes—unless, amounting nearly to the same, it stunningly immobilizes—impasse's near-encounter with a trepanning apparatus in which it hasn't yet been caught, one form of isolation tropaically cambered against another. I should say that at its simplest, however, my attachment to repair has less to do with restoring factitious clarity to the field of Jamesian pain than with the notion of repair-as-return.

As Hamlet writes in a letter to Horatio (to which we are privy only as Horatio reads Hamlet's words aloud), "repair thou to me with as much speed as thou wouldest fly death."[17] In this sense, to repair the "obscure hurt" is to return itself to itself for the sake of forestalling its collation with an interpretive syntax bent on explanation at the expense of inhabiting the slip of its constitutive difficulty. Here, then, is the passage from which the "obscure hurt" has so frequently been extricated, notwithstanding the text's counter-insistent scene of entanglement:

> Jammed into the acute angle between two high fences, where the rhythmic play of my arms, in tune with that of several other pairs, but at a dire disadvantage of position, induced a rural, a rusty, a quasi-extemporised old engine to work and a saving stream to flow, I had done myself, in face of a shabby conflagration, a horrid even if an obscure hurt; and what was interesting from the first was my not doubting in the least its duration—though what seemed equally clear was that I needn't as a matter of course adopt and appropriate it, so to speak, or place it for increase of interest on exhibition. The interest of it, I very presently knew, would certainly be of the greatest, would even in conditions kept as simple as I might make them become little less than absorbing. The shortest account of what was to follow for a long time after is therefore to plead that the interest never did fail. (240–41)

To return the "obscure hurt" to this at once intensely animating and impacting passage is to recover the text's propulsive rhythm, to find one's self alongside James both lost and located in figuration's pull. Philippe Lacoue-Labarthe's remarks on rhythm speak to this implicitly phenomenological dimension of figuration's eddying hydraulic:

> Since rhythm *is* consequently the figure, *essentially* the figure (which itself is perhaps not essentially of the order of the visible), what is missing is the repetition on the basis of which the *repetition of the dance* (the dance as repetition, imitation, and within it, the repetition of figures) might appear. Missing is the repetition from which the division might be made between the mimetic and the non-mimetic: a division between the recognizable and the non-recognizable, the familiar and the strange, the real and the fantastic, the sensible and the mad—life and fiction.[18]

In the case of *Notes of a Son and Brother,* the textual autonomy of figuration, its antirepresentational consistency, all the more activates in readers a mimetic prejudice to which autobiography as a genre is keenly susceptible. Insofar as autobiography is assumed to give an account of its author's life, the latter tends to adumbrate discussion with all the foreclosing influence of an external referent. As de Man writes, the preemptive lure of historicity transforms the autobiographical reader into a "judge, the policing power in charge of verifying the *authenticity* of the signature and the consistency of the signer's behavior."[19] And so reading the "obscure hurt" for many critics too quickly deteriorates into a matter of measuring the germ of James's formulation against the unconfirmable specter of an "actual" injury that James's formulation is said tautologically to obscure.

In the decade following James's death, the Fort/Da prestidigitation of a hurt that is or isn't there foments the uncanny speculation that the injury at hand is nothing so much as a castration. One of the earliest examples of this castration theory appears in "A Sentimental Contribution," Glenway Wescott's contribution to a 1934 issue of Lincoln Kerstein's *Hound and Horn* devoted to Henry James. The third paragraph of Wescott's essay broaches the subject with self-aggrandizing abstruseness: "Lord Byron; incest; Henry James; expatriation and castration; Abélard; George Moore. Which, in over-emphasized sentences, means:—If I were as potent a poet as Byron, would a child have been born of that extreme tenderness?[20] Henry James, it is rumored, could not have had a child. But if he was as badly hurt in the pre-Civil-War accident as that—since he triumphed powerfully over other authors of his epoch—perhaps the injury was a help to him."[21] Tapped out like a string of Morse code, the passage's opening sequence of proper names and semicolons presents literary personages alongside their confirmable and imputed situations, a dossier of proper names wrest from any grammar or relation more nuanced than linear proximity. Wescott, it would appear, offers this series of distillations as a correction to what he appraises as James's opposite tendency toward extravagance: "Embarrassed passion, hinted meaning . . . in excess of the narrated facts."[22] At the same time, of course, his flirtation with the "fact" of castration is nothing if not willfully mannered; even the typographical mark :— (known in England as the dog's bollocks) casts the semicolons that precede it as so much castrative residua, a bit of queer grammarian camp that deflates the scandal of castration in the very moment it's raised. This condensation of readerly apprehension around and as the birth of Jamesian impotence clinches debility as an allegory for its own complex relation to immanence and withdrawal. If this collation of chronic pain and phallic crisis signals the homophobic tenor of the criticism, it also attests, however inadvertently, to the queerness with which James's pain is from the outset implicated.

The semiotic burden of the "obscure hurt" is further encumbered by James's assertion of its coincidence with the start of the Civil War, "the queer fusion or confusion established in my consciousness during the soft spring of '61 by the firing on Fort Sumter, Mr. Lincoln's instant first call for volunteers and a physical mishap, already referred to as having overtaken me at the same dark hour, and the effects of which were to draw themselves out incalculably and intolerably" (239). Even as the hurt's quandary tears the fabric of the prosaic quotidian—"like white lightning, a flash that spread, and spread again, and stayed"[23]—readers of *Notes of a Son and Brother* can't resist darning it back into history's narrative apparatus. Returning the injury to narrative time, however, misrepresents the event of the "obscure hurt" as though it were consubstantial with the world it interrupts, when its difference from the latter is as generically inexorable as poem from prose—as different, in point of fact, as war from peace. Beyond its presumed manipulation or skirting of medical truth, *Notes of a Son and Brother* has to this end been taken to task for playing fast and loose with history at its most cataclysmically staked. Consider, for instance, Peter Rawlings's summation:

> What emerges . . . is the extent to which James's accident, and certainly his subsequent meditations on it, were not simply a contrivance for avoiding the war to become a writer, but the means by which he could compel obscurity and cultivate that discourse and thematics of irony already more than embryonic in the first short stories. In what was soon to become a familiar refrain . . . James repudiates the relevance of mere facts to literature. . . . For James as a writer, battles and casualties are the mere incidents and incidentals of war, and like the so-called facts and events of history, demand to be abused, reversed, and even perverted, if anything worthwhile is to ensue.[24]

The collective effect of Rawlings's vitriol against James's "lingering, perhaps malingering, state of invalidism"[25] is to assert the failure of *Notes of a Son and Brother* in the face of a subject Rawlings takes as his own prerogative to assign—namely, that the injury most clamoring for redress belongs not to James but to "concrete experience . . . mutilated by abstraction"[26]—

while abrogating the autobiography's textual density as so much obfuscatory foofaraw. "In a description that ultimately fails to describe," Rawlings quips, "descriptive excess abounds."[27] In this way, the "obscure hurt" and the constellation of chronic pain to which it speaks registers nothing less than the damning apotheosis of the literary itself. To be sure, I'm not interested in disarticulating the "obscure hurt" from literariness (quite the contrary), from saving or protecting its narrative integrity from what Gregory Phipps terms the "verbose . . . circuitous[ness]" of Jamesian description.[28] I'm drawn instead to the figural substance of obscurity as a form of experience every bit as searchingly candid as anything perceptible from the vantage of conventional medicine, whether that of 1861 or the present. It's against this impasse of factual reduction that I imagine obscurity as a poetics of phenomenology, less a shirking of empirical fidelity than the expansion of a sharper, stranger experiential field.

Writing of difficult poetry, George Steiner posits that there are "intricate, deep-felt contiguities between obscurity and silence on the one hand and loquacity and light on the other."[29] To pursue by contrast the convergences of difficult poetry and chronic pain is to reexamine the intricate contiguities between obscurity and the loquacious.[30] Resisting the anthropomorphosis that would simply give obscurity a voice, contiguity suggests instead that obscurity and language share an edge, "deep-felt," just touching. Pain dwells in this rift between dark and speech; we dwell on it there. Daniel Tiffany's *Infidel Poetics: Riddles, Nightlife, Substance* extends the surface area of obscurity's animacy by implicating in its vividness the vividness of our experience of it. "The problematic of lyric obscurity," Tiffany writes, calls on us to focus "not so much on a poem's composition or construction . . . as on its *reception* by the reader."[31] To this end, Tiffany helps us begin to understand the virtues of thinking about obscurity and chronic pain beyond etiology's attachment to origin as explanation. His insistence that we "reject" obscurity's commonplace association with the "virtuosic, or deliberately experimental"[32] underscores more generally our need to disarticulate the poetics of obscurity from fictions of bravura subjectivity. The point, I think, isn't to divorce obscurity from experiment so much as to recognize the experimental mode at its least deliberate. Obscurity happens. In the case of chronic pain, obscurity, "regarded . . . as an *event*,"[33] doesn't surface so much as sink into the body as what Samuel Vriezen calls a "ritual of contingency."[34] "What," Jean-Luc Marion asks, "does such a contingency mean? Before meaning the mere opposite of the necessary, contingent says what touches me, what reaches me and therefore arrives to me (according to the Latin) or (according to the German) what 'falls like that.'"[35]

Contingency, contiguity: it's not just that "obscurity itself," in Fredric Jameson's words, will be "the object of [our] reading."[36] For the person living with and in duress, thinking about chronic pain's obscurity—rather than etiologically solving it—is inseparable if not indistinguishable from feeling it. As the previous chapter suggested, Emily Dickinson understands this implacable twinning. Consider the following poem, also cited by Tiffany:

> You see I cannot see – your
> lifetime –
> I must guess –
> How many times it ache for
> me – today – Confess –
> How many times for my far
> sake
> The brave eyes film –
> But I guess guessing hurts –
> Mine – get so dim![37]

Ordinarily, vision—what Dickinson, in Steiner's idiom, might call the loquacity of light—denotes an apparatus as perspicuously given as its perceptual object. From chronic pain's tender epicenter,[38] however, it's impossible to see, let alone fathom, its "lifetime," leaving the speaker no recourse but the comparably inexact repertoire of guesswork. Seamlessly as ease of vision inhabits an unimpaired eye, the work of guessing resides in an "Illocality"[39] as difficult for the poem to envision much less mindfully inhabit as the diachrony of a "lifetime," exceeding as the latter does sight's synchronistic purview. After all, the explicitly chronic duress of "How many times it ache" only potentially supplies the direct object of "I must guess –," depending on whether one treats the latter's concluding dash as a pause in thought or the sign of thought's inability to continue. Our ability to speculate on the poem's speculation is only further addled by the opening apostrophe's equivocation, since the "You" to whom "your / lifetime" corresponds could conceivably refer not only to an unnamed person but to a pain internal to the speaker but so "far" removed from her control as to feel like a separate entity. The challenge of calculating the hurt's frequency is compounded by the enjambment of "for / me," indefinitely gesturing as it does toward both an ache felt by the speaker and an ache felt on account of her. Although the poem's ecology of feeling flirts with the implicitly amorous, it resists the trope of erotic pain per se to the extent that it presents hurt and desire as only potentially synonymous variants.[40] The knot of their opaquely indefinitive collusion inflects the first line's doublet of vision—"You see I cannot see"—as the vibrational difference between seeing a poem (reading it without understanding) and thinking one sees what a poem says (risking, in turn, that what one sees will be displaced by what one sees *in* it). If, in the wake of the poem's catalyzing failure, apostrophe and hypothesis operate in tandem, this is because the organ of guesswork ultimately is none other than the folding and unfolding obscurity of the text.

Dickinson's poetry provides a powerful account of figuration as the substance of guessing's incessant ache, of contingent figure's phenomenal life. In its attention to the figurative animacy of obscurity's hurt, Henry James's late writing provides another. Frequently as Dickinson is imagined as James's "nineteenth-century counterpart,"[41] when it comes to their imbricating ordeals of chronic pain, Dickinson follows in James's footsteps. Recall Dickinson's time spent under the care of a Cambridge eye surgeon between 1864 and 1865. In 1861 or, as James remembers in the Sturgis letter, 1862, an eighteen-year-old James (Dickinson would have been thirty-one) visits a Boston surgeon, "the high expert," with a beleaguering injury of his own, the effects of which he will painfully weather for some time to come:

> Agitated scraps of rest, snatched, to my consciousness, by the liveliest violence, were to show for futile almost to the degree in which the effort of our interview with the high expert was afterwards so to show; the truth being that this interview settled my sad business, settled it just in that saddest sense, for ever so long to come. This was so much the case that, as the mere scene of our main appeal, the house from which we had after its making dejectedly emerged put forth to me as I passed it in many a subsequent season an ironic smug symbolism of its action on my fate. That action had come from the complete failure of our approached oracle either to warn, to comfort or to command—to do anything but make quite unassistingly light of the bewilderment exposed to him. In default of other attention or suggestion he might by a mere warning as to

> gravities only too possible, and already well advanced, have made such a difference; but I have little forgotten how I felt myself, the warning absent, treated but to a comparative pooh-pooh—an impression I long looked back to as a sharp parting of the ways. (242).

From the cusp of an adulthood hardly yet able to take itself for granted, how could James not feel this visit as a dismantling embarrassment, what *Notes of a Son and Brother* retroactively cloaks in the hauteur of a "sharp parting of the ways"? Before it learns a literacy of its own, chronic pain is undefended against the blasé medical inference that nothing is the matter, that there is nothing consequently to speak of. A melancholy of broken calibration blooms in this interval between presenting a pain that can't make itself known (the woodman's chest, returned to the queen without the heart) and being told that what fails to meet the criteria of medical expertise can't be treated because it can't properly be said to exist. How does one navigate the exasperating task of making peace with a condition at once so tenuously tethered to and tenaciously splintered at the heart of one's empirical field? How does one learn to improvise living around pain's intractable radius, to speak of much less to demonstrate so disavowed a vibrancy? As the above passage suggests, the confoundment of that "sad business"—"bewilderment" bewildered—lines James's disparaged ailment as a chronicity in its own right, a temporal membrane stretching from the founding dejection ("for ever so long to come") to a middle distance ("an impression I long looked back to") hovering between historical preterition and the autobiography's present scene of writing. As approximate compensation for the expert's nullifying scoff, the figurative repertoire that will characterize James's late style articulates the phenomenal current of pain as it is pervadingly felt from within the medium of consciousness, rather than how it appears (which is to say, fails to appear) to the world outside it. As Oliver Herford remarks, "The 'bad accident'—the back injury James sustained at Newport in 1861, 'a horrid even if an obscure hurt'—thus yields to the 'finer' accident, and in a manner enables it. The very late style is uniquely alive to such fluctuations of contingency."[42]

Timothy Lustig has noted the frequency with which "James's ghost stories feature wounds."[43] In the case of young James's "sad business" with the oracle, the converse is no less true: chronic pain is a ghost story. Leon Edel touches on the spectral influence of the "obscure hurt," its nearly

Gothic economy, vis-à-vis the lubricious enthusiasm that James's account of the injury engenders in its first readers:

> The hurt is "horrid" but it is also "obscure." It is a "catastrophe," but it is in the very same phrase only a "difficulty." . . . James compounds the mystery by giving no hint of the kind of hurt he suffered, although at various times during his life he complained of an early back injury. . . . That he should have chosen to omit all specific reference to his back in his memoirs is significant; in some way he seems to have felt that by vagueness and circumlocution he might becloud the whole question of his non-participation in the Civil War. To the error of omission—"error" because of the consequences of his reticence—must be added the effect of his elaborate euphemisms: the use of the words *intimate, odious, horrid, catastrophe, obscure* and the phrase *most entirely personal.* These had an effect not unlike that of the unspecified "horrors" of *The Turn of the Screw.* His readers were ready to imagine the worst.[44]

Edel is careful to situate the sangfroid of his narration beyond the transmogrifying pull of the hurt itself, countering the overexercised imaginations of fellow Jamesians—Glenway Wescott and F. O. Matthiessen, to name two—with an analysis that confines itself to the halting transcription of James's own terms: "*intimate, odious, horrid, catastrophe, obscure* and the phrase *most entirely personal.*" Edel's paratactic catalog reduces James's source material to a series of keywords meant to ventriloquize the half-metabolized path by which Wescott and others arrive at James's castration as subtext if not solution to the passage at hand. "What, after, all," Edel rhetorically queries, "is the most *odious, horrid, intimate* thing that can happen to a man" if not castration?[45] "The obscure hurt," Edel concludes, "remained obscure to these critics; and to some of them highly ominous," the murkiness of the castration hypothesis—a "theory," Edel notes, "promptly converted into a rumor"—only casting its proponents into further dim.[46]

Edel relishingly meets such tenebrity with the clarity of his own insight, posited as neither claim nor theory so much as the unstated self-evidence of fact. Dispensing with castration's red herring, Edel fixes on a temporal discrepancy in James's account—that is, whether the injury occurs at the start of the Civil War in 1861 or, as James recalls in the letter to Sturgis, 1862—that confirms, for him, the dissembling betrayed by James's "elaborate euphemisms." The peculiarity of Edel's charge suggests a discomfiture at odds with the passage's aspirational levelheadedness. For starters, it's not clear if "elaborate" ought be understood in relation to each item in Edel's list or to the cumulative lexical texture of these words across the paragraph in *Notes of a Son and Brother* from which they're taken. At the same time, the difference between these options is moot, given Edel's interest in elaborateness less as a description of formal complexity than as a metonym for investment, the pains James takes to produce the trick of euphemism in the first place; after all, the more laborious the euphemism, the easier it becomes to argue the consequentiality of what it suppresses. Although it doesn't for Edel's purposes so much matter whether this industry is conscious or unconscious, one senses nonetheless a strain when it comes to his parsing of Jamesian agency, the manifest intent of what James "should have chosen to omit" sliding into the symptomatically hemming periphrasis of what "in some way he seems to have felt" obscurity "might becloud."[47] Again, however, the extent of James's cognizance of the euphemistic function of the "obscure hurt" ceases to register in the face of Edel's equivocation between "omission" and the passage's twice-repeated "effect."

It's not quite that Edel treats James's text and its eventual reception as interchangeable. Rather, his emphasis on effect empties the text of itself, reducing it to the negative space against which its purported omissions might counterintuitively come into relief. This textual disavowal repeats in turn the emptying effected by the charge of euphemism, the alacrity with which obscurity-as-euphemism wishfully shifts our attention to what obscurity obscures. We encounter here a hitch in Edel's logic. Obscurity, after all, isn't a euphemism per se (elaborate or otherwise) so much as it describes, generally speaking, the concealing work achieved by euphemistic substitution. And whereas euphemism depends however asymmetrically on the ability for one substance to stand in for another, James suggests to the contrary, I think, that his (and, in turn, our) experience of the hurt's obscurity emerges from nothing so much as its adamant nonfungibility. In this sense, the obscurity of James's hurt has less in common with the psychical gentrification of euphemism—doesn't, in other words, take the place of some sharper or abashing designation—than it does the deep tenacity of Jean Laplanche's enigmatic signifier, "an internal—external element which, as far as the ego is concerned, acts from the outside."[48] Far from "evading reality or putting the best face on things,"[49] the "obscure hurt" illuminates the closest James can get to the pain, notwithstanding the disparate acuity of pain's reach to him. That it is "non-metabolizable," to borrow from Laplanche, "means that [it] cannot be diluted, and cannot be replaced by anything else."[50]

Edel's charge of euphemism thus enacts the foreclosing violence of converting pain's innate opacity into terms external to it. In treating obscurity as a secondary operation, as the distortion of a malady that might otherwise be named (as though the locative event of naming could solve the awful mystery not only of what pain is but how it feels), Edel and those Jamesians who follow his lead err precisely in the twofold assumption that obscurity's formalism, as articulated in *Notes of a Son and Brother,* can be interpreted before it is analyzed much less read or pondered, and that obscurity's formalism is laid over pain like a scrim or fog when, in fact, obscurity names pain's textually inscrutable substance, through and through. In the manner of enigmatic signifiers, the "highly specific inadequacy of languages"[51] of which the seduction of pain is composed is experienced both as and through duration. If the pain *did* have a name, if its illegibility could sponsor a mode of engagement other than the repetition of its impasse, it might not so luridly *last;*[52] but last it does, the mean alchemy of time causing psychical and somatic life to bleed together, to lose their diacritical value. Pain moves between them like a ghost, a "signifier . . . *designified* . . . without thereby losing its power to signify *to.*"[53] More than the specter of castration, the queerness of obscurity's temporal unflaggingness discomfits Edel's attempt to resolve James's "unaware[ness] of the subjective elements which conditioned and at the same time obscured his hurt":[54]

> The extraordinary case was as mystifying to the doctor as the obscure hurt was to Henry James. . . . [James] gives us a very positive clue in his final account when he asserts "what was interesting from the first was my not doubting in the least its [the obscure hurt's] duration." This is a curious and significant admission. James admits to foreknowledge or to a feeling that his injury would have lasting effects. We can, of course, explain this in part by saying that James was an extraordinarily intuitive person. Still, to know in advance that the hurt would have a "duration" is not intuiton; it is an attempt at prophecy; it suggests in effect a wish that the hurt might endure, or at least betrays an extraordinarily pessimistic frame of mind about it.[55]

From the glum vantage of my own decades with chronic pain, it astonishes me that James's assertion of the duration of the "obscure hurt" could be met with such resounding flummox. Contra Edel's conjecture of James's prophetic posturing, it seems patently plausible that at the time of writing *Notes of a Son and Brother,* James wouldn't *need* clairvoyance to know full well the injury's lastingness, having lived it. And yet more fanciful even than the notion of James's delusion of prophecy is Edel's hypothesis of the latter as an expression of James's desire for the pain to stay, his tsk-tsk of the pain patient's pessimism as though depressive exasperation were so surprising a response to such long duress: even as James's late writing is remarkable for its sustained note of pain's *interest* where one might otherwise expect a wholly warranted despair. Returning to the passage from *Notes of a Son and Brother* already cited, James writes accordingly:

> The interest of it, I very presently knew, would certainly be of the greatest, would even in conditions kept as simple as I might make them become little less than absorbing. The shortest account of what was to follow for a long time after is therefore to plead that the interest never did fail. It was naturally what is called a painful one, but it consistently declined, as an influence at play, to drop for a single instant. Circumstances, by a wonderful chance, overwhelmingly favoured it—*as* an interest, an inexhaustible, I mean; since I also felt in the whole enveloping tonic atmosphere a force promoting its growth. (240–41)

At the risk of tautology, what most interests me about the absorbing interest of James's pain is the way it adopts pain's own temporal principle of chronicity. Like the long horizon of pain's indefinitude, "for a long time after . . . the interest never did fail." In the next sentence, those imbricatingly qualifying clauses so characteristic of James's late writing enact time's tease, insofar as the first two, taken alone, communicate not pain's incessance but its consistent "declin[ation]." It's only in the fourth clause—held apart from the sentence's opening by intermissive turns that invoke the "play" that the text is in the process of enacting—that one is made aware of one's misreading, of having treated "decline" as the sentence's operative verb when in fact it is auxiliary; only in the successive unfolding of the text does the latter's temporal import appear. This shift from a pain that declines to one that "decline[s] . . . to drop" enacts the rhythm of suffering from within which the semblance of relief proves false or at least too achingly short-lived to offer more than a reprieving glint. More succinctly put, James's burgeoning interest in the "obscure hurt" grows all but indistinguishable from the object that transfixes it. The interest *lasts;* what's more, all but ineluctably, this lasting interest "naturally" is "what is called a painful one."

The Emersonian ring of James's favoring "Circumstance" suggests an affinity between Jamesian interest and Emersonian compensation. As Emerson writes in that eponymous essay, "Every act rewards itself, or, in other words, integrates itself, in a twofold manner; first, in the thing, or in real nature; and secondly, in the circumstance, or in apparent nature. Men call the circumstance the retribution. The causal retribution is in the thing, and is seen by the soul. The retribution in the circumstance is seen by the understanding; it is inseparable from the thing, but is often spread over a long time, and so does not become distinct until after many years."[56] It's in this spirit that the circumstance of Jamesian interest—"*circumstance*," Branka Arsić reminds us, "mean[ing] precisely to stand around as a circle"[57]—is inseparable from the pain it notionally (or at least initially) follows and in turn becomes. Whereas Emerson implicitly understands compensation's peculiar duration, its "spread[ing] over . . . time," as lasting longer than the thing that spurs it, pain's especial, compensatory relation to interest is shaped by the synchronized "inexhaustib[ility]" of both. The painful enterprise of drawing a circle around a pain that continues to pulse beyond itself—as Dickinson appositely writes, "No Man can compass a Despair – / . . . Unconscious of the Width – / Unconscious that the Sun / Be Setting on His progress"[58]—pits the phantom of pain's cessation against an exasperatingly concentric ongoingness known only from a temporal distance such as the time of autobiographical writing avails but to which the self in its present-tense throes has no access. The acute, chronic vulnerability of synchronic lucidity to the disappointment of diachronic correction plays out on the level of syntax as the troubled redundancy (*unda:* wave upon wave) of the patient's beleaguered patience.

To retrace our step: I mean to suggest that Edel's brandishing of the hurt's duration as a "very positive clue" leaves him as susceptible to the charge of sensationalizing interference as those Jamesians of whom he alleges the same; the difference between castration and Edel's theory—namely, the back injury's work of "minimiz[ing]" James's "failure during the first six months to spring to the colors with other young men"[59]—being one of degree rather than kind. Edel's insistence on James's "error of omission" as proof of intent recalls no one so much as the governess in *The Turn of the Screw,* who treats as proof of Quint's ghostly visits that Miles and Flora make no mention of him at all. Such fulsome brio likewise characterizes the gauche audience of the frame story's Christmas Eve gathering:

> Mrs Griffin, however, expressed the need for a little more light. "Who was it she was in love with?"
>
> "The story will tell," I took upon myself to reply.
>
> "Oh I can't wait for the story!"
>
> "The story *won't* tell," said Douglas; "not in any literal vulgar way."
>
> "More's the pity then. That's the only way I ever understand."[60]

It's along these lines that Edel presses *Notes of a Son and Brother,* asking questions attuned less to the calibration of the autobiography's textual *desiderata* than to the coarser scope of paraphrasable plot. The frame story between the Christmas Eve party and the story proper nonetheless embeds within it yet another miniature scene of reading, absent the fervor of the governess's misgivings. It's in this frame of the parergon that we find an alternative lesson in chronic pain, one that communicates an ethos that might reach across time to the scene of James's own injury. For most critics, this little anecdote at the start of *The Turn of the Screw* goes unremarked, lost in the macabre of the kernel text's hermeneutic fervor; this is its especial uncanniness, of seeming so slight as to go unnoticed the first time around, as though one's cognizance of it were possible only as recollection. Without overstating the case, the same may be said of chronic pain's revenant blurring of past and present, something so unremittingly, unspectacularly *there* that remembering it becomes impossible, notwithstanding the endless, inescapable ache with which it frames the rest of the world:

> The case, I may mention, was that of an apparition in just such an old house as had gathered us for the occasion—an appearance, of a dreadful kind, to a little boy sleeping in the room with his mother and waking her up in the terror of it; waking her not to dissipate his dread and soothe him to sleep again, but to encounter also herself, before she had succeeded in doing so, the same sight that had shocked him.[61]

And that, abruptly, is the end of the story within a story within a story. In keeping with *The Turn of the Screw*'s commitment to the unconfirmable, we might assume—or, more gently, imagine—that the mother does *not* see the apparition, although to recall Elaine Scarry's discussion of apprehension and effort, not perhaps for lack of trying:

> Thus when one speaks about "one's own physical pain" and about "another person's physical pain," one might almost appear to be speaking about two wholly distinct orders of events. For the person whose pain it is, it is "effortlessly" grasped (that is, even with the most heroic effort it cannot *not* be grasped); while for the person outside the sufferer's body, what is "effortless" is *not* grasping it (it is easy to remain wholly unaware of its existence; even with effort, one may remain in doubt about its existence or may retain the astonishing freedom of denying its existence; and, finally, if with the best effort of sustained attention one successfully apprehends it, the aversiveness of the "it" one apprehends will only be a shadowy fraction of the actual "it").[62]

This inability to be present to someone else's pain immures the latter as a loneliness twice over. The uncrossable loneliness of this empathic failure illuminates the plangence of the boy's impulse, rendering finely perceptible his need for a corroboration surpassing even the need for comfort: the assuagement of *there there,* wishfully restaged as confirming deixis. So long as his mother doesn't see what the boy describes, he will suffer beyond the initial, defenseless dread of the visitation the more ancient, diffuse defenselessness of an unreliable body's privation from the world outside it. Even before the governess's story has begun, the text forewarns that the ensuing ordeal of hauntedness has as much to do with this ache of imperviousness as it does the scandal of penetrability.[63] Inherent in the specificity of the boy's gesture, then, isn't Scarry's dream of seeing what the other sees but the inverse dream of what one sees being seen—and by extension, perhaps, the dream of what one feels being felt.

EPISTEMOLOGY OF THE PAGODA

Eli Clare's meditation on the epistemology (and epistemological limitations) of diagnosis is instructive here. "It's impossible," Clare notes, "to grapple with cure without encountering white Western medical diagnosis . . . a process in the hands of doctors, a system of categorization. I want to read diagnosis as a source of knowledge, sometimes trustworthy and other times suspect. . . . Simply put, diagnosis wields immense power. It can provide us access to vital medical technology or shame us, reveal a path toward less pain or get us locked up. It opens doors and slams them shut."[64] When it comes to diagnosis, James's late idiom (which, of course, doesn't simply appear but evolves rather over time) represents a counter-epistemology attuned to the conundrum posed by the ongoingness of the "obscure hurt." Constituting in part what *Notes of a Son and Brother* terms the "*modus vivendi*" of living with chronic pain, this repertoire finds its apotheosis in the ornately figurative pagoda as which Maggie Verver comes to understand her own shifting epistemology over and against the machismo of her philandering husband's diagnostically inflected epistemology of reduction.[65] I quote the passage at length as its vivifying effects on Maggie's consciousness are inseparable from the time it takes—for Maggie, for us—to unfold:

> It wasn't till many days had passed that the Princess began to accept the idea of having done, a little, something she was not always doing, or indeed that of having listened to any inward voice that spoke in a new tone. Yet these instinctive postponements of reflexion were the fruit, positively, of recognitions and perceptions already active; of the sense above all that she had made at a particular hour, made by the mere touch of her hand, a difference in the situation so long present to her as practically unattackable. This situation had been occupying for months and months the very centre of the garden of her life, but it had reared itself there like some strange tall tower of ivory, or perhaps rather some wonderful beautiful but outlandish pagoda, a structure plated with hard bright porcelain, coloured and figured and adorned at the overhanging eaves with silver bells that tinkled ever so charmingly when stirred by chance airs. She had walked round and round it—that was what she felt; she had carried on her existence in the space left her for circulation, a space that sometimes seemed ample and sometimes narrow: looking up all the while at the fair structure that spread itself so amply and rose so high, but never quite making out as yet where she might have entered had she wished. She hadn't wished till now—such was the odd case; and what was doubtless equally odd besides was that though her raised eyes seemed to distinguish places that must serve from within, and especially far aloft, as apertures and outlooks, no door appeared to give access from her convenient garden level. The great decorated surface had remained consistently impenetrable and inscrutable. At present however, to her considering mind, it was as if she had ceased merely to circle and to scan

> the elevation, ceased so vaguely, so quite helplessly to stare and wonder: she had caught herself distinctly in the act of pausing, then in that of lingering, and finally in that of stepping unprecedentedly near. The thing might have been, by the distance at which it kept her, a Mahometan mosque, with which no base heretic could take a liberty; there so hung about it the vision of one's putting off one's shoes to enter and even verily of one's paying with one's life if found there as an interloper. She hadn't certainly arrived at the conception of paying with her life for anything she might do; but it was nevertheless quite as if she had sounded with a tap or two one of the rare porcelain plates. She had knocked in short—though she could scarce have said whether for admission or for what; she had applied her hand to a cool smooth spot and had waited to see what would happen. Something *had* happened; it was as if a sound, at her touch, after a little, had come back to her from within; a sound sufficiently suggesting that her approach had been noted.[66]

Whether or not the passage's subject extends explicitly to the matter of pain, the impetus for Maggie's epistemological wakening is nothing if not the hurt of infidelity made further harrowing by the quandary of not knowing of what precisely the infidelity—and, by extension, the hurt—consists. Before Maggie "begins to accept" the idea of a change in her own conjugal comportment, she *feels* it. What she feels has less to do with the particular contours of Amerigo's affair with Charlotte—this information ultimately remains as unavailable to Maggie as it proves however counterintuitively gratuitous—than with the sharpening awareness of her body's response to the change in arrangement that the affair effects. From outset, then, though the passage isn't exactly "about" pain—all the more so because the simplifying transparency of diagnosis by which aboutness could be gleaned is precisely that to which Maggie's crisis has no access—its articulation of Maggie's infinitesimally liberating reconciliation with obscurity speaks directly to the predicament of James's own injury.

James and his heroine arrive at this alternative epistemological mode not despite but through the unavailability of diagnostic information. Finding themselves in a universe of sensation more subtly granular than the lower-hanging fruits of detection, Maggie and James alike discover that this new sensorium is inseparable from a capacity for cultivating attention toward it, the autopoesis of its subliminal hum. As Maggie tells it, difference spools quietly onto the loom of prior habit—an ongoingness signaled in that "something she was not always doing"—although the recognition of this difference only arrives "a little," after the fact. From the start of the above passage, the dawning possibility of outward adaptation (of "having done" something different) is balanced by the corresponding possibility of an inner shift (of "having listened" to something new), as though inside and outside could achieve enough of an equilibrium that formal upheaval, however measured, might from certain vantages give the illusion of perfect stasis, of nothing having changed in the quotidian of the novel's politesse.

Maggie doesn't find her attention directed to a new inward voice so much as discerns in the latter a new tone. Again, most salient to her reckoning isn't the quiddity of the tone itself much less what the voice says, or to what inner intelligence or vantage it belongs (hence the generalizing unconcern of "any inward"). Whether troubled, increasingly alarmed, or newly assertive, the new tone matters less than its difference from what precedes it. Precursor to the tactic of ingenious formalism that the pagoda comes to represent, Maggie's perceptual achievement lies in the recognition that this remainder-like interval possesses all the textural density of a phenomenal substance in its own right, irrespective of the reified poles between which it pends. Like the vase-shaped negative space between two facing silhouettes, the interstice onto which Maggie confers her valorizing awareness doesn't displace the tones it mediates, even as the latter perhaps inevitably recede to the background to the extent that the former slides to the fore. If anything, this swinging inversion of perceptual value doesn't displace one version of the actual with another so much as lays bare the way both phenomenal experiences participate in a perceptual trick.

For *The Golden Bowl* no less than *Notes of a Son and Brother,* the work of reimagining epistemology's horizon begins with disarticulating the prestige of certainty from an origin whose material density amounts for all its irretrievability to a hologram of sentience. To say that Maggie's experience mimetically corresponds to James's simplifies the extent to which the substance of pain is felt by both character and author—the pathos of *The Golden Bowl* is galvanized, after all, by an erotic economy unable to rescue any of its four participants from the ineluctable hurt of its currency—as the difficulty of saying where textual vibrancy ends and something like psychical literacy begins. For James, as we will see, the formal scrupulousness from which pain sluices is constitutive, as is the consequent inkling that the hurt's obscurity is unthinkable (however the unthinkable is parsed from the unfeelable) apart from the figurative thickness from which it surfaces, in which it's caught. Here, though, is Maggie's newfound experience of sapience: "Though she tried to deal with herself for a space only as a silken-coated spaniel who has scrambled out of a pond and who rattles the water from his ears. Her shake of her head, again and again, as she went, was much of that order, and she had the resource to which, save for the rude equivalent of his generalising bark, the spaniel would have been a stranger, of humming to herself hard as a sign that nothing had happened to her. She hadn't, so to speak, fallen in; she had had no accident nor got wet; this at any rate was her pretension until after she began a little to wonder if she mightn't, with or without exposure, have taken cold."[67]

The passage's concluding sense of Maggie's vague malaise reclaims the figurative account it follows as coextensive with, thoroughly braided into, the world the novel asks us to believe as Maggie's quotidian, empirical universe. The passage's intentness on this suturing is evident from its opening. Note the jump cut from Maggie as spaniel "rattl[ing] the water from his ears" to Maggie herself "shak[ing] . . . her head, again and again, as she went," the figurative ingeniousness of the passage extending beyond the charm of the comparison to the narration's tendering of the latter as product if not proof of Maggie's interiority, precisely that which *The Golden Bowl*'s first half, told from Amerigo's vantage, had displaced. Maggie's narrative body is thus collated with a textual substance that duplicates the stuff of her psyche as the time of our reading, and it is this collation that lends figuration the etiological prominence of a somatic condition. Like waking up with leaves in one's hair after dreaming of trees, that Maggie is left to wonder "if she mightn't, with or without exposure, have taken cold" reframes James's figurative repertoire as the literacy of self-awareness, not least to those inner elements from which one nonetheless feels decisively barred. Such as the obscure hurt of a pagoda that "rear[s] itself" at "the very centre of the garden" of James's life, whose "strange tall tower of ivory" he approaches like someone rediscovering his own true spine. Or—"carr[ying] on [his] existence in the space left [him] for circulation, a space that sometimes seemed ample and sometimes narrow . . . but never quite making out as yet where [he] might have entered had [he] wished," like pain itself, homeopathically reoriented toward the stenosis of its landscape, blood to bone.

REND AND RIFT

As with Dickinson, it's impossible in the absence of historico-medical accounts to say for how long James's ailment lasts let alone of what, medically speaking, it consists. What James tells us is this: "I came to think of my relation to my injury as a *modus vivendi* workable for the time" (241–42). Even as James's *modus vivendi,* colloquially understood as a "way of life," proffers the autobiography's most distilled statement of the all but unimaginable duration of the "obscure hurt," the aphoristic smoothnesss of the idiom's customary translation, its air of Hesiodic equipoise, falls short when it comes to conveying the rhetorical bristle of *vivendi*'s gerundive. As often as not, the Latin gerundive signals the burden of necessity. In other words, learning to relate to pain, to inhabit that relation, is a mode neither of life nor living per se. On the contrary, the gerundive posits pain as that which must be lived, even as pain descriptively fills the syncope between trying to live and fashioning from that flounder some aesthetic approximation of comportment: of bearing (inextricable as the matter of chronic pain is from the vicissitudes of bearing, weathering, the unbearable). The autopoietic task of forging the imperative one would then aspire to follow brokers a rapprochement achieved, if it's achieved, moment by moment: a Muybridge of arduousness. Not being able to metabolize or otherwise assimilate the injury—unable, that is, to impose his will on a substance whose indifference to coercion amounts effectively to implacable sovereignty—James undertakes or (in consideration of the syntactical fastidiousness of "I came to think of my relation . . ."), at least, orients himself toward undertaking, a truce with the hurt, a Darwinian variant of Foucault's conception of "the cultivation of the self" as an "art of existence."[68] The grammatical particularity of *modus vivendi,* then, refracts itself from within as its own crystalline asymptote, illuminating the Sisyphism of straining to realize a way of being that might feel as though retroactively effortless, that could nearly forget the art by which it is achieved. Occurring somewhere between passive and active voice, this threshold learning's horizon of reconcilement is reached through nothing less than unceasing arrangement. As Emerson writes of "The Conduct of Life," "Beauty is the moment of transition, as if the form were just ready to flow into other forms."[69] James's *modus vivendi* names the ongoing aesthetic practice by which one surrenders the dream of the self's imperviousness to the ceaselessly enacted moment of just readiness.[70] Even as the expression seems to gesture in English toward the holistic span of a life, James will have learned in the interval between 1861 and 1914 that the latter accumulates piecemeal at best: an improvisatory stopgap repeated along an axis of acclimation that never quite falls into place, "workable for the time."

An irrecoverable distance between ontologies of diagnosis and James's own experience as patient impels our own readerly care when it comes to considering the terms of James's condition. No less critically, the latter's terrain according to medicine (and, more generally, the universe external to James's phenomenal/epistemological orbit) can nowise stand in for James's recounting of his "obscure hurt." Moving in the opposite direction, a version of the same is no less true: notwithstanding criticism's persistent citing of the "obscure hurt" as a synecdoche for the event to which it's made to correspond—over and against the formulation's demonstration of nothing so much as its own textually eventive purport—the salience of James's phrasing is nothing apart from the writing from which it's culled:

> Beyond all present notation the interlaced, undivided way in which what had happened to me, by a turn of fortune's hand, in twenty odious minutes, kept company of the most unnatural—I can call it nothing less—with my view of what was happening, with the question of what might still happen, to everyone about me, to the country at large: it so made of these marked disparities a single vast visitation. One had the sense, I mean, of a huge comprehensive ache, and there were hours at which one could scarce have told whether it came most from one's own poor organism . . . or from the enclosing social body, a body rent with a thousand wounds and that thus treated one to the honour of a sort of tragic fellowship. The twenty minutes had sufficed, at all events, to establish a relation—a relation to everything occurring round me not only for the next four years but for long afterward—that was at once extraordinarily intimate and quite awkwardly irrelevant. I must have felt in some befooled way in presence of a crisis—the smoke of Charleston Bay still so acrid in the air—at which the likely young should be up and doing or, as familiarly put, lend a hand much wanted; the willing youths, all round, were mostly starting to their feet, and to have trumped up a lameness at such a juncture could be made to pass in no light for graceful. Jammed into the acute angle between two high fences, where the rhythmic play of my arms, in tune with that of several other pairs, but at a dire disadvantage of position, induced a rural, a rusty, a quasi-extemporised old engine to

> work and a saving stream to flow, I had done myself, in face of a shabby conflagration, a horrid even if an obscure hurt; and what was interesting from the first was my not doubting in the least its duration—though what seemed equally clear was that I needn't as a matter of course adopt and appropriate it, so to speak, or place it for increase of interest on exhibition. The interest of it, I very presently knew, would certainly be of the greatest, would even in conditions kept as simple as I might make them become little less than absorbing. The shortest account of what was to follow for a long time after is therefore to plead that the interest never did fail. (239–41)

This is the heart of the matter, an impossible tableau exactingly strange as a dream. The pain to which the passage bears witness is a supernaturalizing influence: cracking open the world, illuminating like lightning the startling alignment it curates, through which curation it pours. If anything is able to puncture the scene's dense abstraction, it is a queer intensity of time that the text avers with all the acuity of inculcation. How time pulsates from those first "twenty odious minutes" to "hours at which one could scarce have told," returning to the "suffic[ing]" "twenty minutes" and back to "next four years . . . for long afterward": how, in other words, time pulses through James, the text's vigil (almost reading itself being written), like a lightning rod. We are invited in passing to consider the spurious correspondence of sufficing and sufferance, the extent to which the latter fills the interval that the injury cleaves. The text holds tightly onto time, unless time holds onto it—a temporal oscillation suggesting chronometry in disarray, the delicacy with which the prosaic time of the universe is transfigured. This newly figurative temporality doesn't measure the span of time so much as is itself deeply felt. No matter how withdrawn James's pain eventually becomes, no matter the ultimate seabed depth of his absorption in it, it begins, here, as a chrysalis of the outer world. Its "huge comprehensive ache" hangs over time's proceedings like a second smoke-filled sky. James endures the injury's stark coincidence with the outbreak of war as a confusion, in part, of direction; whether the ache's comprehensiveness comes "most from one's own poor organism" or "the enclosing social body" seems—in a moment itself indistinguishable from the ambiguity of unspecifiable "hours"—impossible to say. And beyond the question of where pain originates, the pressing matter of where it goes and how it stays has as *its* answer the text before us.

The tethering of the two Jameses—he who is injured and he who will have lived with the injury—instances just one of the passage's many doublings, all of which overshadowed by the grave, unspoken rift of the country itself.[71] The text is spellbound by its own inability to parse the smoke of Charleston Bay, following the Confederacy's firing on Fort Sumter, from the smoke of the burning Newport barn. The smoke from one becomes the other, the piercing acridity of which lingers in the page too long. In the alignment of injury and war, contingency and fate, the scene described all but drops from historical time; there's no place here, where event touches itself into memory, becomes the writing of it, for the ephemeral. The smoke indelibly hovering over the text's confluent crises no less blurs the soldiers in Charleston with those "willing youths," James included, who work to extinguish the Newport fire. In the manner of *Helen in Egypt* or *Iphigenia at Aulis,* this passage and the pain it holds splits James in two, albeit along temporal rather than spatial coordinates. "Twice and twice," as Hart Crane writes, "(Again the smoking souvenir, / Bleeding eidolon!) and yet again."[72]

Even the fence in which young James (like Turner tied to the mast) is caught doubles over. "Jammed into the acute angle between two high fences" is disarmingly difficult to decipher. What is so pinned in place ought to allow some keener legibility than what the text provides. To recall the "interlac[ing]" way of fortune's hand transforms the fence-work into a loom on which the warp and woof of James is spun, though the force of the jamming also turns James himself into his own prospective subluxation, where the loom goes wrong. Like the acrid smoke before it, the acuteness of the angle sounds within the narrowness of the latter a sharpness shared between it, perhaps, and the pain engendered by the impingement. Beyond this, the arrangement's intimation of geometry—however incompletely realized the geometric plane may be—asserts most forcibly the scene's vigorous abstraction, the corrosion of its mimetic principle. The compositional shift from immobilizing stasis to the frenetically "rhythmic play of my arms" describes in part the analogous ordeal of pain (no longer distinguishable from the ordeal of injury) as the deterritorializing conversion of James's person into an experience of multiplicity. "If we imagined," Deleuze and Guattari write, "the position of a fascinated Self, it was because the multiplicity toward which it leans, stretching to the breaking point, is the continuation of another multiplicity that works it and strains it from the inside. In fact, the self is only a threshold, a door, a becoming between two multiplicities. Each multiplicity is defined by a borderline functioning as Anomalous, but there is a string of borderlines, a continuous line of borderlines (*fiber*) following which the multiplicity changes. . . . A fiber strung across borderlines constitutes a line of flight or of deterritorialization."[73] And so the passage's textual play posits "Jammed" where "James" had been: the past tense of a proper name, noun into participle. If the repeating "m"—a textual doubling of phonemical minuteness—speculatively makes the case for "Jammed" as an amplification of Jamesian substance, we may imagine the pain it begets, that "quasi-extemporised engine," as the galvanizing harbinger-echo of the late writing's *modus vivendi,* its ontologically emptying current.[74]

5. Is the Rectangle a Grave?

Floating Attention, Betweenness in Relief

There is an alternate beginning to queer theory in Leo Bersani's observation that literary characters sometimes are most compelling in their not seeming ontologically compelling at all. I remember feeling thunderstruck upon first encountering Bersani's claim in *Cultures of Redemption* that *Moby-Dick*'s homoerotic coupling of Ishmael and Queequeg was unpersuasive to the extent that Melville's characters seemed unpersuasive as people.[1] Bersani makes such assertions throughout his career. I think of his incisive remark in *A Future for Astyanax* that "it's irrelevant in *The Golden Bowl* that Amerigo and Charlotte were in love before the story began. Their past is a concession on James's part to an order of psychological probability which the novel in fact dismisses. . . . It's as if the geometry of human relations *implied* what we call human feelings into existence."[2] Such moments in Bersani's oeuvre help me understand my fascination with Emerson's exhortation that we "treat the men and women well: treat them as if they were real: perhaps they are."[3] Bersani suggests that if we treat persons well even when they don't seem like persons, it might be on account of the geometry out of which human feelings retroactively come into being; such a geometry would ostensibly become a composition "of human relations" only after the fact. Bersani's insights have bolstered my thinking about chronic pain's responsiveness to queer aesthetics in so often configuring characterological noncredulity or vacancy in terms of an "aesthetic of failure"[4] variously imagined as "immobilizing," "blinding,"[5] or "crippling."[6] Far more interesting than the convergence of critical theory and hackneyed disability tropes is the possibility in Bersani's readings of disability having perhaps felt aesthetic all along.

Bersani's most sustained theorization of our geometric bearings occurs in "Blocked Vision," cowritten with Ulysse Dutoit. One's experience in front of a Rothko canvas, Bersani and Dutoit suggest, involves a catechism in self-diminishment predicated on the erasures of form staged (unless decreatingly unstaged) by the mergers of Rothko's rectangles into each other, the canvas, and in a mutual disappearing, the world. "What is being imitated," Bersani and Dutoit write, "is within our visual field as we look at the painting: it is the rectangular shape of the canvas itself, as well as of the room in which the painting is hung."[7] In this concentrically Emersonian dilation of rectangles, mimesis is involved in absorbingly abdicating what it replicates. The beauty of Bersani's aesthetic vocabulary has to do with a formal attentiveness that keeps at bay the devolutions of erotic vicissitude watchfully traced throughout his writing. If Bersani and Dutoit admire Rothko's work for its resistance to personification, however, it's not because the eventual emergence of persons from Rothko's shapes cannot occur but because the resistance helps us less take for granted how and why they do. Even if aesthetics cannot ensure a break per se from the problems posed by bodies-in-relation, it remains salutarily unclear to what extent aesthetics and sex rethink each other's vantage and vocabulary, if and where the imbrications of aesthetics and sex are figuratively or literally comprised (even as literal and figurative as terms for discussing Rothko seem almost immediately insufficient), or if our ability to imagine sex as aesthetic means the former is becoming something it was not or returning to something it was. These questions drastically energize the closing lines of "Is the Rectum a Grave?" "Male homosexuality," Bersani writes, "advertises the risk of the sexual itself as the risk of self-dismissal, of *losing sight* of the self, and in so doing it proposes and dangerously represents *jouissance* as a mode of ascesis."[8]

According to the above, male homosexuality and "the sexual itself" most differ not in object choice but as opposing terms within a grammar that cagily shuffles our understanding of aesthetic veracity/verisimilitude, as animatingly shaped and undone by assiduous aesthetic praxis. As instrumentalization of the aesthetic, the language of advertisement conjures the fungibility of male homosexuality, in especial relation to the HIV/AIDS epidemic that is the occasion for the special—we may well say *emergency*—

issue of *October* (Winter 1987) in which Bersani's essay first appears. As purposive reframing of the question of what male homosexuality represents, the language of advertisement situates our own aesthetic appetites within a larger economy of prestige, vicariousness and precarity less contestably associated with pornography's demarcation of a desire for fantasy from the fantasies of desire. And yet we are given pause, not least in terms of the truism (contra the boilerplate of truth-in-advertising) that there is no advertisement that doesn't elementally misadvertise both itself and its promissory objects. In this sense, the "risk of the sexual" advertised by male homosexuality suggests the necessary difficulty of distinguishing the titillation of risk, its scenic element, from a "daily terror"[9] at once at the heart of and unabsorbable by our customary erotic routines (even those most bent on the latter's interruption). More than this, however, Bersani's claim frames male homosexuality as itself an aesthetic phenomenon, exploitative and exploitable. "Losing sight of the self"—the psychical circuit through which one disappears if not distributively becomes the art work by which one is captivated—thus amounts less to a banalizing variation on self-loss than distillation of an aesthetic riddle internal to it.

Once attuned to the surface resonances between them, trying to parse Bersani and Dutoit's account of Rothko's rectangles apart from Bersani's earlier remarks on the rectum of a gay bottom (and vice versa) proves a trying business. Consider, for instance, the appearance at the conclusion of "Blocked Vision" of the verb *to enter*—twice intoned, once in quotation marks—and its seeming inscription of us as tops in relation to the art at hand: "It is, then, these risks of disappearance and of appearance—the risk of a dying at once more insignificant and infinitely more consequential than our personal death—which we accept when we 'enter' Rothko's art, when, perhaps, we enter art."[10] The difference between "enter[ing] art" and "'enter[ing]' Rothko's art" suggests in part the difference between *jouissance* for its own sake and *jouissance* as ascetic mode: between losing sight of one's self and learning through ascetic practice an attention to rapture inseparable from its representational constitution. In other words, and notwithstanding our accustomed ease with the disciplinary shorthand of scare quotes, Bersani and Dutoit insist that we experience the entrancement of "enter[ing]" as an ongoing lesson in perceptual rigor,[11] a compositionally spatial awareness evident in Rothko's own understanding of the aesthetic spectator, who "must move with the artist's shapes in and out, under and above, diagonally and horizontally; he must curve around spheres, pass through tunnels, glide down inclines . . . attracted by some irresistible magnet across space, entering into mysterious recesses."[12]

If the sinuousness of this mysticism argues against too quick an equivalence between entering (aesthetically, erotically) and penetration, that entering art entails a movement less literal than somatically stringent is no less articulated in the unfamiliarity of the spaces, within Rothko's work, that we come to inhabit. Exemplary here is the strange commensuration between Rothko's canvases and the otherworldly hush of the Rothko chapel. Along these lines, Bersani and Dutoit note that "some of Rothko's work . . . encourages us to entertain a very different possibility: not only will our looking fail to be rewarded with something significant to see, but the very act of seeing may become irrelevant to the painter's project."[13] Rothko's work thus invites us to entertain entertainment itself along newly deracinated—which is to say all the more etymologically embedded—lines: entrancement in the sense of "keeping (a person)," not least one's own, "*in* a certain frame of mind."[14] It is not insignificant that this account of aesthetic encounter lacks the penetrative bravura often associated with the sexual idiom of entering, such as informs, for instance, Tim Dean's description of an appositely titled early bareback-porn movie *What I Can't See*. "It is as if," Dean remarks, "*What I Can't See* were allegorizing gay life before the discovery of HIV—a life not of sexual hedonism as much as of an inevitable yet temporary blindness to exactly what may be entering one's rectum."[15] One way of gauging the consequence of Bersani and Dutoit's study of Rothko for queer theory is to note that entering—the painting, the chapel—of a sudden opens onto an estrangement usually reserved, as in Dean's account, for what or who is entered.

Bersani writes elsewhere in "Is the Rectum a Grave?" that "Freud keeps returning to a line of speculation in which the opposition between pleasure and pain becomes irrelevant, in which the sexual emerges as the *jouissance* of exploded limits, as the ecstatic suffering into which the human organism momentarily plunges when it is 'pressed' beyond a certain threshold of endurance."[16] Bersani and Dutoit's attention to the geometry of Rothko's compositions a little frees us from the frontal allure of the passage's nominal subjects (*jouissance*, ecstatic suffering, the human organism), drawing us instead to the spatial arrangement, at once scrupulous and exorbitant, in which these terms are relationally implicated. Against a wall, through a sieve, preserved as in an herbarium, the "press[ure]" felt by and exerted on the organism "beyond a certain threshold of endurance" bears upon a sensory field both coextensive with and of a separate order from the momentary tableau of plunging. Notwithstanding pressure's scene of surface and plunging's scene of depth, both modes equally posit a challenge to spectation, our attempt along the "line of speculation" to envision the vicissitudes of relational feeling. The torpedo velocity of the one reduces our vision of the organism to the dynamism of its wake and drag against the oceanic counterflow of plunging medium, besides which the temporal indeterminacy of "momentarily" suggests we strain to witness what may or may not occur faster than our optical apparatus can catch, a speed no less at odds with the asserted resistance of this abstractly aquatic environment, the oceanic feeling's vertical axis.

When it comes to pressure, on the other hand, our vision is differently troubled by the extent to which the scene's expressive minimalism conveys a dermal distress corresponding to a haptic register not so readily translatable in optical terms. In *The Freudian Body*, Bersani turns to the "tensions in [Freud's] work"—a form of buckling or impaction not unrelated to the strain of being "'pressed' beyond"—in hopes they "should help us to see . . . something stranger, something less familiar, than the always necessary adjustments of theory to empirical constraints. I refer," Bersani continues, "to pressures inherent in consciousness itself, pressures which are in fact the object of psychoanalytic reflection. Psychoanalysis is an unprecedented attempt to give a theoretical account of precisely those forces which obstruct, undermine, play havoc with theoretical accounts themselves."[17] If certain prior moments in Bersani's writing suggest an attraction to these erosive shifts in the substance of surface pressure largely dependent on their conscription into more readily demonstrable psychoanalytic paradigms (of desire, shattering, aggression), the recent publication of *Receptive Bodies* argues for the abiding appeal, for Bersani, of compositional surfaces in their own right. Turning to George Herbert Mead's 1932 *The Philosophy of the Present*, Bersani thus voices approbation for the "originality" in Mead's claim "that in pressing against an object we arouse in ourselves the object's 'attitude' of counterpressure."[18] Bersani's early meditation on Rothko suggests that this aesthetically adroit appreciation for a "continuity of the experience of pressure in the organism and of resistance in the physical object"[19] has animated his relational concerns all along. As

Thomas Weiskel observes, "any aesthetic, pressed beyond a certain point, becomes or implies a psychology."[20]

The "line of speculation," for Bersani, describes the object of Freud's interest as much as it does the accumulated force of his insights. The human organism capable of being "pressed" is intelligible as a play of limits, lines, and thresholds, the terms in which Bersani and Dutoit will go on to describe Rothko's paintings. Of Rothko's 1961 painting *Number 207 (Red over Dark Blue on Dark Gray),* Bersani and Dutoit observe "that when one of two rectangles almost merges into the background color, the effect can be just the opposite of what we have been describing. Instead of diminishing the readability of sharply marked contrasts, the blurring boundaries between one rectangle and the background space can make the entire painting seem like a background space to the other rectangle."[21] Almost merging into the background, the rectangle likewise almost merges (spatially if not chromatically) with the other rectangle. The ascesis of this style of looking conduces the surprise of "just the opposite of what we have been describing." The unpredictable pulsing of Rothko's shapes resets our sense of how power, aesthetically coded, moves. We watch and wait.

The discerning humility of the descriptive voice of "Blocked Vision" recalls the speaker's curiosity in Elizabeth Bishop's "The Map," which, like Bersani and Dutoit's essay, articulates with breathtaking calmness the contingency of relational feeling. Bersani and Dutoit's contemplation of Rothko's shifting depths of field echo that poem's opening equivocation: "Land lies in water; it is shadowed green. / Shadows, or are they shallows."[22] And like Bishop, Bersani and Dutoit are experimenting with what we might call a poetics of "or."[23] *Shadows or shallows.* Or as Bersani and Dutoit similarly note, "the foreground-background relation, as in *White and Greens in Blue,* is disturbed by questions the painting raises about which color is above or below the other."[24] Like "The Map," "Blocked Vision" asks its readers to imagine how seeing looks or feels, as extrapolated in the minute and circumstantial evidence of vision struck by Rothko's paintings.

So eminently Jamesian is the quality of this optical practice that it's almost inevitable that Bersani and Dutoit's depiction of it, in their later film study *Forms of Being,* more frequently sounds less like Bishop than James's "The Beast in the Jungle": "The perplexing allusion to a soul that the speaking subject seeks to enter but that is also invited to look at the world it has made through that same subject's eyes—as if the 'I' could be both internal and external to its own soul, and as if this spirit that is his were indistinguishable from that which is external to them both—all this becomes intelligible in terms of an ontology that treats as merely incidental, as a by-product of the illusion of individuality, the opposition between the outside and the inside."[25] Recognizing the fortuitousness of opposition—between object and subject, world and self, outside and inside—doesn't disband ontology altogether but recalibrates ontological difference *as* contingent technique, along the lines by which Bersani reconceives male homosexuality as aesthetic procedure. That a field of perceived interiority could be experienced so discrepantly from its surroundings without being so—that interiority and exteriority could be shown to name at best secondary operations—quickens the Jamesian element in much of Mead's work as well, especially when it comes to the latter's account of "manipulatory area," an interposed space between self and nonself that recalls Winnicott's understanding of transitional space. "There appears in the physical thing," Mead writes, "a content which originally belongs only to the organism, that of pressure, what Whitehead has called the 'pushiness' of things, and the question is how it gets into the thing. . . . The suggestion which I have already made is that the pressures of bodily surfaces against each other . . . are transferred to the object,"[26] what Mead goes on to characterizes as a "something with an inside."[27] Recalling the previous chapter's discussion of James's *The Golden Bowl*, the watchful trepidation on our side of this encounter—gazing on a complementary form we may or may not have fashioned in our own image—rearticulates Maggie's titillated approach of the pagoda as compositional assignation. "At present however, to her considering mind, it was as if she had ceased merely to circle and to scan the elevation, ceased so vaguely, so quite helplessly to stare and wonder: she had caught herself distinctly in the act of pausing, then in that of lingering, and finally in that of stepping unprecedentedly near."[28]

Beyond what threshold of endurance is either rectangle pressed? If the dark blue bottom rectangle "nearly disappears" into the dark gray canvas, into what does it disappear? Furthermore, if it's a gay bottom who most saliently "advertises the risk of the sexual itself as the risk of self-dismissal, of *losing sight* of the self,"[29] then might we imagine some resonance not only between rectangles and recta, but across Bersani's investment in each? "Rothko," Bersani and Dutoit write, "paints the resistance *and* surrender of forms to form-defeating fusions as the principal sign of the very emergence of forms,"[30] which is to say that Rothko's rectangles redistribute Bersani and Dutoit's aspirations for queer relationality from dim bathhouse to dark canvas. In translating the temporality of the bathhouse into the pulsation of only somewhat static shapes, Bersani and Dutoit's Rothko illuminates, in Lauren Berlant's words, the extent to which "structure is a process, not an imprint, of the reproduction of life."[31] In the wake of Rothko's intuition that "process" and the nearly psychical aesthetics of imprinting—the consubsistency of pressure or impingement and the mechanical reproducibility of inaccurate replication—are not mutually exclusive, Bersani and Dutoit invite us to meditate on the ecology of the representation of this transaction as constitutively aesthetic: that this transaction is ontologically representational informs Rothko's practice of painterly mimesis as an experiment in realism. The fidelity of this exchange, recalling Christopher's Bollas's description of Winnicott's good-enough mother as an infant's first aesthetic event,[32] rephrases beauty as an unanswerable question of what Cary Howie calls "hermeneutic propriety."[33]

The relative expressive vacancy of Rothko's art leaves it susceptible to this sort of co-opting, even as susceptibility and co-opting are the very narratives that its ironically mimetic compositions imply. It is in part the suggestion in Rothko's rectangles of the forms to which simultaneously they give rise and from which they emerge that attracts Bersani and Dutoit to them. Rothko's experiment in an art without subjects resonates with Bersani and Dutoit's theorization, if not quite of sex without subjects, then sex as the means by which we're impressed with an idea of desubjectivation. At the same time, Bersani and Dutoit's writing on Rothko brings into focus a continuity between Bersani's meditations on aesthetic being and his earlier accounts of ascesis and self-shattering. The former's receptiveness to formal contingency illuminates aspects of relationality that sometimes risk being occluded by the more glaringly melodramatic elements of erotic management. What follows traces Bersani's fascination with both Rothko's rectangles and the interstice that mediates two rectangles as they approach each other. The interstice becomes a way to visualize the nearliness that underwrites investment. I'm interested less in the extent to which the language of erotic adventure informs a rectangle's contemplation of another rectangle than in the possibility of relations between persons taking on the fastidious spirit of interstitiality and rectangular being.

The particular shape of this interstitial predilection is evident in Bersani's book-length collaborations with Ulysse Dutoit and Adam Phillips. The various forms taken by coauthorship speak to Bersani's long-standing inquiry into where one person ends and another begins, an experiment in epistemological and erotic absorbency evident in Rothko's compulsions. In *Intimacies,* published four years after *Forms of Being,* the delimiting of Bersani's writing from that of Phillips enacts the plausibility (rather than fact) of authorial ipseity. As Phillips writes in that book's preface, "Leo Bersani wrote the first three chapters, and I then responded immediately to what he had written. . . . Bersani then wrote a conclusion prompted, more or less, by my response. . . . The reader can read the book as it was written."[34] By contrast, it is impossible to parse the singularity of discrete author positions in *Forms of Being,* which treats the mystification of how one reads "as it was written" as though it were coextensive with the book's argument for what Bersani and Dutoit call the ontological "implausibility of . . . psychic subject-hood."[35] Read alongside the theories of relation they differently raise, the collaborative dynamics of these books suggest in their complication of formal discreteness a fidelity to the inconsistency of feeling singular in the first place.

The fine variations between these collaborations inform the books' respective cover images, whose similarities and differences alike speak to the perceptual subtlety of proximity made graphic. The cover of *Forms of Being* is composed of two film stills between which hovers the book's title in a white space so nearly equivalent to the rectangles on either side of it that it's hard to say if we are looking at a diptych or triptych. The bottom third of the cover is a production still from Godard's *Contempt.* As Bersani and Dutoit write of this Godard image, "All subjects—human and narrative—are left behind. Nearly everything that would allow us to measure and to distinguish is gone. The horizon line separating sea from sky is much less sharply delineated than in the [earlier] Capri shot; we have nothing—which is almost everything—but the nearly uniform spectacle of blue water and sky."[36] Observing that the jettisoning of "human and narrative" is importantly not the same as their absence, Bersani and Dutoit treat the image like a still to the extent that the diachrony of persons left behind participates in the extended time of a film in which "human and narrative" would have factored. By contrast, their invoking of the "uniform spectacle of blue water and sky" treats the still like the image it synchronically resembles, on some level as it asks to be seen: as an abstract seascape whose bifurcated color fields might well remind us of a Rothko canvas. The image's flickering between genres and interpretations is internally repeated if not anticipated in the "less sharply delineated" horizon line, whose trick of pervious distinction renders it as vivacious as the rectangular sea and sky that it inscribes. The difficulty of saying where sky meets sea shifts the burden of delineation from the inscribed rectangles to us. Our difficulty—what Bersani and Dutoit invoke as the impossibility of measurement—repeats the hazy generic resemblance between film still and painting, anticipation and repeating. Godard's hazy horizon is to be distinguished from the more severely drawn interpersonality announced in the first line of Bersani and Dutoit's chapter on the film: "Contempt cements the couple."[37]

Queen of the Night II, the Barnett Newman painting on the cover of *Intimacies*, reads as an elongated, perpendicular version of Godard's seascape. Its periwinkle zip asymmetrically bisects the violet "like a hinge or spine,"[38] leaving us to ponder the book's titular intimacy as an idea of ligature between asymmetrical but otherwise indistinguishable abstractions. The zip and the horizon convert Bersani and Dutoit's "nothing" into "almost everything," the evacuation of human or otherwise narrative subjects leaving us with a linearity whose intensity at best just approaches subjectivity. Bersani and Dutoit's accounts of desire and subjectivity as aesthetic gambles are unthinkable apart from this asymptotic, interstitial flicker, the proclivity of which drives their study of Rothko's canvases. Newman's painting is instructive here in its rendering of Mozart's coloratura soprano role, the latter's metonymic doubling (dancer from dance) with her notorious aria, "Der Hölle Rache." Although Roger Mathew Grant understands "the Queen (who has no proper name; she is pure role)" in terms of "robotic pyrotechnics,"[39] I'm inclined to imagine her tessitura as soaring counterpart to Bersani's formulation of an organism's "plunge . . . 'pressed' beyond a certain threshold of endurance." In this sense, Newman's painting articulates breath's extremity being cleaved from air. As Deleuze writes of Francis Bacon, "It is not at all a matter of giving color to a particularly intense sound. Music, for its part, is faced with the same task, which is certainly not to render the scream harmonious, but to establish a relationship between the sound of the scream and the forces that sustain it."[40]

In the interplay between this flicker and the chromatic saturation of forms against which it appears, the interest of Rothko's particular geometry migrates to the rectangle's edges. I envision Bersani and Dutoit's gravitation to these shapes alongside Emerson's interest in circles or Sedgwick's interest in Girardian triangles. For present purposes, preference for the rectangle over the triangle speaks to a turn *from* the sharpness of narrative crisis. If the triangle, for Sedgwick, "is useful as a figure by which the 'commonsense' of our intellectual tradition schematizes erotic relations,"[41] the rectangle's conceptual utility is a function of its erotic counterintuitiveness. The rectangle effects, in the manner of Bill Viola, a diffusing and slowing of identification and attraction to the point of unfamiliarity. The triangle is a shape of melodrama to the extent that we are trained to think its geometry in terms of competing vertices and angles; the rectangle's squared corners, by contrast, suspend our assumption of jealousy in enjoining us to consider parallel surfaces and line. Whereas triangular desire, for Girard, is "the basis of the theory of the *novelistic* novel,"[42] the rectangle seems to open onto a theory unmoored from genre. Slightly differently put, a triangle graphically corresponds to imagined hostilities, whereas a rectangle waits to be filled.

Rothko's canvases imply mutually regarding rectangles as repetitions of the parallel lines by which rectangles are themselves construed. Bersani and Dutoit imagine the inexhaustibility less of our reception of this art than its reception of us in terms of blocked vision; latent in this interception is a rectangularly infinite regress returning vision to the spaciousness of these blocks. The interstice offers a ground, so to speak, between that which more conventionally arises as subjects. Already we've encountered one version of the interstice's affective induration as the concretization of contempt. What would it mean to imagine an affect so foregrounded that the couple it joins recedes from (sinks into, is crowded out of) it? What are the phenomenological implications of attaching to affect without persons, or of subordinating attention to foregrounded subjects (seascape, foreboding of shipwreck, whale-spout, etc.) for the slivered sylph hovering within it or beyond?[43]

This account of Bersani's investment in interstitial perspective complicates what strikes me as *Queer Optimism*'s somewhat one-sided critique of his characterization of aggressive intractability.[44] The interstice—whether viewed in terms of affective spaciousness, psychical potentiality, or some equilibrial grace—makes it difficult to trust the intractability of anything so legible as aggression. Further, if *Queer Optimism* wondered about the absence in Bersani's account of psychical violence of Winnicott, Bersani sounds nearly Winnicottian in his curious discovery and rediscovery of the line that holds Rothko's rectangles together and apart. A good-enough mother enters and withdraws from the infant's space (psychical and physical are not yet discernible distinctions) with a subtlety so finessed that the infant misperceives her efforts as inertia, as the pleasantness of needs being met in advance of their being understood as need, let alone deprivation. The interstice serves as a structural analogy for this nonstructuring structure in which space not only is shared between subjects but in which it quite movingly happens. This space and the rectangles it mediates give rise to a set of possible relations between subjects and objects not yet understood as disappointing, rewarding, desirable, repellent. In lieu of evaluation, we encounter *chromatic value,* as though the structure of relation preexisted the affects with which it eventually is inflected. Structure without inflection: Bersani and Dutoit imagine this expectant sliver of moving spaciousness in terms of a shimmer. The vibration between rectangles, as Bersani and Dutoit note in the context of Ellsworth Kelly but no less pertinent to Rothko, "is not a completed movement, and in a sense it is a pseudo-movement. . . . It is as if the color were stretching itself out in order to relate to itself."[45]

Exemplary of Bersani and Dutoit's perceptual delicacy is the following reading of *Green and Maroon* from the Phillips Collection: "a whitish shimmering line between the two rectangles reminds us of the nearly smothering closeness in value of the two rectangles, at the same time that it appears to operate as a kind of barrier of light somehow preventing the somber green mass from descending into and crushing the smaller and more fragile form below it."[46] The *sh* shared—doubled, echoed—between "whitish shimmering" accomplishes in miniature the description's regard for the painting's simultaneous hesitance and quiet. Hesitance: the shimmering line isn't white but "whitish," as the closeness between chromatic values isn't "smothering" but "nearly" so. If the "somehow" by which the shimmer "appears" to operate seems initially at odds with my claim for the passage's fastidiousness, it nonetheless attests to the scruple *of* inexactness, an unwillingness on Bersani and Dutoit's part to force a clarity that the painting forestalls, a clarity understood in this context as meretricious at best. The unwavering of their attention to the corresponding care of the work's compositional waver participates in the shimmer's own paradoxically teeming quiet, insofar as shimmer, as a quality of light, is known equally by its faintness and its tremulousness. Bersani's eye for shimmering animacy repeats Paul's capacity for the same, in D. H. Lawrence's *Sons and Lovers*. "It's because—it's because there is scarcely any shadow in it," Paul says of Miriam's delight in "the last picture" of his sketchbook, "it's more shimmery, as if I'd painted the shimmering protoplasm in the leaves and everywhere, and not the stiffness of the shape. That seems dead to me. Only this shimmeriness is the real living. The shape is a dead crust. The shimmer is inside really."[47]

Green and Maroon will qualify the shimmer's interiority as a relational trick, since its interstice is as much external to the painting's two rectangles as it is internal to the space formed between them. If interiority, here, names a space that might otherwise not quite exist—a protoplasm the rectangles can't entirely contain, or that rises from them like difference dawning on their shared horizon—its shimmer surfaces like first or last breath made visible on the surface of a mirror. Hence the surprising danger of "smothering," whose relation to *smolder* intimates the painting's revelatory making-visible of air itself. "As a result," Rothko writes, "we have the introduction of such things as clouds, smoke, or mist and haze as the only means by which the appearance of existence can be imparted to the atmosphere."[48] For Barthes, "this nuance (this shimmer)" isn't where the Neutral resides, but where it "might reside," the exquisiteness of residing as residue. And so Barthes invokes "the type of 'psychology' we need" (rather than the psychology that we *have*) as "the inventory of shimmers, of nuances. . . . Cf. Walter Benjamin: 'Psychology is but the expression of the borderline nature of human existence.'"[49]

That Bersani and Dutoit's invoking of "a kind of barrier of light" might also have Lacan in mind is hinted in Bersani's subsequent essay, "Psychoanalysis and the Aesthetic Subject," wherein the "invisible, literally unspeakable presence" of "beauty, its blinding brilliance" functions, in Lacan's words, as "an extreme barrier . . . 'forbid[ding] access to a fundamental horror.'"[50] The shimmer of Rothko's line recalls Antigone's "violent illumination, the glow of beauty" through which Lacan understands ethics[51] as an encounter with aesthetic astonishment itself predicated on geometric predicament: "The articulation of the tragic action is illuminating on the subject. . . . It has to do with Antigone's beauty and with the place it occupies as intermediary between two fields that are symbolically differentiated. It is doubtless from this place that her splendor derives."[52] Lacan's understanding of Antigone as the "intermediary between two fields" illuminates in Newman and Rothko something like personification in reverse: it's not that their respective attraction to interstice corresponds to Antigone per se but that Antigone herself assumes eloquence in her desubjectivation *as* shimmering intermediary "between two fields." Lacan is transfixed by Antigone's symbolic crossing of fate, which Sophocles calls *até.* That *até* sometimes is translated as "blind fate," however, confuses the fact that at the center of the tragedy is Antigone's "unbearable splendor" in the face of whose radiance *we* are nearly blinded. Does Antigone cross *até,* or *is* she *até*? "This line of sight," Lacan writes, "focuses on an image that possesses a mystery which up till now has never been articulated, since it forces you to close your eyes at the very moment you look at it. Yet that image is at the center of tragedy, since it is the fascinating image of Antigone herself."[53]

Placed next to "Blocked Vision," Lacan's reading of Sophocles seems to have less to do with what a given figure represents than with the figure's spatial composition itself: this makes sense insofar as the play's tragedy, for Lacan, consists of the afterlife of structure over and against the pulsing fictions of replaceable and irreplaceable signifiers. That the composition both mobilizes and is intercepted by a light source both blind and blinding signals one of several correspondences between Lacan's Antigone and Bersani's Rothko. As Bersani writes of the Houston chapel, the paintings "blind us by visibly working to destroy their own visibility, and they do this by performing an unprecedented act of self-concentration, self-reference, and self-reflection. The religious nature of Rothko's work here, and its confirmation of the Beckettian claim that the artist has nothing to express or communicate, are inseparable from what might be called a suicidal narcissism."[54] Like Narcissus blinded by and lost to his reflection, Antigone embodies an expressly compositional myth that assumes the plangence of personification only after the fact. More interesting than viewing Rothko's work as the personification of one rectangle narcissistically ravished by its reflection is the possibility of Narcissus and Antigone as expressions of rectangular fascination. The reflecting pool's aestheticization of the fictive line between subject and image disturbs the narcissism out of which a narcissism of shapes arises. I think of the Barnett Newman obelisk at the edge of the reflecting pool outside the Houston chapel, the interior of which most recalls the tragedy of Antigone in that being surrounded by these rectangles can sometimes feel like being buried alive.

Bersani returns to this mediating line in spite of himself. The inexorability with which it appears in his writing suggests the intransigence of something other than Freud's death drive or pleasure principle. To be sure, Rothko's interstice answers to neither the death drive's will toward volatility and dissolution nor the pleasure principle's wish for homeostasis. Neither moving per se nor exactly inert, the interstice tautologically inscribes the fields of stasis and motion as a *shimmering* (what Bersani elsewhere calls "vibrating") equilibrium between the two, what Bersani describes in the context of Lawrence as repetition's "deeply paradoxical . . . *activity of inertia*."[55] Even as the interstice operates at a provocatively slight ontological remove from that of the rectangles, its apparent ability to hold, as it were, its own, alters our sense of the rectangles' correspondingly ambient maneuvers.

"This," Bersani writes, "is the virtuality of art which, even when it designates or portrays specific human figures or particular places and acts, has already removed them from the field of actual designation."[56] This "this" describes the thinness of meaning in the characterology of late Henry James, although it may well refer to the virtual virtues of abstract expressionism. James's congruence with Rothko is appreciable in Leon Edel's account of James's 1901 *The Sacred Fount*: "What occurred in the writing, as we see in [James's] second notebook entry, was the introduction of a narrator and the narrator's 'angle of vision'—'I see 2 couples . . . I watch *their* process.'"[57] The abstraction of James's project exceeds the mimetic fidelity of realism. Like the literalism of Rothko's representation of the event of exchange, perhaps it responds to a deeper logic of what in the language of James criticism is understood as an aesthetics of psychological realism. From a novel as early as *Roderick Hudson,* the stunningly abstract interjection of the following gesture into emphatically vacated space anticipates the impersonal ethical framework underlying "Blocked Vision": "Roderick raised his head, but he said nothing; he seemed to be exchanging a long glance with his companion. The result of it was to make him fling himself back with an inarticulate murmur. Rowland, admonished by the silence, was on the point of turning away, but he was arrested by a gesture of the young girl. She pointed for a moment into the blue air. Roderick followed the direction of her gesture."[58]

CRADLING (GEOMETRIES OF TENDERNESS, SANS MIMESIS)

The experience of figurative blinding to which in viewing a Rothko one is vulnerable is heuristically remarkable insofar as its blocked vision is experienced as no less active than seeing itself. Bersani and Dutoit's study of ancient Assyrian palace reliefs offers a way of thinking about this distorting spectatorship as it weathers structural investment in and disappointment by the shifting aesthetic scene. In *The Forms of Violence: Narrative in Assyrian Art and Modern Culture,* Bersani and Dutoit write that "the eye is not passive; it actively fails to dominate its field of vision."[59] Their exploration of the Assyrian reliefs further refines their sense of Rothko's distillations insofar as the reliefs at best approximate the latter's already distilled forms leached of further content. By content, here, I mean the chromatic saturation that sometimes seems to express our own feelings in relation to Rothko's paintings, that suggests what it's like to watch feelings, such slow-moving, deep-sea creatures under glass. Whereas Rothko's work suggests on some level that content (as color) and form (as rectangularity) are inseparable, the Assyrian reliefs give us an endless series of forms both absorbing and emptying out the content of their carvings. Or rather, the unavoidable narrative content of the reliefs assails us less in terms of the violence it represents than in the violence to which it is subjected on the level of form. The "obvious relish with which the defeat, humiliation, and slaughter of Assyria's enemies are portrayed"[60] recircuits through itself the relish taken in the stone carvings' compulsive negative shapes, as though the myriad penetrations recounted in relief spoke to the entrancingly inaccurate replication between the depiction of martial weapons and the chisels that hewed them. The reliefs' gravitation to geometry constantly lures us from our ostensibly primary attention to their rendering of person and scene. Geometric attention atavistically shapes our engagement with these chiseled subjects, whose structural decisiveness only sometimes lines up with our sense of where and how action normatively occurs:

> There are certain curves which produce difference only to reinforce the power of sameness. We are thinking especially of the curves traced by cradling movements back and forth between the same terminal points. To be cradled or to watch a cradling movement is to experience a continual repetition of the same differences. Cradling simultaneously gives us the pleasure of movement and the security of returning to those posi-

> tions where we would still be had we not moved at all. Significantly, the arc produced by cradling hides multiple straight lines. The cradling movement itself is a detour which, without traveling along these straight lines, does nothing but reach, over and over again, their terminal points as half circles on these virtual straight lines.[61]

Bersani and Dutoit's meditation doesn't describe the relief carving so much as the geometric skeleton that subtends it. Cradling operates for both relief and viewer at the same time as our recognition of "scenes of men and animals lying under the stretched bodies of moving horses or camels." This ballet of curvature makes possible what Bersani and Dutoit call an "astonishingly tender violence." Held in the nonnarrativized ebb and flow of "terminal points," "the defeated bodies are enveloped rather than trampled on by the racing animals above them."[62] The same may be said of Rothko's rectangles, which feel (that is to say, look) less trampled by either upper rectangle or canvas than envelopically received, osmosis of swathing.[63]

Narrative mimesis obsolesces in the formality that governs the Assyrian reliefs at hand. While mimesis minimally insists upon some phenomenological distinction between our being in or of the art, the above passage suggests that to "to be cradled" and "to watch a cradling movement" participate in the same shared experience of "continual repetition." Being melts into watching in the reduction of narrative to shape, even as this conjunction of ontology and ocularity will grow ominous in Rothko, "a painter who may not wish to be seen,"[64] producer of an art that "destroys its own visibility through its own self-absorption."[65] The hydraulic by which a painter's troubling of vision becomes our own visual jeopardy is one of many sites at which these pages are attuned to an aesthetics of disability. In an artwork's resistance to the hermeneutics we bring to it, we don't encounter blindness so much as a phenomenology of frustration that softens and shifts into a growing feel for abstraction without horizon, horizon inhabited as immanent. If in their reading of the Assyrian reliefs, Bersani and Dutoit find insidious the cradle's analogous holding into which we are lulled, the expanse of geometric drift in Rothko has more to do with what we are lulled *out of.* The complex passiveness of rectangles sustains the aesthesis by which saturating approach comes to describe not only what we are viewing but what in the absorption we seem to become.

The equivocal generosity of geometry as only potentially insidious establishes a space for imagining personal interaction as it flickers on the compositional apparatus that precedes it. Geometry—the rectangle, the curve, the arc—precedes syntax: in the place of the syntactical we find arrangement. If narrativity coaxes us toward mimetic identification, then geometry recalibrates identification as an experience of inspiring exclusion along the lines of Emerson's transparent eyeball. As consolation for our felt isolation, we learn from and within this compositional scene an identification with the fractures left in narrative's wake. "In the tranquil landscape," Emerson writes, "and especially in the distant line of the horizon, man beholds somewhat as beautiful as his own nature."[66] The beauty of the horizon's distant interstitial line is inseparable from a beholding that is only "somewhat," the Winnicottian nearliness of "inaccurate replication."

Bersani and Dutoit write of Rothko that "art imitates that for which there is no model outside art, since nowhere else can we *see* the ambiguity of boundaries as the noncontingent truth of boundaries," even as we have seen that art—even nonmimetic art—imitates (or initiates?) our understanding of a nonmimetic inhabiting of bodies.[67] There may be no model outside of art, there may be nowhere else where those boundaries are so visible, but in Bersani's contemplation of "aesthetic subjects"[68] the distance between rectum and rectangle blurs as its own contingent truth. Rothko's rectangles, read through Bersani's more recent writings, exactingly strive toward a relationality that doesn't live to tell the tale of its vastation after the fact, so much as testifies to it from within its ascetic eye. Ascesis glimmers in Bersani's work as an inhabitable horizon. In its meditation on ascesis as interstice, "Blocked Vision" anticipates Bersani and Dutoit's speculation in *Forms of Being* of "'a beyond *jouissance*.' . . . [J]ust as the death drive does not eliminate the pleasure principle in Freud, what we have in mind would not erase *jouissance* but might play to the side of it, supplement it with a pleasure at once less intense and more seductive."[69] In this sense, *Forms of Being* and "Blocked Vision" cozen an opening from the conclusion of "Is the Rectum a Grave?" If male homosexuality "dangerously represents *jouissance* as a mode of ascesis," ascesis in this reading shifts to the side like Newman's zip, coming to look less like ultimatum than indefinitely repeatable point of departure.

The longer one spends with Rothko's rectangles, the more it feels like watching life-forms. In the following passage, that "there is usually a differently colored space, however minimal, between the two principal rectangles" implies not only that sometimes the colored space isn't apparent but that sometimes it is unapparent within the very same canvas: indeed, given the sensitivity of most Rothko canvases to external conditions (including sunlight and our own shifting vantage), such speculation of internal variations isn't so far-fetched. To the extent that the contingencies of where and how two rectangles appear to meet recalls the titillating overtures of cruising, I can't help imagining Bersani's watching of the rectangles watching each other in terms of the quiet excitement of a birdwatcher or voyeur:

> There are significant differences in the proximity of the rectangles both to each other and to the canvas edges; there is usually a differently colored space, however minimal, between the two principal rectangles and separating them from the edge of the canvas, although in the late 1960s Rothko did several oil and paper works in which two rectangles appear both to meet with no space between them and to extend to the very edges of the canvas all around the painting. (Even here, however, a thin white strip is detectable as an almost imperceptible frame of the entire painting and as an interstitial horizontal line preventing, so it often seems, the dark upper rectangle from invading the lower one.)[70]

The rectangles watch each other, maybe contemplate meeting without quite meeting, and it's exhilarating for us to witness what may or may not be their own witnessing not in spite of but because there might be just so little—next to nothing—for us to see. The voyeurism of our contemplation of Bersani and Dutoit contemplating rectangles in contemplation is of a piece with the knowing delicacy with which Sedgwick communicates her interest in Proust's narrator's interest in the queer coupling of Charlus and Jupien: "What the narrator has witnessed, however, in the interval is not at all a conquest of this female-gendered self by another self contrastively figured as male. Instead, the intervening pickup between Charlus and Jupien has been presented in two other guises. Primarily it is seen as a mirror-dance of two counterparts 'in perfect symmetry.'"[71] If, as Sedgwick writes, it takes one to know one, we might speculate that her responsiveness to Proust's interest in this Rothko-like mirror-dance registers her own attunement to the queerness of geometry's overture.

Bersani and Dutoit speak of the experience of seeing Rothko's work in terms of an induced blindness, which in light of Sedgwick's and Bersani's own perspicuity comes to describe not the impossibility of seeing so much as a deepening awareness of the possibility of watching abstractions watch other abstractions. The fantasy of blindness, that is, is inseparable from

Bersani's ravishing description of form, as though the ultimate object taken by an aesthetics of failure were itself. If, that is, Rothko's art were more successful at embodying an aesthetics of failure, the blindness it induces in Bersani would ultimately look more like the "all work and no play" repetitions of Stephen King's *The Shining.* This reservation with the terms of failure informs my preference for thinking less about the queer art of failure than an aesthetics of duress. In the above passage, for instance, we note (which is to say, nearly miss noting) the "thin white strip" only as it is conjured in the pulsing blind spot or glancing anamorphosis of a parenthetical. Earlier in the same passage, Bersani and Dutoit write that "there are . . . many paintings with three or even more rectangles. Frequently, one of the three is much smaller vertically than the other two; it can even be reduced to a horizontal strip above, between, or below the other two figures. There is great variety in the placing of these meager elements. Not only does the positioning of the horizontal strip change from painting to painting: the relative sizes of the two main rectangles vary, and we find the larger one sometimes at the top, sometimes at the bottom of the painting."[72] The strip's glimmer visualizes the space between persons, the way we approach each other, the radioisotopic convergence of our meager elements.

PERSPECTIVE ABSENT PERSONS: THE ALMOST PERCEPTIBLE

Rothko's canvas renders the "question of . . . physical position"[73] three-dimensional by mobilizing formal relation in terms not only of top and bottom but foreground and background:

> There are more subtle effects: the showing through of the blue background in the other two rectangles, and, as a crucial element in the partial undoing of the extended blue surface as a background surface, the whitening of some of that blue. The foreground-background distinction is then subverted in both directions: the background advances toward us through the rectangles that the blue at first appeared merely to support, and the rectangle colors spill over into, or recede toward, the background blue. But the very effects of receding and advancing are themselves reduced by interpenetrations that counter our impressions of depth, thereby emphasizing the painting's two-dimensionality. The reduction of differences in hues subverts the fundamental structural difference between foreground and background.[74]

We are invited here to think about the geometrical elements of sex in terms not only of "advancing" and "interpenetration" but receding, supporting, and the enigmatic background on which this "spill[ing] over" transpires. An analogous scene in *Homos* speaks to the "subtle effects" of sex rendered thus as abstract expressionism: "Appropriation has been transformed into communication, a non-dialogic communication in which the subject is so obscenely 'rubbed' by the object it anticipates mastering that the very boundaries separating subject from object, boundaries necessary for possession, have been erased."[75] Although this aesthetic frottage—what Bersani calls a "double rhythm"—reminds him of what *The Freudian Body* depicts as a specifically evolutionary process of masochism, this rubbing friction's biology is coded as intuitively aesthetic, as though we were primed to imagine others, and in turn ourselves, as anciently formal (in the manner, perhaps, of the reliefs). This is the aforementioned gist of Freud's "line of speculation" regarding the line against which the boundaries of organisms are plunged and pressed. This aesthetic of subjectivity-as-impingement echoes an analogous passage in Nietzsche's *Daybreak:* "What do we understand to be the boundaries of our neighbour: I mean that with which he as it were engraves and impresses himself into and upon us?"[76] Like Nietzsche, Bersani and Dutoit turn to a visual vocabulary that "literalizes" the shapes through which they try to understand this strangely obscene rubbing of edges:

> Rothko makes present to us the always tense relation between the distinctness of forms and the indeterminacy of their boundaries. A belief in the distinct nature of boundaries is the precondition of identifying bodies in space, even though we may *know* that our identification of bodies neglects the multiple points at which they are indistinguishable from their contexts. Rothko paints the resistance *and* surrender of forms to form-defeating fusions as the principal sign of the very emergence of forms, and he does this within the framework of what is, apparently, a securely marked-off and privileged aesthetic space.[77]

The beauty of "Blocked Vision," I've argued, involves its sustaining of nonpersonifying vision for the sake of articulating aesthetic relations resistant to the personifying inevitability of what previously might have seemed our only imaginable vista. Bersani and Dutoit's reading of Rothko draws us into this sensorium of enriching ocular difficulty as a stopgap in the compulsively limiting and mutually informing positions from which we ordinarily encounter ourselves and each other. This contemplation of persons receding into relation, the "ontological implausibility of individuality,"[78] is the subject of "One Big Soul," Bersani and Dutoit's 2004 analysis of Malick's *The Thin Red Line,* a film whose response to the ethical trap of believing in persons in turn comes to look like abstract composition. In its mobilization of the terms of "Blocked Vision," "One Big Soul" speaks directly to Bersani's claim from "Is the Rectum a Grave?" that "being on top can never be just a question of physical position."[79] Rothko problematizes what seems unimpeachable (all the more so in the context of a film like Malick's) in the statement that "as soon as persons are posited, the war begins."[80] If it seems like suddenly there are too many Bersani texts and terms at play, it is in the deceptive elegance of "Blocked Vision" that these differing accounts of aesthetics, sex, and war come together.

One of the two characters in Malick's "so-called war film"[81] in whom Bersani and Dutoit are most interested is Sean Penn's Sergeant Top. Top makes sense as a top less in terms of aggression than his negotiation of other characters as formal complexity. More to the point, Bersani is drawn to Penn's sergeant for the same reasons he is drawn in "The Jamesian Lie" to an early James character like Eugenia of *The Europeans*. Bersani writes of Penn's character that "although this complexity is magnificently embodied in Sean Penn's performance, Top's function in the film is more interesting than his implied psychic richness. He has the *relational* function of putting into relief Witt's *un*intelligibility."[82] Eugenia is similarly instructive as relationality emptied of content: "Eugenia's 'dishonesty,' as Richard Poirier has indicated . . . is the margin she leaves for her own and for other people's absorbing possibilities. If she lied she would say the opposite of what she means, but 'between' her words and her meanings lies the *prospect* that the beneficently strenuous conjectures of another mind may offer some views of her meanings rich enough to make a relation seem appealing. . . . The idea of her fibbing hides her psychological originality (her emptiness)."[83] Whereas Eugenia thrives in the comic burgeoning of relations (which, James notes, "was one of a certain number of words that [she] often pronounced in the French manner"),[84] Top's response to the fact of relationality is guardedness. Like "the darker upper rectangle . . . invading the lower one,"[85] Malick's Top (the "darkest point of view in the film")[86] speaks to a fantasy of rectangularity as self-sufficiently identical to itself rather than absorbed by the world to which it corresponds. Top's top-ness, as Bersani writes, depends on there being "no world but this one, a world of madness and evil where wars are fought for property and those in charge 'want you dead or in their lie.'"[87] This singularity of vision requires (more precisely, is inseparable from) an interminable vigilance that differently describes what sometimes makes Rothko's canvases exciting. To imagine the rectangles evolving into something capable of aggression is to conjure something like an indefinitely deferred shootout.

"In addition to its other virtues," Bersani and Dutoit write, "Penn's acting is at times a masterpiece of squinting. His response to what he has seen is to try to see less."[88] Bersani and Dutoit have insisted from the start of *Arts of Impoverishment* that "the Rothko of the Houston chapel appears to have painted in order to keep us from seeing his painting, to make us blind."[89] Or later: "And yet that willful insistence on this simplest of truths about painting—it is an art to be seen—depends for its originality not on the reintroduction of another type of subject, but on a kind of unprecedented demonstration of the difficulty of the very act of seeing."[90] In their introduction to *Arts of Impoverishment,* Bersani and Dutoit note that "we will frequently see Beckett, Rothko, and Renais—all masters of their media—engage in certain sacrificial or crippling moves."[91] Or to indulge a false etymology, in making us "masterpieces of squinting" they leave us, like Newman's *Queen of the Night II,* periwinkled.

Top exists as a rectangle in relation to Witt's interstitiality but likewise functions as a viewer of Rothko-like rectangularities. His aesthetic and ontological function doesn't blur so much as suggest that aesthetic subjectivity entails the necessary difficulty of trying to see oneself as the aesthetic subject one is, doing justice to the weather of interstices rather than the bounded shapes which the former only sometimes delineates or avails. To be viewer and viewed, both blinding and blinded, or in the case of Top, squinting and squinted, is to perceive one's self as literally figurative. Rather than not seeing, we find the possibility of almost seeing, a squinting given over on the squinter's part to seeing differently.

While "Is the Rectum a Grave?" can't not pair a top's vision of supremacy with a bottom's obliteratingly heroic masochism, *The Thin Red Line*'s extension of soldiers "individuated not as personalities but as perspectives on the world"[92] instead pairs Top with Witt, a figure who allegorizes an interstitial rather than rectangular relation to the world. Witt counters

Top's belief in an evil world not with some symmetrically obverse optimism but with a belief in openness itself, complicating Top's "Manichean vision," by which to "bring one [world] into contact with the other is either to have the evil destroy the good, or to have the good penetrate the evil just enough to be evoked as a tantalising but essentially unreachable paradise. Witt asks, 'Why can't we reach out and touch the glory?'"[93] Witt personifies this possibility of "reaching out," which is of a piece with his final words of the film, "all things shinin.'" Witt's words, like Witt himself, illuminate the "all" that they absorb by "never ceasing to locate him within it."[94] Witt's ethical openness corresponds to the relational function of what we have already encountered as the "whitish shimmering line [that] . . . appears to operate as a kind of barrier of light somehow preventing the somber green mass from descending into and crushing the smaller and more fragile form below it."[95] The shimmering line makes possible an ethical encounter not only between or among rectangles and an interstice's surveillance of them but between the shimmering light and the canvas itself (and us). Witt's noninvasive inhabiting of the world recalls Bersani and Dutoit's earlier insistence that the eye—in this case, Witt's eye—"is not passive; it actively fails to dominate its field of vision."[96] Interstitial being allows Witt to represent formal immanence as an antiformal disposition toward self-disintegration and absorption. "Surfaces blurred," Bersani and Dutoit write, "made somewhat indeterminate by the light shining on them, are visual metaphors for the indeterminate identity conferred on all things by inaccurate replication."[97] Witt, interstitially, is both a surface and the light that blurs it. Like Antigone, Witt seems to be *até* in the moment that he enters it.

The Emersonian force of being what one sees makes our identification with Witt both critical and trivial, since "Witt's look . . . receives us in the same way it receives the rest of the world. . . . [A]nd since that world is inseparable from Witt's look, we are also being called upon to share Witt's looking."[98] Perhaps most telling in terms of Bersani's theorization and practice of coauthoring, our shared looking with Witt is described by Bersani (which is to say by Bersani and Dutoit) as a "collaborat[ing]."[99] One of the impediments to understanding Rothko's interstice as corollary to Witt's riveting and expansive vision has to do with the difficulty of not perceiving it as though from the vantage of a rectangle. The shimmering strip surfaces from the imagined depth of the canvas, or seems to float above it, but how to experience it nonrectangularly as Witt's Whitmanian spaciousness?[100]

What does the world look like when viewed from the horizon? I see it as the fractally explosive simultaneity of Rothko's interstice and the "world seen as a vast reservoir of correspondences, of surfaces always ready to 'open,'"[101] something like the coincidence of promontory and horizon in Caspar David Friedrich's *Wanderer above the Sea of Fog*. I look out onto what may or may not be separate from myself, less to be taken than taken in.

ASCETIC ECHO, AESTHETIC BEING

In *The Freudian Body*, Bersani avers that "we are, ontologically, implicated in violence almost from the beginning."[102] Rectangularity, in giving shape to the observation's slippery but potentially crucial "almost," treats ecstasy, to paraphrase Dickinson, as a fundamentally formal feeling:

> *Jouir* is the French word for coming, for having an orgasm. Lacanian *jouissance* unavoidably evokes orgasmic pleasure, but it pushes pleasure beyond itself, to the point of becoming the enemy of pleasure, that which lies "beyond the pleasure principle." "My neighbor's *jouissance*," Lacan states, "his harmful, malignant *jouissance*, is that which poses a problem for my love"—the insurmountable problem of an ecstasy dependent (for both my neighbour and myself) on my being destroyed. *Jouissance* accompanies the "unfathomable aggressivity" which is what I find at the heart of both the other's love for me and my love for the other. . . . To follow Freud in [*Civilization and Its Discontents*] is, as Lacan claims, to conclude that "we cannot avoid the formula that *jouissance* is evil."[103]

Jouir may well "unavoidably" evoke orgasmic pleasure, but as a coming, it compositionally signals the questions of approach and nearness that inform Bersani's watching of the rectangles. In the moment of *jouissance*, we find an "unfathomable aggressivity," conjuring not only an aggressivity that cannot be thought but an aggressivity without bottom. The latter formulation returns us to a version of Top's bottomlessness—the extent to which Top, in Malick's film, approaches not a Bottom but an incandescently questioning Witt. When one calls, *I'm coming*, one locates oneself in a Winnicottian confusion of proximities; by the time one announces one is coming, one is often usually there. Bersani's gloss of Lacan insists on both ecstasy and aggression as constitutively compositional issues. The neighbor is neither a lover nor spouse nor stranger nor friend. What matters more than how well one knows or loves the neighbor is their physical proximity. Are they near or far? How near must they be to be considered neighborly? The neighbor's pure relationality can be heard in the nearness of its etymon, the "nigh" of neighbor pushing toward one form of space and one's coming indicating another. Pushing pleasure beyond itself.

"Pleasures of Repetition," a chapter in *The Freudian Body,* ends with a passage lifted almost verbatim from the concluding section of *The Forms of Violence,* whose titular interest in "'betweenness' in the Palace Reliefs" anticipates Bersani's long-standing investment in the "near-rectangle" as "a cage which imprisons nothing."[104] "The nearly indefinable quality of 'betweenness' in the palace reliefs—and, consequently, our interpretive suspension between narrative and nonnarrative readings—may manifest an impressive hesitation or even ignorance, on the part of these ancient anonymous artists, about the forms of disruption and of violence which they had chosen to love."[105] "Nearly indefinable," like the earlier "almost from the beginning," asks us to think further not only about "betweenness" but about the "impressive hesitation" that so well describes the phenomenology internal to much of Rothko's work. Like Whitman's constellation of homosexuality alongside cradling and impressiveness,[106] Bersani's attachment to hesitation is energized not only by hesitation's almost-withdrawing flutter but by its capacity to be impressive, to leave, quite literally, a mark. Published twelve years after *The Freudian Body, Caravaggio's Secrets* (1998) seeks further to elaborate this betweenness between the fictive sovereignty of palatial reliefs. Recalling the cradling motion that absorbs us into the work of art (its own version perhaps of finding ourselves, like Antigone, caught in stone), Caravaggio "shows, and he is part of what is being shown."[107] In his compulsive insertion of himself—variously disabled, castrated, decapitated—into his own paintings, Caravaggio literalizes the fantasy of viewing oneself as aesthetic subject. Maud Ellmann is exactly right that "in *Caravaggio's Secrets* the authors seem to recognise the limits of their previous ascetism."[108] But recognition of limits isn't impasse so much as the grounds for less ineluctably aggressive an intimacy. Here is Bersani and Dutoit's account of the Brera *Supper at Emmaus:*

> There are several pairings in the work, pairings that ignore the boundaries not only between persons but also between living human beings and inanimate matter. Christ's raised right hand is paired with the raised left hand of the figure to his right; his left hand is resting on the table next to

> the similarly positioned right hand of the other seated disciple; there are two pieces of bread, one already broken, the other intact; and there is the curious repetition of the folds of wrinkles on the old woman's brow in the ribs of meat on the plate she is carrying. Each member of each couple remains distinct. Even the two hands resting on the table are contiguous without touching. Indeed, the possibility of contiguity as the subject of this painting is suggested by the miniscule space separating the sharply outlined little finger of the apostle to Christ's right from the unbroken piece of bread. A *space between* keeps all these paired objects apart. The couple never becomes one; each member of each pair echoes its partner without sacrificing any parcel of its own space, of an individuality that can be paired but that cannot essentially be repeated.[109]

Bersani and Dutoit likewise articulate "the between-ness Caravaggio emphasizes" in *The Resurrection of Lazarus* in terms of a "between-ness [that] means that Lazarus is neither dead nor alive, or that he is both."[110] *The Resurrection of Lazarus* brings to mind Bersani's insistence that "if the rectum is the grave in which the masculine ideal (an ideal shared—differently—by men *and* women) of proud subjectivity is buried, then it should be celebrated for its very potential for death."[111] In taking rectangularity as a model for less proud, less self-apparent a structure of subjectivity, the gravity of recta cedes to a lightness of being that doesn't displace rectal spectacle so much as yields a differently infiltrating echo of it.

"Art," Bersani and Dutoit write, "illuminates relationality by provisionally, and heuristically, immobilizing relations. A light we never see appears, as being, momentarily 'trapped,' designates itself to us . . . by the prominent strip of light . . . that has no function other than to make illumination literally the center of the painting."[112] What, again, seems a description of a Rothko in fact comes from a reading of Caravaggio's *Betrayal of Christ.* To uncouple the rectum from "the internalized phallic male,"[113] to recouple a rectum with a rectangle, is to anticipate the impressive hesitation shining between the two. Rectum and rectangle, curiously pondering the new aesthetic and ontological scene in which they find themselves, "float because they have not 'chosen' the direction in which they will move. Floating, then, would be a special effect of immobility; it is the vibratory relation among the various directions that forms have not yet taken, between the different points not yet designated as their goals."[114]

6. Weaver's Handshake

The Aesthetics of Chronic Objects

> We are the photometers, we the irritable goldleaf and tinfoil that measure the accumulations of the subtle element. We know the authentic effects of the true fire through every one of its million disguises.
>
> —RALPH WALDO EMERSON, "SPIRITUAL LAWS"

> "an important writer of
> fiction and poetry,—"
>   of *criticism*
> and poetry, of course it's meant to say,
> but "fiction," in this empty register,
> scans, so 'fiction' in my head it always is. . . .
>
> Waking as an adult, now, who has an art.
>
> —EVE KOSOFSKY SEDGWICK, "A POEM IS BEING WRITTEN"

In his 1836 essay "Nature," Emerson invokes what he calls a "theory of nature,"[1] inviting us to think about a theory as problematic and surprising as nature itself. Beyond the boilerplate of the double genitive, the flexibility of this "of" between theory and nature speaks to Emerson's interest in minimizing the ontological distance between the theorizing and the thing being theorized. The unabsorbable appeal of this "of" recalls Paul Grimstad's account of what in Emerson most lends itself to the radical empiricism of William James.[2] "For such a philosophy," James writes, "*the relations that connect experiences must themselves be experienced relations, and any kind of relation experienced must be accounted as 'real' as anything else in the system.*"[3] If the "of," as an object, belongs to theory and nature alike, it's not entirely clear how one might best think through this category of objects between, as Lacan might say, the glove and the hand.[4]

As a grammatical unit, "of" ordinarily vanishes into the words it holds together. Here, it is an experience as much as theory is an expression and act of nature. In the wake of "our Cartesian moment,"[5] the difficulty posed to thinking by objects about which one doesn't quite know how or what to think describes the neither-quite-subject-nor-object of a particular strain of queer theory connecting the work of Emerson to that of Eve Kosofsky Sedgwick. Along related lines, Jordy Rosenberg has recently analyzed queer theory's involution with theories of materialism, informed by William James no less than Whitehead or Spinoza. Rosenberg argues that this ontological turn conceals a primitivism bound to the separation of objects from the social sphere. Of queer theory's recent fascination with "the object"—specifically, that queerly, aleatorily resistant object, the molecule—Rosenberg asks, "Would it be unorthodox to suggest that what was once a methodological question attending queer theory at its outset—what is theory's relation to its object?—has now taken on the character of an a priori answer? In other words, we no longer ask: *what is the object of queer studies?* Rather, the object of queer studies—at the present moment—appears to be *the* object."[6] The slippery nonequivalence of "[queer] theory's relation to its object" and "the object of queer studies" suggests the shiftlessness of the shift that Rosenberg describes, an unresolved set of remainders that equally subtend and undermine what Emerson calls our most unhandsome condition.

Elsewhere in *Contingent Figure* I have asked what difference genre makes in terms of Elaine Scarry's inclination in *The Body in Pain* to think about pain as a question of narrative rather than poetics. I similarly wonder how a turn from narrative to poetics might open along an edge of Rosenberg's thinking a place for the kind of Emersonian objects that sustain Sedgwick's attention. For instance, in reminding us that "'the object' has been a foundational question for queer studies," Rosenberg points to Judith Butler's "unsettling the appearance of [the] ontological reality" of the "object" that "was sex/gender."[7] An inverting of Emerson, Butler's reading takes an object previously supposed natural—through an atavism strategically posited beyond the social frame—and restores our sense of its theoretical constitution. Butler's analysis yields a performative object consigned to constant iterations of what in the guise of the natural it had professed to be. Even as performativity and iterability are no less essential to the following lines from Sedgwick's early essay "Privileges of Unknowing," the object to which they accrue, by contrast, isn't theoretical or abstract so much as figuratively vivid:

> In fact, the delineation of "the sexual" in this convent, in this reading, is done by a process that resembles gravestone-rubbing. The dense back-and-forth touch of the crayon leaves a positive map not of excrescences but of lines of absent or excised matter. And the pressure of insistence that makes a continuous legibility called sexual knowledge emerge from and take the shape of the furrows of prohibition or of stupor is, most powerfully, *the reader's* energy of need, fear, repudiation, projection.[8]

Notwithstanding its correspondence to the object that is Butler's "sex/gender," "the sexual" here is all but eclipsed by the passage's translation of it into the continuous present tense—what I am inclined to call the chronic object—of the aestheticized and aestheticizing figure of gravestone-rubbing. That the predicate of the sentence under way is "the sexual" gratuitously amplifies the erotic energy inherent to the process that these lines describe. Sedgwick's metaphorical vehicle and tenor catch and drag, even as the fidelity of the gravestone-rubbing—if not as vehicle then as nonfigurative practice—depends on the maintenance of the uniformity of the hand that effects it. Sedgwick seems to introduce gravestone-rubbing as an approximately transparent medium; we are asked, after all, to read the furrows as though they were "made legible," rather than written. And yet, the ingenious extravagance of the comparison also implies that the more it helps us see what is otherwise occluded, the more what we are seeing might be on account of the weight of a hand. If, in the case of Butler's "sex/gender," what had seemed material reappears at the end of a process of reading as abstract, Sedgwick's comparison demonstrates the interesting difficulties that arise when such inversions become the coefficients of an analogy. This difficulty of knowing how to distinguish the properties of the sexual from "the sexual" from the equivocally material and only somewhat transparent medium out of which either appears returns us to the

Emersonian project of minimizing if not quite dissolving the differences between theory and nature.

The dense "back-and-forth touch" of Sedgwick's analysis anticipates the activity at the lightning-rod heart of *Tendencies'* notorious chapter, "Jane Austen and the Masturbating Girl," in which Sedgwick juxtaposes passages from *Sense and Sensibility* with lines such as the following from "Onanism and Nervous Disorders in Two Little Girls": "In addition to the practises already cited, X . . . provoked the voluptuous spasm by rubbing herself on the angles of furniture, by pressing her thighs together. . . . One night she succeeds in rubbing herself till the blood comes on the straps that bind her."[9] While Sedgwick doesn't entirely discount the authenticity of this "narrative structured as a case history,"[10] or for that matter its 1881 publication, I expect that the frisson that her writing registers for these lines actually is intensified by their implicit (and eventually, confirmed) fraudulence.[11] The text's tantalizing frustration of a reader's assumption of veracity leads me to think about the counterfeit Foucauldian document in terms of what Daniel Tiffany, following Susan Stewart, calls the distressed genre of the imitation ballad. The lurid recoil of not being able to tell an authentic text from a sham generates, for Tiffany, the flinch of kitsch.[12]

The possible imbrication of kitsch with the surveillant rise (circa 1881) of the Foucauldian sexual subject is an important context for Sedgwick's own influential articulation of kitsch's relation to queerness. As I note in this chapter's next section, that Sedgwick's writing has given us a theory of kitsch is not separable from the frequency with which she seems to have induced something like a kitsch response in many of her critics. Sentimental and florid: a way of describing both the theory and the style of the writing in which the theory occurs. It is arguably in this confluence (of, we might say, radical empiricism and aesthetics) that Sedgwick's queer theory is most Emersonian. But to return to the rubbing at hand: that the girls waver in and out of seeming real as subjects of history in general and medical scrutiny in particular isn't incidental to how Sedgwick helps us think about their rubbing themselves to bloody distraction. Like Hawthorne's "discovery" of the artifact that is the scarlet letter, Sedgwick's attention to this spurious text is all the keener on account of the possibility that its insatiably rubbing subjects—stand-ins, not insignificantly, for Sedgwick herself—might not be "real" at all. That the rubbing surveilled in the fake case study could seem ontologically compatible with the rubbing which Sedgwick describes as the sexual lends this flickering connection between scenes the feel of substantial presence, at once established and hollowed out by a chronicity figured in and across both scenes as out of thin air.

Even though this scene does not belong to the object world in the sense understood by Rosenberg and the OOO (object-oriented ontology) theorists she critiques, it's an object world nonetheless. Its terms resonate with those of Rosenberg's admonitory claim that "the turn to ontology" is an "origin narrative . . . that takes the form of appearance of a methodology, but that is, in essence, driven by a figural logic."[13] And yet the figural logic by which Sedgwick's lines are driven is of a different granular order than the one Rosenberg describes in part because it is, in a certain sense, literal. To adapt Bersani's formulation, "the dense back-and-forth touch of the crayon" is an inaccurate replication of Sedgwick's pen or her fingers on an early computer keyboard. Nonetheless, it's hard not to imagine Sedgwick inside the scene being conjured. This is all the more the case insofar as gravestone-rubbing, somewhere between writing and craft, uncannily compresses her evolution to and from the high stylistic verve associated with *Epistemology of the Closet* and *Tendencies,* of which this passage is exemplary. Far more than is usually acknowledged, Sedgwick's investment as a critic in her own writerly style is unthinkable apart from her lifelong sense of poetry as a first calling. At the same time, Sedgwick's eventual migration to the differently capacity-making medium of textiles—precipitated by what she sometimes describes as a waning investment in authorial control—is as much an intensification of her long-standing attachments as it is a turning away. What follows traces some of the continuities between her earlier and later conceptions of herself as poet, theorist, and artist.

First, though, I want to return to Emerson and the Orphic chant that concludes *Nature.* As a mythology of the fall of man *as* the birth of objects, the chant complements Sedgwick's attention to what in the gravestone passage she hauntingly calls "excised matter." In its conjuring the cutting off of a limb or organ, Sedgwick's "excised" is homologous with what in "Experience" Emerson calls "caducous": "So is it with this calamity: it does not touch me: some thing which I fancied was a part of me, which could not be torn away without tearing me, nor enlarged without enriching me, falls off from me, and leaves no scar. It was caducous. I grieve that grief can teach me nothing, nor carry me one step into real nature."[14] The disorienting alacrity of this caducous falling away is a variation on the Orphic chant's myth of externizing:

> Man is the dwarf of himself. Once he was permeated and dissolved by spirit. He filled nature with his overflowing currents. . . . The laws of his mind, the periods of his actions externized themselves into day and night, into the year and the seasons. But, having made for himself this huge shell, his waters retired; he no longer fills the veins and veinlets; he is shrunk to a drop. He sees, that the structure still fits him, but fits him colossally. Say, rather, once it fitted him, now it corresponds to him from far and on high. He adores timidly his own work.[15]

I appreciate this passage next to Sedgwick's account of "the sexual" because it suggests that the spatial relations literalized in gravestone-rubbing's paper over stone belong to a spectrum of the ever-dilating centrifugal distance between correspondences. Unlike Sedgwick's figurative words "magically" arising in the feel of a crayon for what it passes over, Emerson's myth of the waters retiring is like a *Trauerspiel* that never quite comes to life. That it doesn't come to life is precisely the point. The extravagance of the myth is an amplifying symptom of the exaggeration the myth describes, as though hyperbole and observation were different in degree rather than kind.

What this pathos of cosmic estrangement is least able to conjure is what Sedgwick, following Henry James, calls the middle range. In Emerson's lines, the middle range is experienced, if at all, as the cavernousness of its qualities grown imperceptible. It is like air—neutral, abstract—or like *like,* or *of.* Bearing in mind the botany of caducousness, we might say that Emerson encounters the textures of the world as if they were phantom pains. "The wholeness we admire in the order of the world," Emerson writes in "The Method of Nature," "is the result of infinite distribution. Its smoothness is the smoothness of the pitch of the cataract. Its permanence is a perpetual inchoation. Every natural fact is an emanation, and that from which it emanates is an emanation also, and from every emanation is a new emanation."[16] Another way of describing the situation in for which this cataclysm hyperbolically stands is that that the suffering of the loss of a relation to an object isn't distinguishable from suffering the loss of the object is symptomatic of the loss itself. This confusion of categories pervades the strangeness of Emerson's claim in "Experience" that he grieves that grief can teach him nothing: as though the loss of his son were mistakable for the grief that follows the loss of his son, in turn mistakable for grief over the insufficiency of grief.

Although the Orphic chant doesn't explicitly mention feeling, it's nonetheless "permeated and dissolved" by it insofar as feeling, like reading, is so often synonymous for Emerson with the intractable perception of distance between one's self and the world for which one feels. It's not that Emerson is asking us to believe in the primordial ruin as a historical fact, not least because the logic of facts is coextensive for him with confronting the world as though it were a set of objects and we the scrutinizing subject.[17] Rather, I take Emerson to be suggesting that this scalarly disorienting vision is how a certain relation to objects *feels.* I've elsewhere discussed chronic pain as a realism of hyperbole; even if these lines don't mention pain per se, they illuminate how pain shapes a world that is neither internal nor external to it. Lacan thinks about pain—chronic pain in particular—in analogous terms, as an inhabiting of the landscape one has become:

> The complex character of pain, the character that, so to speak, makes it an intermediary between afferent and efferent, is suggested by the surprising results of certain operations, which in the case of some internal illnesses, including some cancers, allow the notation of pain to be preserved, when the suppression or removal of a certain subjective quality has been effected, which accounts for the fact that it is unbearable. . . .
>
> I will . . . limit myself to suggesting that we should perhaps conceive of pain as a field which, in the realm of existence, opens precisely onto that limit where a living being has no possibility of escape.
>
> Isn't something of this suggested to us by the insight of the poets in that myth of Daphne transformed into a tree under the pressure of a pain from which she cannot flee? Isn't it true that the living being who has no possibility of escape suggests in its very form the presence of what one might call petrified pain? Doesn't what we do in the realm of stone suggest this? To the extent that we don't let it roll, but erect it, and make of it something fixed, isn't there in architecture itself a kind of actualization of pain?[18]

Not only does Lacan, like Emerson, imagine pain as both more and less than the object it might otherwise have been. He also, like Emerson, thinks about the vicissitudes of the objects of pain in terms of the poet, who, for Emerson, "stands one step nearer to things, and sees the flowing or metamorphosis."[19] Looking ahead to Sedgwick's predilection for lyric, chronic objects, the poet's "insight" is most salient for Lacan because it intuits a relation between trying to imagine the experience of pain and the experience (such as that might be) as though it were inseparable from the pulsation—perpetual inchoation, incessant capsizing of unending movement into stasis—of anthropomorphosis.

SCOURING, SMUDGING: FAULTS IN THE STYLE

The eventual decision to take notes in my original copies of Sedgwick's books in ink instead of pencil felt surprisingly drastic.[20] Floating beside the new marks are the earlier ones in pencil, from when trying to make sense of her writing had all the imagined, *Nachträglichkeit* urgency of learning the language of the country unfolding from under me. What was the language, that first summer, for carrying *Epistemology of the Closet* less as book than transitional object, like the volume with which Charlotte Stant steels herself—"the dark cover . . . that was to explain her purpose in case of her being met with surprise"[21]—fleeing unsuccessfully to a garden's canicular heat from the terms, strictly speaking, she no less than James at some earlier point might have claimed proudly as her own? What was the language for having brought with me, that afternoon of reading on the UC Berkeley campus, a neon yellow and quickly fading neoprene messenger bag bought at the gift shop from my first and only visit to the Louvre; or, as I sat under a tree absorbed in the woeful and fruitless first efforts of cruising, for coming to the mortifying realization that the bag, surely flung with the insouciance of some new variation on the inveterate rhythms of the compensatory, was lying in a new pile of dogshit, as though the olfactory under the right conditions were as affectively susceptible to slow motion as vision or sound? The language and the country, it turns out, belonged to what Sedgwick, several years following *Epistemology,* would call queer performativity: that of the demolishing interruption of self-spending theatricality both by and as an experience of shame transformable perhaps only by a subsequent version of the readerly self of which that younger one up until this very moment was unaware.[22]

In ink, even desultory marks seem to contradict note-taking's spirit of off-the-cuff, what Sedgwick following Flaubert might call note-taking as *idée reçue:* "The interpretive paths by which there is any sense to be made of him are completely paved, as I'm afraid I may be unable to stop demonstrating, with the *idées reçues* of homophobic 'worldly wisdom.'"[23] In other hands, this peppering of English with French might register as cacozelia, "a stylistic affectation of diction, such as throwing in foreign words to appear learned."[24] *Cacozelia,* from the Greek κἄκοζηλία, meaning "unhappy imitation," sounds like something Sedgwick would appreciate: after all, it names a species of the snobbish habit that makes minor James and Proust characters recognizable as such.[25] Contra Austin's sense of theatricality as performatively nullifying (e.g., a wedding performed within a play), "unhappy imitation" bespeaks the inseparability of style from thinking about the performative felicity of mimetic acts. More generally it calls our attention to the affective gamut on which any given imitative act might fall. That some forms of imitation are unhappy or make us so (and some are/make us happy) recalls in its deceptive simplicity the empirical vigor, revolutionary as Luther's theses on the sale of indulgences, of the axioms at the outset of *Epistemology of the Closet.* In the manner of indulgences, my speculation on what Sedgwick might hypothetically appreciate helps me appreciate among other things the difficulty sometimes of telling imitations apart.

Insofar as Quintilian's definition of *cacozelia* conjures the lavishness toward which Sedgwick's critics and devotees equally gravitate, it's maybe unsurprising how closely it lines up with the spoken and unspoken criteria of *Philosophy and Literature*'s "bad writers of the year." "Unhappy imitation" manages to describe the potential indistinguishability of what Denis Dutton calls "kitsch theorists"[26] from the real thing. The fault line that sets Quintilian's definition apart from Dutton's is that of sincerity. Amid all the licenses bad writing might take, one of Dutton's few requirements for contest entries is that they "be non-ironic," since "deliberate parody cannot be allowed in a field where unintended self-parody is so widespread."[27] Like Jack Spratt's wife (although stylistically speaking, Dutton and Quintilian alike inhabit the non-uxorious position of *eat-no-fat*), Quintilian oppositely insists that cacozelia is allergic to sincerity, even as the prodigiousness of Sedgwick's style seems nothing if not sincere. Cacozelia, Quintilian writes,

> or perverse affectation, is a fault in every kind of style: for it includes all that is turgid, trivial, luscious, redundant, far-fetched or extravagant, while the same name is also applied to virtues carried to excess, when the mind loses its critical sense and is misled by the false appearance of beauty, the worst of all offences against style, since other faults are

> due to carelessness, but this is deliberate. This form of affectation, however, affects style alone. For the employment of arguments which might equally well be advanced by the other side, or are foolish, inconsistent or superfluous, are all faults of matter, whereas corruption of style is revealed in the employment of improper or redundant words, in obscurity of meaning, effeminacy of rhythm, or in the childish search for similar or ambiguous expressions. Further, it always involves insincerity, even though all insincerity does not imply affectation. For it consists in saying something in an unnatural or unbecoming or superfluous manner. Style may, however, be corrupted in precisely the same number of ways that it may be adorned.[28]

If Sedgwick suggests that the difference between kitsch and camp is the difference between *who on earth would ever want that* and *this has my name all over it,*[29] then somewhere between these modes, to borrow one of Sedgwick's *mots justes,* is the vicariating impulse of *this has* her *name all over it* (she would *love* that), which this passage does.

The finality of the blue ink sets into relief the pencil's earlier scenes of reading, which retrospectively seem both mystified and trusting, tentative and zealous. To move from *Epistemology of the Closet* to Sedgwick's essay on queer performativity: "The first of these scouring depressions was precipitated in 1895 by what James experienced as the obliterative failure of his ambitions as a playwright, being howled off the stage at the premiere of *Guy Domville.*"[30] No pencil there. The pencil is waiting for "narcissism/shame circuit," which it circles. It underlines "in the prefaces is using reparenting or 'reissue' as a strategy for dramatizing and integrating shame, in the sense of rendering this potentially paralyzing affect narratively, emotionally, and performatively productive."[31] The blue pen circles "scouring," whose economy conjures the upstairs-downstairs drama of feeling's textural relation to the person who feels it. As a singular verb of exasperatingly repetitive action, scouring choreographically forces depression to its hands and knees—unless depression does this to James—immersed (physically if not otherwise), red-knuckled, in a labor whose *fata morgana* terminus we hear in *Annie*'s "And if this floor don't *shine like the top of the Chrysler Building,* your backsides will." At the same time, scouring won't tell us if depression is being compared to a scullery maid or the Bon Ami (signature combination of tallow soap and feldspar) at her side, the hermeneutic challenge of which, Sedgwick suggests in *A Dialogue on Love,* is constitutive:

> "It's just so much easier for me to envision things in discrete parts. But then you come along and smudge up the barriers, and it's really different. It's important for you to keep doing that—I really think I am getting it."
>
> Deconstruction 101, I do *not* say impatiently.
>
> Then he asks, when I was involved in these scouring devaluations of myself, could I tell whose voice it was that I was hearing in my head?
>
> Me: "I think that's an important question"—meaning I can't answer it—"but there's something else I want to say about it."[32]

Perhaps because the image in my head is of *Guy Domville* wiping James's floors clean, my first inclination is to think of scouring in terms of detergent, the root of which, *tergo,* denotes both the wiping and the backside in need of it. Only subsequently do I remember scouring's less abrasive, epistemological register, the scavenging of a landscape as for clues.

As Beatrix replies to Trollope in Sedgwick's Victorian novella in verse, *The Warm Decembers,* "Oh, Uncle Cosmo will stay out / Nimrodding while there's light anywhere— / scouring his horizons."[33] Sunlight and Cosmo alike are scourers, as are acolytes of cacozelia, "childishly search[ing]" for expression. As object of scrutiny, the horizon (let alone "horizons") illuminates the rigor with which scouring searches out texture in a field of vision worn epistemologically smooth: in the case of James, a smoothness itself the diachronic result of depression's scrubbing fervor. Epistemologically, scouring locates texture where there had been none (the stubble of a field, versus "the flat, the blueless / aerated tones of earth—and glazed, like pastry"[34] as which the field appears on the horizon), even as scouring detergently wears down buildup to a smooth polish.

EYE OF THE NEEDLE, RUB OF THE REAL

In an essay approximately contemporary with Sedgwick's "A Poem Is Being Written," Jonathan Culler distinguishes between two modes of reading, the lyrical and the descriptive. Culler's terminology clarifies my understanding of Sedgwick's high critical style, its gregarious enactment of charisma, its bottomless carpetbag of rhetorical intensities. Specifically, the lyrical—and in "A Poem Is Being Written" the lyrical as inextricable from Sedgwick's sense of herself as a poet—provides a way of thinking about style in terms of its relation to the objects it mobilizes. "Critics," Culler writes, "have characteristically translated apostrophe into description ('O rose, thou art sick,' is an intensified way of describing the rose as sick), but what the lyric or a lyrical reading (to use de Man's term) does is to translate description into apostrophe and anthropomorphism."[35] If "scouring depression" operates "not as truth or assertion but as dramatized experience of a consciousness," the scouringly "corrosive but magical substance" of this consciousness belongs to neither James nor Sedgwick but to the scouring, an exemplarily tergiversating quilting point between read and written texts.[36]

Lacan's quilting point—"the point at which the signified and the signifier are knotted together, between the still floating mass of meanings"[37]—describes a space imaginable as having been expansive only in the precise moment of being compressed to an approximation of that single point. I take this to be the force, in part, of Lacan's observation that its "point of convergence . . . enables everything that happens in this discourse to be situated retroactively and prospectively."[38] The quilting point incessantly converts what it holds together from two dimensions to three and back again; this back-and-forth between dimensions corresponds to the quilting point's own pulsation between being a word and being an object, an animation not unrelated to Culler's understanding of anthropomorphosis. Its simultaneous implication in and collapse of intermediate space repeats the play of pressure and surface from which emerges the gravestone-rubbing, the scouring's pulverizing crystallography. Lacan's own attention to these fractal dimensions of the materiality of language is evident throughout his seminars, as in the possibility of "see[ing] in isolation the various dimensions in which the phenomenon of the sentence—I am not saying the phenomenon of meaning—unfolds."[39]

This dimensional mutability helps us differently visualize the oddness of figuration when it seems neither quite metaphorical nor literal. Such is the coalescing, animating force of "the weaver's handshake," a gesture that Sedgwick describes in "Making Things, Practicing Emptiness," published posthumously in *The Weather in Proust:*

> But really I've always loved textiles. I used to sew my own clothes (though ineptly), back in college when I had time for it and no money, and the feel of any kind of fiber between my thumb and fingers—in a gesture I probably got from my grandmother, who also taught me to crochet and embroider—just is the rub of reality, for me. It's funny that the same brushing-three-fingers gesture is mostly understood to whisper of money, the feel of the coin, as a bottom-line guarantee of reality. I've

> learned that this gesture is also called "the weaver's handshake," because of the way a fabric person will skip the interpersonal formalities when you're introduced and move directly to a tactile interrogation of what you're wearing.[40]

As a Masonic salute of sorts between textiles and the tactually sensitive people who love them, this not quite clandestine greeting recalls Sedgwick's account in *Between Men* of "Whitman" as a "Victorian homosexual shibboleth": "Photographs of Whitman, gifts of Whitman's books, specimens of his handwriting, news of Whitman, admiring references to 'Whitman' which seem to have functioned as badges of homosexual recognition, were the currency of a new community that saw itself as created in Whitman's image."[41] We find in this "currency of a new community" a way of making sense of the gesture's "whisper of money." The resemblance between these two forms of address is striking not only in the way each functions in tacit exchange but in Sedgwick's intuition of the shibboleth as a kind of quilting point caught in the act of making fiber art. "In England," Sedgwick writes, "to trace the path of individual copies of the book, beginning with the remaindered copies of the 1855 *Leaves* scattered abroad by an itinerant pedlar, would be to feel like the eye of a needle that was penetrating from layer to layer of the literate social fabric . . . around the connecting thread of manly love."[42]

This plangent and bizarre passage reads like the activation of a heterogeneous vision only subsequently reduced to a series of discrete movements from poet to critic to theorist to fiber artist. "We begin" in a periphery or interruption of literary history, the sort of lost days that Emerson describes as "intercalated."[43] In this nearly unimaginable moment, not least in terms of the Emersonian approbation with which the 1855 *Leaves of Grass* is greeted, Whitman's work wakes (if we might allow it even this animating percipience) to discover itself unread and undesired: remaindment in England as dead letter office. It's in this incapacity that it appears as an object other than the one as which it has been imagining itself. What is most startling in Sedgwick's passage isn't that Whitman's poetry is no longer being handled like a body; after all, by the last lines of "Song of Myself" the poem foresees a version of this ghostliness: "I bequeath myself to the dirt to grow from the grass I love, / If you want me again look for me under your bootsoles."[44] What it *can't imagine* (even redistributed as dead leaves or "drift[ed] . . . in lacy jags") is not having a body, not having a voice, as though dropped from an anthropomorphosis that may well have been the figurative move least possible for Whitman himself to shake.

The voice that narrates Sedgwick's tableau is as little a reader as the book, in Whitmanian terms, is a book. Thus the eye that traces the book's path (rather than reads its pages) so quickly gives way to the unseeing eye of a needle. These lines are as much a reversal of Emerson's transparent eyeball as the mute, insensate book is a reversal of Whitman's Emersonian agenda. They are disorienting in part because they treat words, texts, and names as though they were objects without quite knowing how best to navigate a relation to them; we might, for that matter, say that the experience of words as objects speaks directly to this unmooring. What is the ideal distance or vantage from which to read becomes a question of how many vantages one can sustain more or less at the same time. The sinuous terrain of Sedgwick's sentence does not ask us to choose between the long view of tracing a transatlantic path and the micro-attention by which a needle is threaded. Rather, the coincidence of these ocular orders suggests that as early as *Between Men,* Sedgwick is thinking about simultaneities of reading in terms of fractals, and thinking, more specifically, about fractals as the mutual constitution across multiple figurative registers of textile and text. This is not least the case in the turbulence of a reader's eye as it tries to imagine as continuous what otherwise is experienced as the jolts of distance and dimension. What on earth would it "feel like" to be the eye of this needle as it penetrates "layer to layer of the . . . social fabric?" The Whitman with which we are familiar would keen at the touch let alone pierce of a needle. But can this remaindered, transatlantic *Leaves of Grass,* the one without a voice (which is to say, at least in Sedgwick's imagination of the scene, without consciousness), still feel this sharpness to which we, at least, as readers, are privy?

Taking *Leaves of Grass* in terms of the first titular half of *Fat Art, Thin Art,* we might also imagine Sedgwick's vision of Whitman as a reparative engagement with James's preface to "The Beast in the Jungle," a text never far, it seems, from Sedgwick's mind, "where every object was as familiar to [her] as the things of [her] own house and the very carpets were worn with [her] fitful walk very much as the desks in old counting-houses are worn by the elbows of generations of clerks."[45] As James writes, "It takes space to feel, it takes time to know, and great organisms as well as small have to pause, more or less, to possess themselves and to be aware. Monstrous masses are, by this truth, so impervious to vibration that the sharpest forces of feeling, locally applied, no more penetrate than a pin or a paper-cutter penetrates an elephant's hide."[46] The relations between the social fabric, the poem, the poem's readers, the thread and needle—they all blur and bleed together at the precise point at which the needle, such as it is and we are, makes contact. Turning to a trope so similar one wonders if Sedgwick is playing homage, James writes in the preface to *Roderick Hudson* that "really, universally, relations stop nowhere,"

> and the exquisite problem of the artist is eternally but to draw, by a geometry of his own, the circle within which they shall happily *appear* to do so. He is in the perpetual predicament that the continuity of things is the whole matter, for him, of comedy and tragedy; that this continuity is never, by the space of an instant or an inch, broken, and that, to do anything at all, he has at once intensely to consult and intensely to ignore it. All of which will perhaps pass but for a supersubtle way of pointing the plain moral that a young embroiderer of the canvas of life soon began to work in terror, fairly, of the vast expanse of that surface, of the boundless number of its distinct perforations for the needle, and of the tendency inherent in his many-coloured flowers and figures to cover and consume as many as possible of the little holes.[47]

It is in the spaciousness of these relations (including those between Sedgwick and Whitman and James), rather than the comparably obvious overdetermination of "penetrating," that Sedgwick locates the queerness of the sexual. Over and against the de-apostrophization of Whitman's book, the needle translates the social into fabric and that fabric into an art we are unable to name. In the manner of Dickinson's fascicles, is the fabric becoming a book, or a garment? Or something else altogether?

Like Whitman-as-shibboleth, the weaver's handshake occurs in the text as a double movement between absorption and outward interest. Alongside the gravestone-rubbing, I try to take the needle and the weaver's handshake on their own terms. Even as these are the sorts of passages that most bear for me Sedgwick's signature, we don't yet have an idiom for conceptualizing just how fundamental their singularity is to the quality of her thinking. As an attempt to treat this figurative elaborateness as nonornamental or, at least, nonsubsidiary, this chapter is an effort to think about style as theory as the latter looks from one vantage onto poetry and from another onto textiles. The compressed emblem of this practice, for me, is the weaver's handshake, the unfamiliarity of which brings to mind the question that opens "Pedagogy of Buddhism": "What does it mean when our cats bring small, wounded animals into the house?"[48] Cross between *Hamlet*'s play within a play and a Buddhist koan, the question posits a scene of pedagogy about a scene of pedagogy. Our balking at the little carnage is an inflexible extension of the narcissism that presupposes it is a gift. Like Reagan not knowing French, we are ungrateful when our obstinate language of gratitude misses the point of the cat—to be sure, an imperious creature conversant only in *its* language—who isn't proffering an object for us to accept so much as heuristically performing an action for us to repeat. We are (unaware that we are) being treated, that is, as kittens in need of training rather than masters or parents deserving tribute. "Is it true," Sedgwick asks, "that we can learn only when we are aware we are being taught? How have we so confused the illocutionary acts of gift giving and teaching?"[49]

Adopting what Sedgwick calls "the relations of near-miss pedagogy,"[50] I try to take the weaver's handshake, like the cat's mouse, on its own terms. Whereas strong theory, as Sedgwick understands it, corresponds to the graspiness of Emerson's "clutch[ing] hardest," the weaver's handshake seems to propose a new, necessarily minor chirography. I would be inclined to describe the latter's endgame as incompatible with strong theory's language of possession were the weaver's handshake not so resolutely nonteleological. The rubbing back and forth of thumb and fingers translates grasping into a motion potentially as chronic as scouring or gravestone-rubbing. What's more, the gesture's intervention in other, more aggressive forms of handling is inseparable from its replicability. The pleasure that Sedgwick finds in the gesture has less to do with its secrecy than its self-pollinating ubiquity. Analogously, when someone in Victorian England unexpectedly works Whitman into polite conversation, it's not quite the *beginning* of friendship or otherwise between like-minded souls so much as the effortless extension of a sodality almost magically already in place. That one falls gently into a sympathy one has done little to achieve likewise conjures the felicitous meeting, one afternoon in Weatherend, of John Marcher and May Bartram. (That the friendship that follows seems so asymmetrically May's doing is another story.) It's possible that something momentous had been conveyed between them in the past to account for their present inimitable intimacy, but it's also as plausible that their relation is founded on the unspoken, shared belief that something along those lines *might* have happened. We can almost imagine Sedgwick's description, "between my thumb and fingers," of the "brushing-three-fingers" gesture, anticipating the irresistibility with which its future readers will try the gesture out themselves.

As I type (or rather, more precisely, in the interstices between typing), I find myself performing the weaver's handshake in front of the passage that incessantly teaches it to me. And yet: what most strikes me about the passage's rub of reality is that it comes on the heels of the following lines:

> Actually it was just before this diagnosis that I was finding I had fallen suddenly, intrusively, and passionately in love with doing textile work. That is, before the *diagnosis,* but I think it may have happened after I'd started having the neck pains that were misdiagnosed for several months before they turned out to represent the cancer recurrence. I can't exactly remember the order in which things happened, actually. I just found myself cutting up fabrics, especially old kimonos, which I've always been fond of, to make into other fabrics—appliqués, collages . . . and an odd kind of weaving that used scraps of already-woven cloth as its weft material.[51]

This neck pain is another kind of quilting point. In the fall of 2005, Sedgwick and I (along with my then-partner and Sedgwick's friend and former student, John Emil Vincent) meet in Cambridge, Massachusetts, where she is undergoing an experimental procedure at Brigham and Women's and I'm having nerves in my neck cauterized at Harvard's Pain Clinic. After our respective treatments, the three of us end up, I think, in the candy aisle of Walgreens. The neck pain is a relay switch, as powerful a site of identification and cross-identification as the lyric and narrative sensitivities of the backside through which Sedgwick understands her "identification 'as' a gay man; and in among its tortuous and alienating paths are knit the relations, for me, of telling and of knowing."[52] We risk losing the textural specificity of pain and desire alike (not to mention that of textural specificity itself) in straining to make this earlier figurative knitting too much line up with the later "odd kind of weaving that used scraps of already-woven cloth as its weft material." And yet I can't help but think that something of the literal and figurative vicissitudes of figuration can be gleaned in pondering such felicitous correspondences.

"So I've always loved textiles," Sedgwick tells us again, "without doing much about it, but something different was happening right around then, something that kept kidnapping me from my teaching and writing tasks and pinning me to my kitchen table with a mushrooming array of 'arts and crafts' projects and supplies. Why? Here's one thing that was different: I think I was finally giving up the pretext of self-ornamentation, to which my love of textiles had always clung before."[53] The complexity of such a claim begins "right around then" in the simultaneously specific (*before the* diagnosis) and slippery (*I can't exactly remember the order in which things happened*) temporality of a pain whose diagnostic elusiveness conjures its own scene of near-miss pedagogical encounter. We can perhaps hear the echo of a lyric poem being written inside "Making Things, Practicing Emptiness" in the pleasure of its sound pattern: how the *app* of *happening* becomes the second syllable of *kidnapping,* how the double *p* of both becomes the opening sound of *pinning,* whose double *n* amplifies the one in the middle of those previous words. The reservation of *perhaps hear the echo of* responds to what de Man might call the phenomenal difference between the compression of "scouring" and this triple rhyme, which nonetheless arguably belongs less to the domain of anthropomorphism than description. The difference is telling.

"A Poem Is Being Written" stitches together at least four temporally specific Eves: the nine-year-old poet who masters "two-beat Untermeyer rhythm"; the "eleven-year-old redhead"[54] who experiments with the further lyrical resistance of enjambment; the "twenty-four-year-old graduate student" at Cornell for whom the narrative poem "enacts . . . the generic leap . . . to the social and institutional framing as narrative of exactly the same scene";[55] and finally—and ultimately, not final at all—the thirty-five-year-old assistant professor at Amherst who presents "A Child Is Being Beaten" at a Columbia University colloquium. "In Making Things, Practicing Emptiness," the Sedgwick who has spent "two decades of thinking, lecturing, and writing [queer theory]"[56] finds herself not in Amherst or Durham but a few streets up from Washington Square in New York. That the fantasy is one of being kidnapped evokes the crossed wires of masochism and self-infantilization, the particular richness of what Sedgwick has elsewhere taught us about her fantasy life. While "pinn[ed] to the kitchen table" quivers with the excitement of being held turning into being held *down,* it no less strikingly intimates that the fantasy on some other fractally synchronic level involves becoming the very kind of fabric scrap that this other self, having pinned it, might stitch to something else. As tellingly, we find in the fantasy's proliferation of gerunds—*doing, kidnapping, teaching, writing, mushrooming, giving*—the temporal preference that marks so much of Sedgwick's work, including "A Poem Is Being Written," *Touching Feeling,* and the essay at hand, "Making Things, Practicing Emptiness." The ongoingness of the verb formation is an expression of Sedgwick's longstanding investment in the chronic, a point all the more emphatically made in the formulation, "kept kidnapping." It's not quite that the kidnapping's reiteration follows the logic of repetition compulsion. After all, it's not that the fantasy repeats, but that the fantasy itself is one of repeating, the kidnapping happening chronically, again and again, within the single moment of the fantasy's frame.

"A WOVEN THING WITH JUST A WOVEN DEPTH" (RESISTANCE AS FORM)

This forty-six-year-old Sedgwick isn't discovering so much as remembering the art most saliently present in that earlier essay in lines quoted from "Two Arts," the last chapter of *The Warm Decembers:*

> It *is* strange:
> the way the art of our necessity
> makes precious, the vile things—
> the finger's-breadth by finger's-breadth
> dearly bought knowledge
> of the body's lived humiliations,
> dependencies, vicarities
> that's stitched into the book
> of The Sexualities, wasteful
> and value-making specificity.[57]

"Finger's-breadth by finger's-breadth," a version of the once and future fabric lover's thumb-against-fingers. If we think about "fat art, thin art" in terms of "criticism and poetry" (although as strong a case can be made for the correspondence of "poetry and criticism"), how then to make sense of this third art that governs the stitching, knotting, and weaving of the literal figures embedded in *The Weather in Proust*? What has happened—what was happening—involves an ontological shift away from an experience of writing (as ambitious, spoiled, spoiling, ebullient, effervescent) as a scene (both source and expression) of power. In her preface to *Tendencies,* Sedgwick writes that "for me, a kind of formalism, a visceral near-identification with the writing I cared for, at the level of sentence structure, metrical pattern, rhyme, was one way of trying to appropriate what seemed the numinous and resistant power of the chosen objects."[58] "A Poem Is Being Written" further articulates this specific power of poetic utterance as eventful and immanent: "But I was genuinely in love with something in this poem: it gave me power, a kind of power I still feel, though I no longer feel it in this poem. The name of that power—I know it now, and I knew it not long after I got this [Untermeyer] anthology at age nine—is, enjambment."[59] But what happens to this notion of poetic power in the obsolescing wake if not of power itself than power at that particular frequency? Compare these passages, for instance, to this one from *A Dialogue on Love:*

> SHE FEELS THAT ONE OF THE THINGS SHE HAS GOTTEN IN THERAPY IS A MORE REALISTIC SENSE AND UNDERSTANDING OF HER POWER. SHE FEELS LESS AND LESS THAT POWER (INTELLECTUAL, SPIRITUAL, ARTISTIC, ETC.) IS EITHER BOUNDLESS OR NOTHING, EITHER THE OVERBLOWN BALLOON OR THE SUDDENLY DEFLATED BALLOON. "MORE LIKE A SLEEPING BAG WITH MANY SEPARATE AIR COMPARTMENTS—A SINGLE PUNCTURE WON'T FLATTEN IT." RELATES THIS TO EMPHASIS ON TALENTS RATHER THAN GENIUS. ALSO RELATED TO HANDICRAFT PASSION?[60]

"As Cyndi Lauper might put it," Sedgwick writes apropos Milly Theale, "illness changes everything."[61] Milly was never a writer (that calling falls at least notionally to Densher), but when James's dying heroine—famously, scathingly, heartbreakingly, triumphantly—"turn[s] her face to the wall," she is being radicalized not as poet but as a lyric poem, insofar as this is precisely the embodiment of lyric's paradigmatically apostrophic gesture.

That it's hard to read Sedgwick's essay on "The Beast in the Jungle" without imagining her "as" May Bartram is as much to say that it's hard not to imagine Sedgwick imagining herself "as" May Bartram. Having *had* imagined? Which Sedgwick does one imagine when, by her own count, there are so many? *The death of the author* never seemed so mathematically simplifying. Sedgwick, after all, has told us countless times that the place of her own "will-to-live . . . often aggressively absent" is "taken, when it is taken at all, partly by an also aggressive will-to-narrate and will-to-uncover, each with a gay male siting."[62] For Sedgwick to identify with Bartram is for her to identify, in part, with a will-to-live that is ontologically fused with the ideally interminable project of carving out—locating, claiming, lighting, inhabiting—the space in which she and Marcher together might meditate on the queer contingency of what might have been the past on what might become the future. This meditation, founded as it is on a cultivated practice of lavish attention, is a respite if not for Marcher then for us from Marcher's comparably foreclosing, melodramatic idiom of girding-for and deliberation. The queerness of this contingency, as conceivably interminable (and interminably conceivable) as the meditation on it, is in turn a respite from the comparably terminating "diagnosis" of homosexuality that waits in the story's wings, as different from the rigors of May's interminability as the coercion of an over-firm handshake from the weaver's deft rubbing.

James writes that "it was only May Bartram who had, and she achieved, by an art indescribable, the feat of at once—or perhaps it was only alternately—meeting the eyes from in front and mingling her own vision, as from over his shoulder, with their peep through the apertures."[63] Marcher's "mask" of "the social simper" is haunted (and not entirely unhappily) not only by Bartram over Marcher's shoulder, but James over Bartram's, and Sedgwick over James's, and like Marcher's interminable queerness, this leapfrog pajama game—"the chain stretched and stretched"[64]—could go on forever. Kevin Ohi is right to align the mask's dissimulating properties with those of a Janus-faced closet; that the mask in the first place is chronically, mendaciously enabling gives way to a new pleasure whose brazenness marks precisely the extent to which the mask no longer tethers Marcher to the social world, no longer renders, like a scuba mask, that world's air as at least fleetingly breathable. Rather, Bartram's appearance on either side of it takes it out of social circulation, thereby repurposing its capacity as interface. In the manner of Charlie Chaplin's flagrant and ingenious repurposing of objects, Marcher and Bartram take advantage of the mask's ability to refine the contours of proximity. If the mask's incipient function (Marcher less aware of it than we) still bears some relation to the chronically prevaricative, its import is less ontic than ontological. To this end, the mask's outpacing of its original use resembles the literal creativeness of what Bersani indispensably calls the Jamesian lie. "But what James suggests is that this reality—so ominously final elsewhere in his work—is not a fact prior to artfulness but, like all human activities, is rather a possible development of some artful design and can be replaced by other possible developments. . . . Because experience is never without design, it's impossible to locate an original design, that is, an absolute fact or motive which could not itself be recomposed, whose nature would not be changed by changes in its relations."[65] Ohi writes that "'Perhaps . . . only alternately' prevents this multifaceted gaze from being 'merely' figural—or merely 'figural.'"[66] This attention to dissimulation's movement from the logic of true/false to some more slippery coupling of literal/figurative illuminates the mask's newly calibrated aesthetic import. As importantly, the difference between "at once—or . . . only alternately" is also one of chronicity. "Only alternately" breaks down the staring-contest mesmerization of a sustained glance and alchemizes it into motion, a back-and-forth. Just as the mask literalizes an evolving of the properties of space, the back-and-forth literalizes the repetitive labor not of literal but figurative action. And if Bartram alternates between both sides of the mask, she might in the scopic feat blurringly manage to catch a glimpse of herself, catching a glimpse, around the corner.

Of "The Beast in the Jungle," Sedgwick notes the story's "negative virtue of not pretending to present [May] rounded and whole," insofar as not articulating May's desire seems preferable to displacing it with the normative proscription, in Sedgwick's words, of "what she Really Wanted and what she Really Needed."[67] To entertain the possibility of May catching a glimpse of herself from behind Marcher's fractally recalibrated mask is to imagine May's roundedness not in terms of psychical complexity so much as Emersonian sphericity, as being dimensional enough for her to go behind herself. The possibility of going behind not just other characters—"for routing the authorial point of view austerely through the eyes of characters as they in turn view other characters"[68]—but one's self illuminates, in part, what strikes Sedgwick as most enigmatic in an early characterization of Kate Croy in *The Wings of the Dove:* "A striking phrase, 'her eyes aslant no less on her beautiful averted than on her beautiful presented oval.' But, as my favorite Linda Barry character would say, what does it even mean? Is Kate looking at her butt in the mirror? Is she watching the back of her head? . . . A moralistic formulation would be that the pressure of want and disgrace has made her two-faced. And that's not far from true, if you can subtract *its* punitive patness: the simple fact of *sidedness,* double-sidedness, presented and averted, recto and verso, seems not just to be lodged in Kate's person but to radiate out from it across the novel."[69] Bearing the alternations of Marcher's mask in mind, we may also envision Kate's eyes, aslant, catching a glimpse of themselves through themselves, or Kate, in her roundness, perceiving her own roundness, as though turned oval in the slant speed of anamorphosis.

Going behind one's self is an apt way of describing James's relation, in both his prefaces and his tripartite autobiography, to himself. The idiom figures a capacity for an author to go behind his younger self with the acquired ability, through the differently dimensionalized distance of years, to see what that younger self couldn't. In this sense, the anal erotics of going behind that Sedgwick traces in "Is the Rectum Straight?" speaks also to the possibility of selves treated in the text not as characters per se but as three-dimensional, "rounded" objects, capable not so much of being penetrated as going 'round. This dimensionalizing of one's relation to one's self is as literally revolutionary as James's conversion of shame over his earlier self into pleasure. We ought, in this context, recall the source of the shame that is the nominal subject of Sedgwick's essay on queer performativity. In Sedgwick's words, the younger James is abashed by "his mortifyingly extravagant miscalculations concerning the length of (what he had imagined as) a short story: 'Painfully associated for me has "The Spoils of Poynton" remained, until recent reperusal, with the awkward consequence of that fond error. The subject had emerged . . . all suffused with a flush of meaning; thanks to which irresistible air, as I could but plead in the event, I found myself . . . beguiled and led on.'"[70]

I quote this passage at length because the lines Sedgwick cites from the preface to *The Spoils of Poynton* exemplify the figuratively elaborate language from which, mortifyingly, James's textual excrescency is inseparable. After all, the James who writes *The Spoils of Poynton* in 1896 isn't going over the word limit because he can't resist just one more element of plot. James's stories are most susceptible to "going over" on account not of too much action but of too much of the "too much" that characterizes James's and Sedgwick's writing alike. As James writes in the preface to "The Lesson of the Master" of his liberating lack of word limit in *The Yellow Book:*

> I was invited, and all urgently, to contribute to the first number, and was regaled with the golden truth that my composition might absolutely assume, might shamelessly parade in, its own organic form. . . . One had so often known this product to struggle, in one's hands, under the rude

> prescription of brevity at any cost, with the opposition so offered to its really becoming a story, that my friend's emphasised indifference to the arbitrary limit of length struck me, I remember, as the fruit of the finest artistic intelligence. We had been at one—that we already knew—on the truth that the forms of wrought things, in this order, *were,* all exquisitely and effectively, the things.[71]

That "the forms of wrought things . . . *were,* all exquisitely and effectively, the things" isn't an argument for understanding Jamesian style as non-ornamental. Rather, the repetition of "things" suggests that when it comes to Jamesian style, the ornamental is constitutive. Such a claim is unsurprising in the context of *The Spoils of Poynton,* given the novel's distinction not between the ornamental and non-ornamental but between the ornamental and the decorative. The flush of prodigiousness is as fundamental to James's sentences as the ivory to Mrs. Gereth's Maltese cross.

When *Poynton*'s narrator notes that "Maltese," as ascription of provenance, is "technically incorrect,"[72] he echoes a self-reproach related to James's inability to keep his stories short: he frequently can't remember the anecdote or "real-life" person or place out of which any given tale emerges. As James notes of "The Lesson of the Master," his stories "make together, by the same stroke, this other rather blank profession, that few of them recall to me, however dimly, any scant pre-natal phase." Or as he notes of "The Beast in the Jungle," "I remount the stream of time, all enquiringly, but . . . come back empty-handed."[73] In the context of the necessarily unverifiable origin of Marcher and Bartram's relationship, the missing provenance of the stories, like that of the Maltese cross, acquires a specifically psychical value, which is as much to say treats style and psychical value as though they were one and the same. It's along these lines that I think of James's prose in conventionally lyrical terms. Unlike an origin story of *who did what to whom* but like a lyric poem, the Jamesian line isn't paraphrasable. "Let it pass that if I am so oddly unable to say here, at any point, 'what gave me my idea,' I must just a trifle freely have helped myself to it from hidden stores."[74] The line's scare quotes mark the difference between a paraphrasable sense of plot and the sensibility of text freed from the burdens of synopsis. We might, in fact, hear "what gave me my idea" not in James's own voice at all but rather that of a devoted reader not quite launched into the difference between the "idea" and the ideationally saturating objects of which James's work in so many ways is composed. The thing is the thing is the thing, and if shame arises in response to its largesse it has less to do with miscalculation than the eminently queer sense of style as altogether irrevocable, because it's as much a thing as the things it describes, a theory of nature pitched at a level of grandeur ambitious enough to do both Emersonian theory and nature justice.

James's writing resists paraphrase for the same reasons a poem resists paraphrase, namely, because its descriptive value is inextricable from the abstractions it enacts. I borrow these terms from Culler, who distinguishes, recall, between a criticism that "translate[s] apostrophe into description," and "lyric or lyrical reading," which "translate[s] description into apostrophe and anthropomorphism."[75] Along these lines, "The Beast in the Jungle" might be said to translate the description of a mask into an anthropomorphosis of one. For that matter, we might analogously say that Bartram herself translates—*enacts*—Marcher. In both cases, the transformation involves a multiplication of the modes of relation one might sustain in, around, or with a given object. The object—even Marcher, who implicitly thinks about himself as though he were a (nonrhetorical) question—becomes an answer different from what it was not because it changes but because the questions we ask it change. In moments such as these, Jamesian text salubriously breaks free from the air of omnipotence that Sedgwick comes to associate with writing, and in terms of which she describes her evolving detachment from it in favor of the wabi-sabi of textile art. "Unlike making things," Sedgwick writes, "speech and writing and conceptual thought impose no material obstacles to a fantasy of instant, limitless efficacy. Nor for that matter is there anything to slow down the sudden, utter spoiling of such fantasy."[76] This desire for obstacles is inseparable from the real-toads-in-imaginary-garden desire of materiality embedded in the texture of fantasy, from the more general, tacit counterfantasy of inefficacy and limit. James's writing seems most persuasive not in its mimetic fidelity to a world outside itself but in the sense that it is self-responsive, self-negotiating unto itself.

The near-simultaneous pedagogical and erotic exhilarations of constraint are evident in Sedgwick's writing from outset. Consider these lines from the opening of *Epistemology of the Closet,* which on first and second read I knew I loved without understanding why. Here was my first encounter with Sedgwick's transfixing theatricalizing of a need for and magnetizing justification of our readerly attention:

> Accordingly, one characteristic of the readings in this book is to attend to performative aspects of texts, and to what are often blandly called their "reader relations," as sites of definitional creation, violence, and rupture in relation to particular readers, particular institutional circumstances. . . . It has felt throughout this work as though the density of their social meaning lends any speech act concerning these issues—and the outlines of that "concern," it turns out, are broad indeed—the exaggerated propulsiveness of wearing flippers in a swimming pool: the force of various rhetorical effects has seemed uniquely difficult to calibrate.[77]

Not having worn flippers in a pool for some time, I can only imagine (which is precisely the point) the particular form of attentiveness that they ostensibly bring to and encounter in Sedgwick's swimming pool library. Another name for this attentiveness is resistance, as though the prosthetic appendages made one newly or differently aware of the neither-attraction-nor-repulsion of one's feet, ankles, shins in and against the (somewhat euphemistically) appreciated wear of the water. This flipper effect speaks not only to the density of social meaning but to the incessant grip and pulsive give of Sedgwick's own writing as a site where writing itself—some illuminated exchange between its most material and phantasmatic selves—experiences its own campy, complexly lovable torpor. The fantasy of *feeling writing* as both more and less than itself, of trusting the vitality of a text to the extent that one feels its (or is it one's own?) strain, suggests the mutual constitutiveness for Sedgwick of resistance's outer valence as it flickers in and out of literal and figurative registers. "The book aims to resist in every way it can the deadening pretended knowingness by which the chisel of modern homo/heterosexual definitional crisis tends, in public discourse, to be hammered most fatally home."[78] Sedgwick's writing, that is, seeks to resist the velocity (and instantaneous-seeming hurt) of knowledge-as-chisel by exposing scenes to as well as being an environment where the physics of resistance more visibly occurs. To paraphrase Melville's Claggart, resistance is as resistance did it. Or as that text's narrator says of Vere, "No more trying situation is conceivable than that of an officer subordinate under a captain whom he suspects to be not mad, indeed, but yet not quite unaffected in his intellects. To argue his order to him would be insolence. To resist him would be mutiny."[79]

The problem against which Sedgwick's mutiny of resistance arises isn't that knowingness is pretending but that this specific form of pretend lacks the non-abstracting feeling that resistance confers:

> Then, of course, I am disquieted at this tectonic shift in what I've presumed were the fixed zones of permission and prohibition.
>
> Also, though, I feel somehow restored to an adult size—in relation, that is, to the spectral figure of my fear and rage. Which I've always associated with my father in his own rage: a figure who's abstract to me in the particular sense that it could never have occurred to me to resist or push back against him, or to wrestle him to a standstill or to anything else.[80]

As Sedgwick observes in the eponymous essay of *The Weather in Proust,* "It's worth noting here that in requiring support from the elements, the subject also lays a claim on their reliable ability to resist pressure from it or damage by it. In Barbara Johnson's paraphrase of Winnicott, 'The object becomes real because it survives, because it is outside the subject's range of omnipotent control.'"[81] Sedgwick's observation translates the Cartesian cogito into something along the lines of "I resist, therefore I am," a haptic vividness in comparison to which the Winnicottian "I survive, therefore I am" tautologically pales in comparison. Sedgwick's gravitation to an ontology of resistance makes sense insofar as it slows down and expands a terrain of writing at risk of being otherwise reduced to the dualisms of active and passive, subject and object. "Any verb, aside from the verb 'to be,' generates a doer and a done-to. And by this simple, built-in grammatical feature it thus makes it almost impossible for any language user to maintain a steady sense of the crucial middle ranges of agency: the field in which most of consciousness, perception, and relationality really happen."[82] Even as Sedgwick's investment in a "'wabi-sabi' aesthetic that prefers funky craft to finely done craft" marks a turn, for her, away from her "vocation as a writer and theorist,"[83] it also rearticulates the love of resistance that had been there all along. In this context, Sedgwick's practice of *suminagashi* and *shibori* is an experiment in resistance's middle ranges of literal and figurative expression, even as this surprise of the middle range regularly collates figuration's specifically haptic unpredictability with not only resistance but a capacity to feel and be felt: "I used a resist to cover the shape of each letter. . . . I wanted reading it to involve a series of hypotheses."[84] "Here the mark of the scissor works as the marks of dye and resist do in shibori: they gain a kind of material purchase, in one moment and dimensionality, that persists, albeit transformed and even unrecognizable, into a changed one. And neither folded nor unfolded state can be called realer than the other."[85] Imagining Bartram as anthropomorphically enacting Marcher is thus to encounter lyric reading as it approaches the patience (as opposed to finished perfectibility) of the middle ranges of craft:

> The rest of the world of course thought him queer, but she, she only, knew how, and above all why, queer; which was precisely what enabled her to dispose the concealing veil in the right folds. She took his gaiety from him—since it had to pass with them for gaiety—as she took everything else; but she certainly so far justified by her unerring touch his finer sense of the degree to which he had ended by convincing her. *She* at least never spoke of the secret of his life except as "the real truth about you," and she had in fact a wonderful way of making it seem, as such, the secret of her own life too. That was in fine how he so constantly felt her as allowing for him; he couldn't on the whole call it anything else.[86]

The meticulousness with which Bartram "dispose[s] the concealing veil in the right folds" both literalizes the middle range that her relation to Marcher occupies and figures the particular care that I imagine Sedgwick may have imagined between herself and others (broadly and infinitesimally conceived). Like the resists, such folds become a way of inhabiting a theory of writing from which Sedgwick's subsequent interest in textile art isn't a departure so much as a rededication. Sedgwick's thinking about artistic folds in terms of the dimensionality of fractals corresponds to James's account of Bartram's indescribable art, insofar as the art by which she is able to peep through the mask's apertures translates the mask's two-dimensional surface enough into three that she can go behind it. "The fractal, the fractionally dimensional, seems like, among other things, a language invented exactly to talk about texture."[87] It's this three-dimensionality of Bartram's art that makes it possible for Marcher's "finer sense"—"that was in fine how he so constantly felt her as allowing for him"—to be "justified by her unerring touch."

In both Sedgwick's earliest and last writings, the difficulty of doing justice to the pathos of dimensionality (reflected back to itself as the dimensionality of feeling) arises in or as the waver of perspective. "In pictorial terms," the above passage continues, "a fractured dimensionality might be a way of describing the struggle staged in perspectival realism, between the receding space of illusion and the frontal space of the picture plane."[88]

In "A Poem Is Being Written," Sedgwick imagines the feel of this struggle between telescopingly complex, competing visions as the "'thud / of longing' with which the contracted, bodily siting of the drama of enjambment is displaced back outward onto the sheepish hungry gaze from the wedged-open door."[89] Analogous scenes appear throughout Sedgwick's poems. Here's the opening of a 1973 poem titled "An Essay on the Picture Plane," whose surficial preposition converts the notion of subject (an essay about a given topic) into a Magritte-like encounter between differently dimensioned media:

> The vertical plane makes the absence present
> to you, who are absent both from the horizon
> and from the fabric itself before you
> which is too articulate. Be thankful
> for the absence is at least here, because it is stretched,
> stretching clear to the edges, and immobile.
> Be grateful too when sometimes it resolves
> as a woven thing with just a woven depth.[90]

That the relation between Marcher and Bartram is structured, as Bersani suggests, like an analytic encounter[91] makes it all the more tempting to hear in a later poem titled "Snapsh" the susurrus by which Sedgwick refers in writing to her therapist, Shannon, as "Sh." The last lines of "Snapsh" take the form of two questions whose emotional and aesthetic proximity to "The Beast in the Jungle" foresees Sedgwick's affection for a fractal's capacity both to expand and contract along a single fold:

> Why won't the proffer of such comforts
> comfort me?
> Why mask out, at each viewing, with my hand,
> the smooth, huge foreshortening of his own?[92]

Such points of contact between genres, authors, and years complicate our sense of the relation between Sedgwick's insatiably various career and itself. It illuminates my sense that if Sedgwick "fastens" on a photograph of Judith Scott and if this identification "is less as the subject of some kind of privation than as the holder of an obscure treasure, or as a person receptively held by it,"[93] it's not quite because Scott's embrace of her art traces the same curve as Bartram's embrace of Marcher. Not quite, to the extent that the causal narrative of "because" overlooks the irresistible, middle-range textures we've been tending. Although we are told that the beginning of Scott's sculptures is often a central object, I think rather that her work no less begins when the possibility of a core is enough swaddlingly buried that its never having been there strikes us as no less plausible than its being. In this manner would Scott's sculptures repeat the pattern of Bartram and Marcher's art of friendship, predicated on the possibility rather than fact of their having met before.

Scott's sculptures rewrite Galatea as an aesthetic of ongoing attention. That Galatea and Pygmalion make each other out of each other makes me think of the aestheticizing self-distance inherent to what Sharon Cameron calls "beautiful work": "To be competent to speak of pain is to speak of pain that isn't yours. This requires experiencing pain that is yours. Pain experienced," so Cameron exquisitely observes, "*as if* it were your own."[94] The moment at which the sculpture seems to come to life is the endlessly repeatable, scouring, scrubbing, flickering of aesthetic duress, the expression of both one's calling and one's resistance to it. To turn this screw one thread more: Judith Butler writes of the heroine of James's *Washington Square* that if Catherine Sloper "takes up life 'as it were,' we are asked to understand the life she takes up as a figural one, a life that is as proper to fiction as, say, the life of a fictional character must be."[95] Catherine's earlier gluttony—"In her younger years she was a good deal of a romp, and, though it is an awkward confession to make about one's heroine, I must add that she was something of a glutton"[96]—leads to the falling curtain of the novel's last line with an air almost of inevitability. "Catherine, meanwhile, in the parlour, picking up her morsel of fancy-work, had seated herself with it again—for life, as it were." The life we take up in the end is not the life of a fictional character but of a lyric figure. And figuration is what happens in the blur between what at once again and again makes one one's self and what keeps one from becoming:

If the night finally

comes when you and I, one sleepless darkness
mimicking another darkness, penetrate
from room to room, or into breathless

room, I needn't wonder if your voice
hollows under mine, sounding delicate, or absent,
the glutted body of that voice being here.[97]

Acknowledgments

Portions of this project were presented at Brown University, McGill University, Penn State, SUNY Cortland, the University of Chicago, and the University of Texas Austin. Early versions of its material appeared in *Qui Parle; Melville's Philosophies,* ed. Branka Arsić and K. L. Evans; *Rethinking Ahab,* ed. Meredith Farmer and Jonathan Schroeder; *The New Emily Dickinson Studies,* ed. Michelle Kohler; *Leo Bersani: Queer Theory and Beyond,* ed. Mikko Tuhkanen; and *Reading Sedgwick,* ed. Lauren Berlant.

With inordinate thanks to the University of Houston, and to my colleagues and students in the Department of English. I'm indebted to the Corporation of Yaddo and the James Merrill House Residency for halcyon stretches of time and vivifying sodality that sustained me through the long solitudes between. Especial thanks to Elaina Richardson, Christy Williams, Candace Waite, and the Callahans.

For friendship, interlocution, and example, most abiding gratitude to Branka Arsić, Margot Backus, Ian Balfour, Lauren Berlant, Leo Bersani, Michael Berubé, Brian Blanchfield, Tyler Bradway, Nathan Brown, Susan Brynteson, Kristen Case, Ann Christensen, Cassandra Cleghorn, Peter Coviello, Nan Z. Da, Theo Davis, Colin Dayan, Barbara Dixon, Sarah Ehlers, Marianne Ehrlich, Maud Ellmann, Kim Evans, Meredith Farmer, Laurel Farrin, Frances Ferguson, Elaine Freedgood, Elizabeth Freeman, Erica Fretwell, Ben Friedlander, Jamie Gabbarelli, Jordan Greenwald, Elizabeth Gregory, Christian Haines, Lanny Hammer, Elizabeth Hanson, Martin Harries, David Hobbes, Daniel Hoffman-Schwartz, Eileen Joy, Beena Kamlani, Laura Karetzky, Pat Kiley, Michelle Kohler, Anna Kornbluh,

Regina Kunzel, Wendy Lee, James Lilley, Thomas Loebel, Heather Love, Jacki Lyden, Janet Lyon, Missy Mazzoli, William McDugald, Maureen McLane, Maryse Meijer, Cristanne Miller, Zenyse Miller, Lisa Lynn Moore, Richard Morrison, Barbara Nagel, Maggie Nelson, Edgar Oliver, Bergin O'Malley, Cormac O'Malley, Samuel Otter, Don Pease, Jayne Anne Phillips, Ailís Ní Ríain, Elaina Richardson, Julie Rivkin, Leslie Roberts, Lisa Ruddick, Andrew Salomon, Ellen Samuels, Karen J. Sanchez-Eppler, Jonathan Schroeder, Brian Teare, Roberto Tejada, Rei Terada, Daniel Tiffany, Robert Tobin, Pat Towers, Mikko Tuhkanen, John Emil Vincent, Candace Waite, Jason Weidemann, Marta Werner, Eric Wertheimer, Dara Wier, Christy Williams, Elizabeth Willis.

For Kevin, this peridot & pearl.

And for Lynn, truest friend, ad astra.

Notes

PREFACE

1. *Oxford English Dictionary,* s.v. "lux, v."

2. *Oxford English Dictionary,* s.v. "sumpter, n."

3. Michel Foucault, *The History of Sexuality, Volume 1: An Introduction,* trans. Robert Hurley (New York: Vintage, 1990), 123–24.

4. "With the same movement by which the subject advances towards jouissance, that is to say, towards what is furthest from him, he encounters this intimate fracture, right up close." Jacques Lacan, *Anxiety: The Seminar of Jacques Lacan, Book 10,* ed. Jacques-Alain Miller (New York: Polity, 2014), 11.

5. Foucault, *The History of Sexuality,* 96.

6. Elizabeth Freeman, *Time Binds: Queer Temporalities, Queer Histories* (Durham: Duke University Press, 2010), xvi–xvii. See also her essay "Hopeless Cases: Queer Chronicities and Gertrude Stein's 'Melanctha,'" *Journal of Homosexuality* 63, no. 3 (March 2016): 329–48, not least for its conceptualizing of chronocatachresis as an individual's queer experience of and capacity for temporal waywardness.

7. Henry James, *Roderick Hudson* (New York: Penguin Books, 1987), 386.

8. James, *Roderick Hudson,* 220.

9. Henry James, *The Golden Bowl* (New York: Penguin Books, 1987), 488, 492–93. Hereafter cited parenthetically in the text.

10. Wallace Stevens, *The Collected Poems* (New York: Vintage Books, 1982), 61.

11. Leo Bersani, *Receptive Bodies* (Chicago: University of Chicago Press, 2018), 9–10.

12. Here and elsewhere, my appreciation of excrescence (and the latter's pulsive knack for capsizing plot) is indebted to Colin Dayan. See, for instance, her "'Israel Potter'; or, the Excrescence," *Los Angeles Review of Books,* December 19, 2017.

13. Erich Auerbach, *Scenes from the Drama of European Literature* (Minneapolis: University of Minnesota Press, 1984), 17.

14. Elaine Scarry, *The Body in Pain: The Making and Unmaking of the World* (New York: Oxford University Press, 1987), 22. Scarry's italics suggest the extent to which "story," unitalicized, fades into the background of taken-for-granted.

15. Mel Y. Chen, *Animacies: Biopolitics, Racial Mattering, and Queer Affect* (Durham: Duke University Press, 2012), 195.

16. Fred Moten, *In the Break: The Aesthetics of the Black Radical Tradition* (Minneapolis: University of Minnesota Press, 2003). Consider also Moten's meditation on genre: "But how do we address that privileging of narrative that might rightly be seen to emerge from a certain politics, a certain theory of history, a certain desire? Not by opposition; by augmentation. This means an attention to the lyric, to the lyric's auto-explosion, to the auto-explosion the lyric gives to narrative." *Black and Blur: Consent Not to Be a Single Being* (Durham: Duke University Press, 2017), 3.

INTRODUCTION

1. Nathaniel Hawthorne, *The Scarlet Letter* (New York: Norton, 1988), 8. Hereafter cited parenthetically in the text.

2. See Michael D. Snediker, "Whitman on the Verge: Or the Desires of Solitude," *Arizona Quarterly: A Journal of American Literature, Culture, and Theory* 61, no. 3 (2005): 27–56.

3. Roland Barthes, *The Grain of the Voice: Interviews, 1962–1980,* trans. Linda Coverdale (Evanston: Northwestern University Press, 1981), 231.

4. Michel Foucault, *Herculine Barbin,* trans. Richard McDougall (New York: Vintage Books, 2010), xiii. Judith Butler takes Foucault's account of Barbin to task for its "sentimental indulgence in the very emancipatory discourse his analysis in *The History of Sexuality* was meant to displace" (*Gender Trouble* [New York: Routledge, 1990], 96). Whereas Butler's assertion that "smiles, happinesses, pleasures, and desires are figured here as qualities without an abiding substance to which they are said to adhere" (24) presumes from the outset figuration's incompatibility with "abiding substance," *Contingent Figure* entertains the prospect of figuration's surface area, its capacity for lasting, as an element of psychical life in its own right. To the extent that *Gender Trouble* suggests we experience the trouble with gender as a problematic *of* abidingness, we would do well to consider the latter's phenomenological texture unto itself.

5. Gilles Deleuze, *Francis Bacon: The Logic of Sensation,* trans. Daniel W. Smith (Minneapolis: University of Minnesota Press, 2002), 56.

6. Emily Dickinson, *The Poems of Emily Dickinson,* ed. R. W. Franklin (Cambridge: Harvard Belknap Press, 1998), F372. Unless otherwise specified, references to Dickinson are to this edition and cited parenthetically in the text, according to Franklin's numbering system.

7. Forest Pyle, *Art's Undoing: In the Wake of a Radical Aestheticism* (New York: Fordham University Press, 2013), 106.

8. Herman Melville, *The Piazza Tales and Other Prose Pieces, 1839–1860,* ed. Harrison Hayford, Hershel Parker, and G. Thomas Tanselle (Evanston: Northwestern University Press, 1987), 197. Hereafter cited as *PT.*

9. Kristen Roupenian, "Cat Person," *New Yorker,* December 11, 2017, 64–71.

10. See Elizabeth Renker's *Strike through the Mask: Herman Melville and the Scene of Writing* (Baltimore: Johns Hopkins University Press, 1997), 49–68.

11. Samuel Otter, "Introduction: Melville and Disability," *Leviathan: A Journal of Melville Studies* 8, no. 1 (March 2006): 8. Hereafter cited parenthetically in the text.

12. Renker, *Strike through the Mask,* 60.

13. Erving Goffman, *Stigma: Notes on the Management of Spoiled Identity* (New York: Simon and Schuster, 1963), 1.

14. Goffman, *Stigma,* 1.

15. Heather Love's account of the accord between Goffman's work and queer theory —especially in terms of the former's own "corrosive attitude toward identity" (248)—informs my effort to pursue a line of thought that loosens the suture between disability theory and characterological convention. Love, "Reading the Social: Erving Goffman and Sexuality Studies," in *Theory Aside,* ed. Jason Potts and Daniel Stout (Durham: Duke University Press, 2014). The difficulty, meanwhile, of imagining a relation between disability studies and stigma in "the original literal sense" that isn't haunted by the word's prior figurative thresholds puts me in mind of Cynthia Chase's work on "accidents of disfiguration" in Wordsworth's *Prelude:* "The spot is a scene of effacement, the erosion of the remnants of an execution, itself the effacement of a murder. Calculated to coincide and cancel each other, the matched annihilations rather leave remains—a residue which, strangely, consists not in the instruments or objects of annihilation . . . but in its site, the spot 'Whose shape was like a grave.' Nature here, the 'long green ridge of turf,' is figured as the remnant of repeated effacements." Chase, "The Accidents of Disfiguration: Limits to Literal and Rhetorical Reading in Book V of 'The Prelude,'" *Studies in Romanticism* 18, no. 4 (Winter 1979): 553.

16. David T. Mitchell and Sharon L. Snyder, *Narrative Prosthesis: Disability and the Dependencies of Discourse* (Ann Arbor: University of Michigan Press, 2000), 126.

17. David Mitchell, "'Too Much of a Cripple': Ahab, Dire Bodies, and the Language of Prosthesis in *Moby-Dick,*" *Leviathan* 1, no. 1 (March 1999): 7.

18. Ellen Samuels, "My Body, My Closet: Invisible Disability and the Limits of Coming-Out Discourse," *GLQ: A Journal of Lesbian and Gay Studies* 9, no. 1 (2003): 236.

19. Todd Carmody, “Rehabilitating Analogy,” *J19: The Journal of Nineteenth-Century Americanists* 1, no. 2 (Fall 2013): 432–33.

20. Carmody, “Rehabilitating Analogy,” 438.

21. Jennifer L. Nelson and Bradley S. Berens, “Spoken Daggers, Deaf Ears, and Silent Mouths: Fantasies of Deafness in Early Modern England,” in *The Disability Studies Reader,* ed. Lennard Davis (New York: Routledge, 1997), 53.

22. Samuels, *Fantasies of Identification: Disability, Gender, Race* (New York: New York University Press, 2014), 221n7.

23. Robert McRuer, *Crip Theory: Cultural Signs of Queerness and Disability* (New York: New York University Press, 2006), 207.

24. Rosemarie Garland Thomson, *Extraordinary Bodies: Figuring Physical Disability in American Culture and Literature* (New York: Columbia University Press, 1997), 10.

25. Auerbach, *Scenes from the Drama,* 26–27.

26. Jacques Derrida, *On Touching—Jean-Luc Nancy,* trans. Christine Irizarry (Stanford: Stanford University Press, 2005), 58.

27. With an ear for the etymologies with which the preface opens, I'm pleased to have discovered that *easel* comes from the Dutch word *ezel,* meaning “ass” (notwithstanding its resemblance to “ease”), as in a canvas propped against an easel like a burden loaded on a donkey.

28. Garland Thomson, *Extraordinary Bodies, 10-11.*

29. Garland Thomson, *Extraordinary Bodies,* 12.

30. Auerbach, *Scenes from the Drama,* 17.

31. Cary Wolfe, *What Is Posthumanism?* (Minneapolis: University of Minnesota Press, 2010), 137.

32. Compare to Elaine Scarry's observation in *The Body in Pain* that “to have a body, a body made emphatic by being continually altered through various forms of creation, instruction (e.g., bodily cleansing), and wounding, is to have one's sphere of extension contracted down to the small circle of one's immediate physical presence. Consequently, to be intensely embodied is the equivalent of being unrepresented and . . . is almost always the condition of those without power” (207).

33. Mitchell and Snyder, *Narrative Prosthesis,* 120.

34. Michael Bérubé, “Pressing the Claim,” foreword to Simi Linton, *Claiming Disability: Knowledge and Identity* (New York: New York University Press, 1998), vii.

35. Or as Bérubé observes, “[Disability] is a category whose constituency is contingency itself” (“Pressing the Claim,” vii).

36. Claudia Rankine, *Don't Let Me Be Lonely* (Saint Paul, Minn.: Graywolf Press, 2004), 56. Hereafter cited parenthetically in the text.

37. John Ashbery, “The Impossible,” *Poetry* 90, no. 4 (July 1957): 250.

38. Frederick Douglass, *Narrative of the Life of Frederick Douglass, an American Slave, Written by Himself*, ed. David W. Blight (New York: Bedford/St. Martin's, 2003), 51.

39. www.law.nyu.edu/sites/default/files/upload_documents/louima%20 trascript.pdf.

40. "And does terrorism have to work only through death? Can't one terrorize without killing? And does killing necessarily mean putting to death? Isn't it also 'letting die'? Can't 'letting die' . . . also be part of a 'more or less' conscious and deliberate terrorist strategy?" Jacques Derrida, "Autoimmunity: Real and Symbolic Suicides—A Dialogue with Jacques Derrida," in Giovanna Borradori, *Philosophy in a Time of Terror: Dialogues with Jürgen Habermas and Jacques Derrida* (Chicago: University of Chicago Press, 2004), 108.

41. Jasbir Puar, *The Right to Maim: Debility, Capacity, Disability* (Durham: Duke University Press, 2017), xiv.

42. Puar, *The Right to Maim*, xiv.

43. Samuel Taylor Coleridge and William Wordsworth, *Lyrical Ballads*, ed. M. Gamer and D. Porter (Buffalo, N.Y.: Broadview Editions, 2008), 100.

44. Frances Ferguson, *Solitude and the Sublime: The Romantic Aesthetics of Individuation* (New York: Routledge, 1992), 164.

45. Ralph Waldo Emerson, *Essays and Lectures*, ed. Joel Porte (New York: Library of America, 1983), 21.

46. Anthony Reed, *Freedom Time: The Poetics and Politics of Black Experimental Writing* (Baltimore: Johns Hopkins University Press, 2014), 112.

47. Maurice Blanchot, *The Space of Literature*, trans. Ann Smock (Lincoln: University of Nebraska Press, 1989), 258. Hereafter cited parenthetically in the text.

48. Agnes Martin, *Schriften* (Berlin: Hatje Cantz, 1998), 62.

49. Leo Bersani, *Is the Rectum a Grave? and Other Essays* (Chicago: University of Chicago Press, 2009), 3.

50. Leo Bersani, *A Future for Astyanax: Character and Desire in Literature* (New York: Columbia University Press, 1984), 148.

1. MELVILLE'S IRON CROWN OF LOMBARDY

1. Judith Butler, *Senses of the Subject* (New York: Fordham University Press, 2015), 20.

2. Herman Melville, *Moby-Dick, or The Whale*, ed. Harrison Hayford, Hershel Parker, and G. Thomas Tanselle (Evanston: Northwestern University Press, 1988), 79. Hereafter cited parenthetically in the text.

3. "[In an annealing furnace] there's a round hole through which the flame

and heat passeth into the tower; this hole is call'd *Occhio* or *Lumella*, having an Iron ring encircling it call'd the Cavalet or Crown." Antonio Neri, *The Art of Glass: Wherein are Shown the Wayes to Make Art and Colour Glass, Pastes, Enamels, Lakes, and Other Curiosities*, trans. Christopher Merrett (London: Printed by A.W. for Octavian Pulleyn, 1662), 243. See *Oxford English Dictionary*, s.v. "cavalet."

4. Scarry, *The Body in Pain*, 3.

5. Herman Melville, *Correspondence*, ed. Lynn Horth (Evanston: Northwestern University Press, 1993), 219.

6. *Oxford English Dictionary*, s.v. "trifle."

7. *Oxford English Dictionary*, s.v. "about."

8. *Oxford English Dictionary*, s.v. "wale."

9. Levi R. Bryant, "The Ontic Principle: Outline of an Object-Oriented Ontology," in *The Speculative Turn: Continental Materialism and Realism*, ed. Levi R. Bryant, Nick Srnicek, and Graham Harman (Melbourne: Re.Press, 2009), 271.

10. "For if this is what time is, it is nothing that I see from without. From without, I would only have the trail of time; I would not be present at its generative thrust. So time is myself; I am the duration I grasp, and time is duration grasped in me." Maurice Merleau-Ponty, *Signs*, trans. Richard C. McLeary (Evanston: Northwestern University Press, 1964), 184.

11. Graham Harman, *Guerrilla Metaphysics: Phenomenology and the Carpentry of Things* (Peru, Ill.: Open Court//Carus, 2005), 162.

12. "I say then that likenesses of things and their shapes are given off by things from the outermost body of things, which may be called, as it were, films or even rind, because the image bears an appearance and form like to that, whatever it be, from whose body it appears to be shed, ere it wanders abroad." Lucretius, *On the Nature of Things*, trans. Cyril Bailey (Oxford: Clarendon Press, 1921), 144.

13. Eyal Peretz, *Literature, Disaster, and the Enigma of Power: A Reading of "Moby-Dick"* (Stanford: Stanford University Press, 2003), 148n1.

14. Harman, *Guerrilla Metaphysics*, 214.

15. E. L. Grant Watson, "Melville's *Pierre*," *New England Quarterly* 3, no. 1 (1930): 198.

16. For further consideration of the rhetorical materialism of "throughness," see Michael D. Snediker, "Minute Effulgencies: Language as Gesture and the Spires of Form," *J19* 1, no. 2 (Fall 2013): 228–40.

17. Herman Melville, *Pierre, or the Ambiguities*, ed. Harrison Hayford, Hershel Parker, and G. Thomas Tanselle (Evanston: Northwestern University Press, 1992), 37. Hereafter cited parenthetically in the text.

18. Harriet Hustis, "'Universal Mixing' and Interpenetrating Standing: Disability and Community in Melville's *Moby-Dick*," *Nineteenth-Century Literature* 69, no. 1 (2014): 27.

19. R. P. Blackmur, *Language as Gesture* (London: Allen and Unwin, 1954), 285.

20. Susan Sontag, *Illness as Metaphor and AIDS and Its Metaphors* (New York: Picador/Farrar, Straus and Giroux, 2001), 3.

21. Garland Thomson, *Extraordinary Bodies,* 11–12.

22. Sharon L. Snyder and David T. Mitchell, *Cultural Locations of Disability* (Chicago: University of Chicago Press, 2006), 51.

23. See Leo Bersani's indispensable account of Ishmael and Queequeg in *Culture of Redemption* (Cambridge: Harvard University Press, 1990), 145–47.

24. Wai-Chee Dimock, *Empire for Liberty: Melville and the Poetics of Individualism* (Princeton: Princeton University Press, 1989), 137.

25. Gilles Deleuze, *The Fold: Leibniz and the Baroque,* ed. and trans. Tom Conley (Minneapolis: University of Minnesota Press, 1993), 4.

26. Eve Kosofsky Sedgwick, *Epistemology of the Closet* (Berkeley: University of California Press, 1990), 22.

27. Michael D. Snediker, "*Pierre* and the Non-Transparencies of Figuration," *ELH* 77, no. 1 (Spring 2010): 217–35.

28. Emerson, *Essays and Lectures,* 473.

29. Maurice Merleau-Ponty, *The Merleau-Ponty Aesthetics Reader: Philosophy and Painting,* ed. Galen A. Johnson and Michael B. Smith, trans. Michael B. Smith (Evanston: Northwestern University Press, 1993), 125.

30. William Wordsworth, "Fidelity," in *Poems of Wordsworth,* ed. Matthew Arnold (London: MacMillan, 1892), 36.

31. I. A. Richards, *The Philosophy of Rhetoric* (Oxford: Oxford University Press, 1965), 100.

32. Blackmur, *Language as Gesture,* 285.

33. Leo Bersani, *A Future for Astyanax: Character and Desire in Literature* (New York: Columbia University Press, 1984), 138.

34. Eugenie Brinkema, *The Forms of the Affects* (Durham: Duke University Press, 2014), 2.

35. Brinkema, *The Forms of the Affects,* 19.

36. Roland Barthes, *Camera Lucida: Reflections on Photography,* trans. Richard Howard (New York: Hill and Wang/Farrar, Straus and Giroux, 1982), 26–27.

37. Plato, *The Dialogues of Plato,* ed. and trans. Benjamin Jowett (London: Oxford University Press, 1892), 457. Hereafter cited parenthetically in the text.

38. Michael D. Snediker, "Melville and Queerness without Character," in *The New Cambridge Companion to Herman Melville,* ed. Robert S. Levine (New York: Cambridge University Press, 2013), 155–68.

39. Maurice Merleau-Ponty, *The Visible and the Invisible,* ed. Claude Lefort, trans. Alphonso Lingis (Evanston: Northwestern University Press, 1968), 12.

40. Nathan Brown, "Absent Blue Wax (Rationalist Empiricism)," *Qui Parle* 19, no. 1 (2010): 100.

41. Herman Melville, *Clarel: A Poem and Pilgrimage in the Holy Land,* ed. Harrison Hayford, Alma A. MacDougall, Hershel Parker, and G. Thomas Tanselle (Evanston: Northwestern University Press, 1991), 186.

2. QUEER PHILOLOGY AND CHRONIC PAIN

1. Friedrich Nietzsche, *The Anti-Christ, Ecce Homo, Twilight of the Idols, and Other Writings,* ed. Aaron Ridley and Judith Norman, trans. Judith Norman (Cambridge: Cambridge University Press, 2005), 51.

2. Nietzsche, *The Anti-Christ,* 51.

3. Friedrich Nietzsche, *The Anti-Christ,* trans. H. L. Mencken (New York: Knopf, 1920), 148; Alan Schrift, *Nietzsche and the Question of Interpretation* (New York: Routledge, 1990), 164; Richard Weisberg, "De Man Missing Nietzsche: *Hinzugedichtet* Revisited," in *Nietzsche as Postmodernist: Essays Pro and Contra,* ed. Clayton Koelb (Albany: SUNY Press, 1990), 119.

4. Roland Barthes, *The Neutral,* trans. Rosalind E. Krauss and Denis Hollier (New York: Columbia University, 2005), 12.

5. Leo Bersani, "Is the Rectum a Grave?," in *Is the Rectum a Grave? and Other Essays* (Chicago: University of Chicago Press, 2010), 3. Hereafter cited parenthetically in the text.

6. Jean-Luc Nancy, *Corpus II: Writings on Sexuality,* trans. Anne O'Byrne (New York: Fordham University Press, 2013), 2.

7. "Beyond Redemption: An Interview with Leo Bersani," with Nicholas Royle, in *Is the Rectum a Grave? and Other Essays,* 193.

8. Leo Bersani, "Sociability and Cruising," in *Is the Rectum a Grave? and Other Essays,* 50.

9. A more straightforwardly aggressive version of like's epistemological trickiness subtends much of the hostility of *Who's Afraid of Virginia Woolf:*

GEORGE: Good, better, best, bested! How do you like that for a declension? You didn't answer my question. Don't condescend. I asked you how you liked that declension.

NICK: I don't know what to say.

GEORGE: You don't know what to say?

NICK: Shall I say it's funny, so you can say it's sad? Or shall I say it's sad so you can say it's funny?

In the cases of both Bersani and Albee, *like*'s particular responsiveness to irony derives in part from what I've described as its metaphysical relation to affect. Or rather, liking disingenuously implies that we ought to be able to respond to its question with the celerity of affect when in both cases our needing to think about it puts us in the position of not knowing whether or in what ways liking does our "feelings" justice.

10. On the Red Carpet, "Sally Field's 'You Like Me' Oscar Speech," https://youtu.be/u_8nAvU0T5Y.

11. Foucault, *The History of Sexuality,* 121.

12. Frances Ferguson, "Philology, Literature, Style," *ELH* 80, no. 2 (2013): 325.

13. Lauren Berlant, *Cruel Optimism* (Durham: Duke University Press, 2011), 24.

14. Lauren Berlant and Lee Edelman, *Sex, or the Unbearable* (Durham: Duke University Press, 2014), 25.

15. Anne-Lise François, *Open Secrets: The Literature of Uncounted Experience* (Stanford: Stanford University Press, 2008), 2–3.

16. Emerson, *Essays and Lectures,* 473.

17. A related interest in expanding the vocabulary of phenomenologies of grasping pervades George Oppen's "The Gesture," the first section of his 1972 "Five Poems about Poetry," which distinguishes between holding something "In the mind which he intends / To grasp" and holding "a bauble he intends / to sell" (*New Collected Poems,* ed. Michael Davidson [New York: New Directions Press, 2008], 97). My sense of these lines as Emersonian is indebted to Branka Arsić's important supposition that "to have better hands . . . would repair and love what they touch." If a "nonviolent hand," for Arsić, "is a hard thing to conceive," it might be the case that the onerousness of the fantasy of reparation is in part what makes us clutch hardest in the first place (*On Leaving: A Reading in Emerson* [Cambridge: Harvard University Press, 2010], 82).

18. Eve Kosofsky Sedgwick, *Tendencies* (Durham: Duke University Press, 1993), 201.

19. Jonathan Culler, "Anti-Foundational Philology," *Journal of Aesthetic Education* 36, no. 3 (2002): 52.

20. Berlant, *Cruel Optimism,* 25.

21. François, *Open Secrets,* 3.

22. Culler, "Anti-Foundational Philology," 51.

23. Eve Kosofsky Sedgwick, "Shame in the Cybernetic Fold: Reading Silvan Tomkins (Written with Adam Frank)," in *Touching Feeling: Affect, Pedagogy, Performativity* (Durham: Duke University Press, 2003), 96.

24. Lee Edelman, *Homographesis: Essays in Gay Literary and Cultural Theory* (New York: Routledge Press, 1994), 10.

25. Edelman, *Homographesis,* 13.

26. John Ashbery, "The Impossible," *Poetry,* July 1957, 250.

27. Gertrude Stein, *Stanzas in Meditation: The Corrected Edition,* ed. Susannah Hollister and Emily Setina (New Haven: Yale University Press, 2012), 216.

28. Stein, *Stanzas in Meditation,* 166.

29. Werner Hamacher, "95 Theses on Philology," *Diacritics* 39. no.1 (2009): 29.

30. Stein, *Stanzas in Meditation,* 165.

31. Herman Melville, *The Piazza Tales and Other Prose Pieces, 1839–1860* (Evanston: Northwestern University Press, 1987), 47. Hereafter cited parenthetically in the text.

32. Herman Melville, *Billy Budd, Sailor (An Inside Narrative)* (Chicago: University of Chicago Press, 1962), 98. Hereafter cited parenthetically in the text.

33. Barbara Johnson, "Melville's Fist," in *The Critical Difference: Essays in the Contemporary Rhetoric of Reading* (Baltimore: Johns Hopkins University Press, 1980), 92.

34. Lynne Huffer, "Foucault and Sedgwick: The Repressive Hypothesis Revisited," *Foucault Studies* 14 (2012): 30.

35. Emily Dickinson, *The Poems of Emily Dickinson: Reading Edition* (Cambridge: Belknap Press, 2005), F372.

36. Hamacher, "95 Theses," 28.

37. Barthes, *The Neutral,* 45.

38. Walt Whitman, *Leaves of Grass: The First (1855) Edition,* ed. Malcolm Cowley (New York: Penguin Books, 1986), 117.

39. Barbara Johnson, "Bringing Out D. A. Miller," *Narrative* 10, no. 1 (2002): 5.

40. Johnson, "Bringing Out D. A. Miller," 5.

41. As Giorgio Agamben observes, "there is no escape [from acedia] because one cannot flee from what cannot even be reached." Agamben, *Stanzas: Word and Phantasm in Western Culture,* trans. Ronald L. Martinez (Minneapolis: University of Minnesota Press, 1993), 6.

42. Jonathan Flatley, "Like: Collecting and Collectivity," *October* 132 (Spring 2010): 73. Hereafter cited parenthetically in the text.

43. I appreciate Brian Glavey's attention to the "wear and tear" that accompanies if not partly constitutes Warhol's aesthetic, itself inseparable from receding as performative apprehension. Glavey, *The Wallflower Avant-Garde: Modernism, Sexuality, and Queer Ekphrasis* (New York: Oxford University Press, 2016), 131.

44. Hamacher, "95 Theses," 29.

45. Walter Benjamin, "Unpacking My Library: A Talk about Book Collecting," in *Illuminations,* trans. Harry Zohn, ed. Hannah Arendt (New York: Schocken Books, 1968), 60.

46. Maurice Blanchot, "Two Versions of the Imaginary," in *The Station Hill*

Blanchot Reader, trans. Lydia Davis et al. (Barrytown, N.Y.: Station Hill Press, 1999), 421.

47. Blanchot, "Two Versions of the Imaginary," 421–22.

48. Paul de Man, *Aesthetic Ideology* (Minneapolis: University of Minnesota Press, 1996), 45.

49. Hawthorne, *The Scarlet Letter,* 31.

50. I understand this doubling in terms of Hawthorne. Insofar as the letter by the end of *The Scarlet Letter* has rewritten Hester's ontology as aesthetic, she is experienced less as a character than a pulsing whose back and forth calibrates coterminousness as a throb. "On this public holiday, as on all other occasions for seven years past, Hester was clad in a garment of coarse gray cloth. Not more by its hue than by some indescribable peculiarity in its fashion, it had the effect of making her fade personally out of sight and outline; while, again, the scarlet letter brought her back from this twilight indistinctness, and revealed her under the moral aspect of its own illumination" (153).

3. "THE VISION – PONDERED LONG"

1. Sharon Cameron, *Lyric Time: Dickinson and the Limits of Genre* (Baltimore: Johns Hopkins University Press, 1979), 23.

2. This movement away from a hermeneutically overfamiliar relation to Dickinsonian unfamiliarity follows the bracing bon voyage of R. P. Blackmur's 1954 proposal "first to examine a set of prejudices which are available as approaches to Emily Dickinson, and then to count—and perhaps account for—a few staring facts: obvious, animating, defacing facts about the verses as they now appear," since "depend[ing] on prejudice for the nature of time or poetry . . . allows for mistakes, and in the present condition of Emily Dickinson's poetry, it is imperative to allow for continuous error, both in the facts and . . . in the prejudices by which we get at them" (*Language as Gesture,* 26–27).

3. This project's interest in pain's seeming responsiveness to our attention to it arises in part from a dissatisfaction with extant critical descriptions of pain's place within the Dickinson canon; I address a related set of concerns in *Queer Optimism: Lyric Personhood and other Felicitous Persuasions* (Minneapolis: University of Minnesota Press, 2009), 79–125. Consider Marianne Noble's suggestion that "the experience of affliction . . . is intrinsically transgressive. While contentment quietly remains within the confines of the law, pain will not stay in its place. It defies laws and the boundaries that regulate them and (as Scarry demonstrates) the language that articulates them" (*The Masochistic Pleasures of Sentimental Literature* [Princeton: Princeton University Press, 2003], 161). Noble is able to insist on pain's juridical abruption because pain, for Noble, has no laws of its own. Her paraphrase

of "A nearness to Tremendousness" turns pain into something more Byronically roguish than the poem is willing to confirm. After all, pain doesn't "def[y] laws" (a pun on *loss*, to be sure), but lies in vicinity to them; its closeness to explanation or principle—and it's worth noting that the third and fourth definitions for *vicinity* in Dickinson's 1844 *Webster's Dictionary* are "obedience; compliance"—invokes far subtler a quandary. Similarly, to my eye, "It's Location / Is Illocality" doesn't quite mean it "will not stay in place" but that where it lives seems to exist as a cartographic blur or sylph, innavigable (rather than merely piratical) in the manner of Emerson's hermetically intercalated days. As Dickinson (and anyone, for that matter, living with chronic pain) would know all too well, pain frequently *does* stay in place (hoveringly, pulsingly) like a ghost in the bone no technology or procedure can deliver let alone resolve.

4. My recent work on Dickinson's poetic practice seeks to distinguish figurative difficulty's propulsive density from the static visual lure of metaphor. Whereas metaphorical meaningfulness is tethered to an expectation of objectual intelligibility, Dickinson's most autonomous figurative gestures are neither scrutable nor inscrutable so much as semicharismatically transcrutable (impacted and impacting). It's along these lines that I think of figuration's suspensive substance as transmaterial. This present sense of figuration's phenomenological pressure resonates hopefully with Dana Luciano's claim that "the point of historicizing materiality, and the range of responses thereto, would ultimately be to question our own assumptions about what qualities count as 'material,' what the purpose of transmateriality or transobjectivity might be, why we have come to equate vibrancy and activity with agency, and what we might do when things don't work out that way" ("Sacred Theories of Earth: Matters of Spirit in *The Souls of Things*," *American Literature* 86, no. 4 [December 2014]: 730). See also Daniel Tiffany's *Toy Medium: Materialism and Modern Lyric* (Berkeley: University of California Press, 2000).

5. Emerson, *Essays and Lectures*, 473.

6. Thomas H. Johnson, *Emily Dickinson: An Interpretive Biography* (Cambridge: Belknap Press of Harvard University Press, 1955), 124.

7. Emily Dickinson, *The Letters of Emily Dickinson*, ed. Thomas H. Johnson, vol. 2 (Cambridge: Belknap Press, 1958), L290. Hereafter cited parenthetically in the text, according to Johnson's numbering.

8. Donald L. Blanchard, MD, "Emily Dickinson's Ophthalmic Consultation with Henry Willard Williams, MD," *Archives of Ophthalmology* 130, no. 12 (2012): 1594.

9. Following Richard B. Sewall's 1974 *The Life of Emily Dickinson*, Kerry McSweeney notes that while it "is not clear whether during these stays [Dickinson] was operated on," surgery was "the standard treatment in severe cases" (*Language of the Senses: Sensory-Perceptual Dynamics in Wordsworth, Coleridge, Thoreau,*

Whitman, and Dickinson [Montreal: McGill-Queen's University Press, 1998], 148). In the absence of corroborating sources, Diana Fuss's claim that Dickinson was "eventually cured . . . of her temporary blindness" (21) seems less authoritative than wishful (*The Sense of an Interior: Four Writers and the Rooms That Shaped Them* [New York: Routledge, 2004], 21).

10. Contra James R. Guthrie's more sanguine assessment of the scarcity of this pain dossier: "Although references to her optical illness faded away from letters and poems written after 1866, some of the tropes Dickinson had adopted perhaps as a result of having been ill persisted, yet in contexts that are distinctly more positive. For example, the carcerative images we saw her associate in her poems with sickroom confinement reappear in her communications with Judge Lord in a completely different guise, as a form of erotic play" (*Emily Dickinson's Vision: Illness and Identity in Her Poetry* [Gainesville: University Press of Florida, 1998], 155). Suffice it to say that I find Guthrie's heterosexualization of Dickinson's chronic illness—here and elsewhere in his investigation—puzzling to say the least. That Dickinson's distress might spur in the critic a homophobic discomfiture soothed only by heterosexuality's appearance on the horizon of pain's abatement speaks to the occult intervolutions of queerness and chronic pain traced (however obliquely) throughout the work at hand.

11. Allen Tate, "New England Culture and Emily Dickinson," in *The Recognition of Emily Dickinson: Selected Criticism since 1890*, ed. Caesar R. Blake and Carlton F. Wells (Ann Arbor: University of Michigan Press, 1964), 153–66. See also Michael D. Snediker, "Emily Dickinson's Queer Pain: 'One Claw Opon the Air,'" in *Queer Optimism*, 79–125.

12. Emerson, *Essays and Lectures*, 10.

13. Michelle Kohler's monograph *Miles of Stare: Transcendentalism and the Problem of Literary Vision in Nineteenth-Century America* analyzes a Dickinsonian ocular poetics that in many ways overlaps with my own concerns. For another phenomenologically attuned account of Dickinson's vision, see Marianne Noble's "Dickinson on Perception and Consciousness: A Dialogue with Maurice Merleau-Ponty," in *Emily Dickinson and Philosophy*, ed. Jed Deppman, Marianne Noble, Gary Lee Stonum (New York: Cambridge University Press, 2013), 188–206. See also Jed Deppman's *Trying to Think with Emily Dickinson* (Amherst: University of Massachusetts Amherst Press, 2008), 71–74; Joanne Feit Diehl's *Dickinson and the Romantic Imagination* (Princeton: Princeton University Press, 1982), 10; and Guthrie's *Emily Dickinson's Vision* (discussed above).

14. To be sure, Scarry herself is deeply interested in pain's extrasomatic life, the ways its "felt-characteristics [. . .]—one of which is its compelling vibrancy or its incontestable reality or simply its 'certainty'—can be appropriated away from the body and presented as the attributes of something else" (*The Body in Pain*, 13).

Though the genres at play in *The Body in Pain* may be largely prose, Scarry's theorization of pain's centrifugal vibrancy in terms of "analogical verification" hints at a figurative principle above and beyond literature's mimetic terms.

15. Jean-Luc Marion, *In Excess: Studies of Saturated Phenomena,* trans. Robyn Horner (New York: Fordham University Press, 2002), 92.

16. Cameron, *Lyric Time,* 14.

17. Cameron, *Lyric Time,* 262n31.

18. Cameron, *Lyric Time,* 27.

19. Emily Dickinson, *The Poems of Emily Dickinson: Reading Edition,* ed. R. W. Franklin (Cambridge: Belknap Press, 1999), F425. Hereafter cited parenthetically in the text, according to Franklin's numbering (unless stated otherwise).

20. Cameron, *Lyric Time,* 95.

21. Nathaniel Hawthorne, *The Scarlet Letter* (New York: Norton, 1988), 34.

22. Herman Melville, *Moby-Dick, or The Whale,* ed. Harrison Hayford, Hershel Parker, and G. Thomas Tanselle (Evanston: Northwestern University Press, 1988), 573.

23. Cameron, *Lyric Time,* 95.

24. Helen Vendler, *Dickinson: Selected Poems and Commentaries* (Cambridge: Harvard University Press, 2012), 198–99.

25. Cameron, *Lyric Time,* 53, 28.

26. Scarry, *The Body in Pain,* 4.

27. Scarry, *The Body in Pain,* 4.

28. Scarry, *The Body in Pain,* 172.

29. "That this record of the imagination's activity occurs here in the form of narrative event and story would only in error be called allegory, for the act it describes, the reflex and outcome of the action whose design it traces, is overtly presented as the act and action of the imagination. There is, as suggested earlier, no veiled language here; for maker, making, hurting, believing, working, creating, are the wholly undisguised terms of the story. Furthermore, the categories in which its activity is followed, categories encountered throughout the first half of the present study—body and voice (or, in the language of the Christian scriptures, flesh and word)—are not categories read into the text but the categories in which the text announces itself directly" (Scarry, *The Body in Pain,* 182).

30. Judith Butler, *Antigone's Claim* (New York: Columbia University Press, 2000), 57. See also the epilogue of *Queer Optimism,* 213–18.

31. Allen Grossman, *The Long Schoolroom: Lessons in the Bitter Logic of the Poetic Principle* (Ann Arbor: University of Michigan Press, 1997), 92–96. See also Grossman's *True-Love: Essays on Poetry and Valuing* (Chicago: University of Chicago Press, 2009), 71–126.

32. https://www.edickinson.org/editions/1/image_sets/238955.

33. Emerson, *Essays and Lectures,* 471.

34. Ralph Waldo Emerson, "Beauty," in *Select Writings of Ralph Waldo Emerson,* with an Introduction by Percival Chubb (London: Walter Scott, 1888), 168. Not coincidentally but no less provocative in light of this present exploration of a figurative aesthetics elemental rather than applied to the life of chronic pain, one word that Emerson supplies for such a model is beauty, whose own "pungency" of light against eye returns us to the pang of Dickinson's haunted, antipastoral experiment. Here is the passage at hand, in full: "Into every beautiful object there enters somewhat immeasurable and divine, and just as much into form bounded by outlines, like mountains on the horizon, as into tones of music, or depths of space. Polarized light showed the secret architecture of bodies; and when the *second sight* of the mind is opened, now one colour, or form, or gesture, and now another, has a pungency, as if a more interior ray had been emitted, disclosing its deep holdings in the frame of things" (168).

35. *The Bible, Authorized King James Version with Apocrypha* (New York: Oxford University Press, 1997), 1 Peter 2.24.

36. Stephanie A. Tingley, "My Business Is to *Sing*: Emily Dickinson's Letters to Elizabeth Holland," in *Dickinson and Audience,* ed. Martin Orzeck and Robert Weisbuch (Ann Arbor: University of Michigan Press, 1996), 189.

37. Maurice Merleau-Ponty, *The Visible and the Invisible,* ed. Claude Lefort, trans. Alphonso Lingis (Evanston: Northwestern University Press, 1968), 230.

38. Merleau-Ponty, *The Visible and the Invisible,* 201.

39. Maurice S. Lee, *Uncertain Chances: Science, Skepticism, and Belief in Nineteenth-Century American Literature* (Oxford: Oxford University Press, 2012), 184.

40. Emerson, *Essays and Lectures,* 47.

41. Ralph Waldo Emerson, *Letters and Social Aims* (Boston: James R. Osgood, 1876), 10.

42. Lee, *Uncertain Chances,* 187.

43. Lee, *Uncertain Chances,* 188.

44. Merleau-Ponty, *The Visible and the Invisible,* 263.

45. Duane H. Davis and William S. Hamrick, eds., *Merleau-Ponty and the Art of Perception* (Albany: State University of New York Press, 2016), xvii.

46. Merleau-Ponty, *The Visible and the Invisible,* 263–64.

47. Gertrude Stein, *Lectures in America* (Boston: Beacon Press, 1957), 13.

48. Theo Davis, *Ornamental Aesthetics: The Poetry of Attending in Thoreau, Dickinson, and Whitman* (New York: Oxford University Press, 2016), 108.

49. Davis, *Ornamental Aesthetics,* 108.

50. Virginia Jackson, *Dickinson's Misery: A Theory of Lyric Reading* (Princeton: Princeton University Press, 2005), 25.

51. Jackson, *Dickinson's Misery*, 132.

52. Jackson, *Dickinson's Misery*, 147.

53. D. W. Winnicott, "The Theory of the Parent-Infant Relationship," in *Essential Papers on Object Relations*, ed. Peter Buckley (New York: New York University Press, 1986), 242–43.

54. D. W. Winnicott, "Aggression in Relation to Emotional Development," in *Winnicott: Through Paediatrics to Psychoanalysis*, intro. M. Masud R. Khan (New York: Basic Books, 1975), 212.

55. Emerson, *Essays and Lectures*, 20.

56. Democritus Junior, *The Anatomy of Melancholy, Volume 1* (London: Thomas McLean, 1826), 325.

57. Cecila Sjöholm, *Doing Aesthetics with Arendt: How to See Things* (New York: Columbia University Press, 2015), 17.

58. David Brewster, *Memoirs of the Life, Writings, and Discoveries of Sir Isaac Newton*, Vol. 1 (Edinburgh: Thomas Constable, 1855), 378.

59. Christopher Smith Fenner, *Vision: Its Optical Defects, and the Adaptation of Spectacles* (Philadelphia: Lindsay and Blakiston, 1875), 121.

60. Max Born, *Einstein's Theory of Relativity*, trans. Henry L. Brose (New York: E.P. Dutton & Company, 1922), 75.

61. Maurice Blanchot, *The Book to Come*, trans. Charlotte Mandell (Stanford: Stanford University Press, 2003), 244.

62. Jackson, *Dickinson's Misery*, 219.

63. Jackson, *Dickinson's Misery*, 219.

64. Jackson, *Dickinson's Misery*, 22.

65. Jackson, *Dickinson's Misery*, 25.

66. Paul de Man, *The Rhetoric of Romanticism* (Minneapolis: University of Minnesota Press, 1984), 257.

67. De Man, *The Rhetoric of Romanticism*, 256.

68. De Man, *The Rhetoric of Romanticism*, 254.

69. De Man, *The Rhetoric of Romanticism*, 262.

70. De Man, *The Rhetoric of Romanticism*, 261.

71. Jackson, *Dickinson's Misery*, 109.

72. Jackson, *Dickinson's Misery*, 228.

73. https://www.edickinson.org/editions/1/image_sets/240053.

74. Davis, *Ornamental Aesthetics*, 139.

75. Davis, *Ornamental Aesthetics*, 19.

76. Barthes, *The Neutral*, 17–18.

77. William Wordsworth and Samuel Taylor Coleridge, *Lyrical Ballads, 1798 and 1802* (New York: Oxford University Press, 2013), 107.

78. Walter Pater, *Appreciations, with an Essay on Style* (London: Macmillan, 1895), 16.

79. Davis, *Ornamental Aesthetics,* 91.

80. Quoted in Paul Guyer, "What Is It Like to Experience the Beautiful and Sublime," in *Kant and the Faculty of Feeling,* ed. Kelly Sorenson and Diane Williamson (New York: Cambridge University Press, 2018), 149.

81. Davis, *Ornamental Aesthetics,* 91. In addition to admiring its attention to Dickinson's phenomenal surfaces, I'm drawn anecdotally to Davis's gloss in terms of the baffling number of times I've attempted capsaicin creams to assuage the neck's irascible unhappiness, turning for relief to a burning meant to distract from pain's competing intensities.

82. Blackmur, *Language as Gesture,* 36–37.

83. Melville, *Pierre,* 41.

84. Ian Balfour, "Figures in Excess and the Matter of Inversion in the Discourse of the Sublime," *ELH* 84 (2017): 331.

85. Quoted in Balfour, "Figures in Excess," 316–17.

86. Blackmur goes one step further, in fact, conceiving plushness itself as a metonym for the loss of textual control. "We have the word *plush* in different poems as follows. 'One would as soon assault a plush or violate a star . . . Time's consummate plush . . . A dog's belated feet like intermittent plush . . . We step like plush, we stand like snow . . . Sentences of plush.' The word is on the verge of bursting with wrong meaning, and on account of the bursting, the stress with which the poet employed it, we are all prepared to accept it, and indeed do accept it, when suddenly we realize the wrongness, that 'plush' was not what was meant at all, but was a substitute for it. The word has been distorted but not transformed on the page; which is to say it is not in substantial control. Yet it is impossible not to believe that to Emily Dickinson's ear it meant what it said and what could not otherwise be said" (*Language as Gesture,* 46).

87. Compare to Robert Weisbuch's foundational observation, speaking of a different plushness, that "most often, the boundary of a Dickinson poem is not a particular scene or situation but the figure of the analogy as it moves from scene to scene. Dickinson gives us a pattern in several carpets and then makes the carpets vanish." Weisbuch, *Emily Dickinson's Poetry* (Chicago: University of Chicago Press, 1981), 16.

88. Auerbach, *Scenes from the Drama,* 17.

89. Gillian Osborne, "Dickinson's Lyric Materialism," *Emily Dickinson Journal* 21, no. 1 (2012): 57–78.

90. Leo Bersani and Ulysse Dutoit, *The Forms of Violence: Narrative in Assyrian Art and Modern Culture* (New York: Schocken, 1985), 46.

91. Osborne, "Dickinson's Lyric Materialism," 66.

92. Osborne, "Dickinson's Lyric Materialism," 71.

93. Gilles Deleuze, *Difference and Repetition,* trans. Paul Patton (New York: Columbia University Press, 1994), 23.

94. Deleuze, *Difference and Repetition,* 23.

95. Emerson, *Essays and Lectures,* 474.

96. https://www.edickinson.org/editions/1/image_sets/240281.

97. Allen Tate, "New England Culture and Emily Dickinson," in *The Recognition of Emily Dickinson,* ed. Caesar R. Blake and Carlton F. Wells (Ann Arbor: University of Michigan Press, 1968), 153–67.

4. INVETERATE PAGODA

A Pentimento, for KH

1. Edmund White, "Portrait of a Sissy," *New York Review of Books,* March 6, 2008, 15.

2. See Ross Posnock, *The Trial of Curiosity: Henry James, William James, and the Challenge of Modernity* (New York: Oxford University Press, 1991), 193–220.

3. Henry James, *Letters,* ed. Leon Edel, vol. 4, *1895–1916* (Cambridge: Belknap Press, 1984), 105–6.

4. Henry James, *Notes of a Son and Brother* and *The Middle Years: A Critical Edition,* ed. Peter Collister (Charlottesville: University of Virginia Press, 2011), 240. Hereafter cited parenthetically in the text.

5. Sheldon M. Novick, *Henry James: The Young Master* (New York: Random House, 1996), 79.

6. Novick fillips the above supposition with a footnote, "*NSB* 300–301" (*Henry James,* 466n21), whose laconic redirection to James's autobiography treats the relation of the "obscure hurt" to "private existence" as all but self-explanatory. Although Novick doesn't directly cite the "obscure hurt" in the body of his work, he borrows from the formulation—"[James] was beginning to feel obscurely that the pain was a permanent condition" (78)—in a paraphrase that lays bare the biography's indifference toward James's own textual painstaking. The mutation of James's "obscure hurt" into Novick's "feel obscurely" registers the temporal errancy that paraphrase introduces, falsely transforming the epithetical obscurity authored by James in 1914 into its own retroactive referent. As I hope to show, that the formulation asks to be evaluated as a signified in its own right means its antecedent can't so readily be supplied, whether in terms of the "actual" physical condition James is said to suffer or the obscurity such a condition is said to occasion.

7. As if James's incomparable achievement were the work, so Leon Edel

rightly quips, of "a young Mozart or . . . Paganini." Edel, "Oh Henry!," https://slate.com/news-and-politics/1996/12/oh-henry.html.

8. Sedgwick, *Epistemology of the Closet,* 205.

9. Again, this demarcation of queerness and chronic pain as separate grammatical entities is largely heuristic, convinced as I am of the frequent impossibility of knowing where one ends and the other begins.

10. The word's brazen Gallicism is signature Sedgwick (*Epistemology of the Closet,* 195).

11. Blanchot, *The Infinite Conversation,* 291. "Weariness is the most modest of misfortunes, the most neutral of neutrals; an experience that, if one could choose, no one would choose out of vanity. O neutral, free me from my weariness, lead me to that which, though preoccupying me to the point of occupying everything, does not concern me.—But this is what weariness is, a state that is not possessive, that absorbs without putting into question.

"As long as you reflect upon what you call your weariness (1) you show complacency with regard to your weary self; (2) you miss your object, for you encounter no more than the sign of your intention; (3) you attenuate and efface it, drawing meaning and advantage from what is vain, you become interested instead of disinterested.—That is true, but only partially true: I do not reflect, I simulate reflection, and perhaps this manner of dissimulating belongs to weariness. I do not really speak, I repeat, and weariness is repetition, a wearing away of every beginning; and I not only efface, I increase as well, I exhaust myself in pretending to have still the strength to speak of its absence.—All of this is vain, quite true. You work, but at what is in vain. I leave you to work, then, since it is the only way for you to realize that you are incapable of working" (*The Infinite Conversation,* xx).

12. Deborah Esch, "A Jamesian About-Face: Notes on 'The Jolly Corner,'" *ELH* 50, no. 3 (Autumn 1983): 595.

13. Esch, "A Jamesian About-Face," 604n23.

14. Blanchot, *The Infinite Conversation,* 45. As I mention in an earlier chapter, Blanchot's *The Infinite Conversation* has influenced my thinking about chronic pain for nearly as long as I've been aware of my neck's degenerative persistence. From the outset, the extent to which Blanchot's idiom seemed to lie beyond the immediate purview of chronic pain or disability was its draw. Its conception of an aesthetics of broken objects presented my own travail with the language it seemed most keenly lacking, of which, those first years, it felt most in need. If the work of composing a theory adequate to those early inklings has taken longer than I could have imagined, Blanchot's example has long felt navigationally instrumental; if not quite steadying as a North star, then something more curious, a Viking sunstone.

15. Sedgwick, *Touching Feeling,* 146.

16. Berlant and Edelman, *Sex, or the Unbearable,* 40.

17. William Shakespeare, *Hamlet*, ed. Neil Taylor and Ann Thompson (New York: Bloomsbury Arden Shakespeare, 2016), 422.

18. Philippe Lacoue-Labarthe, *Typography: Mimesis, Philosophy, Politics*, ed. Christopher Fynsk (Cambridge: Harvard University Press, 1989), 194.

19. Paul de Man, "Autobiography as De-Facement," in *The Rhetoric of Romanticism* (New York: Columbia University Press, 1984), 71. I think, too, of de Man's tantalizing suggestion that "the mimesis here assumed to be operative [in autobiography] is one mode of figuration among others" (69). De Man thus understands the crisis of disability less as a subject of autobiographical industry than a figure for it. "But the question remains," he insists, "how this near-obsessive concern with mutilation, so often in the form of a loss of one of the senses, as blindness, deafness, or, as in the key word of the Boy of Winander, *muteness*, is to be understood and, consequently, how trustworthy the ensuing claim of compensation and restoration can be" (73–74). One answer suggested toward the end of de Man's essay is that Wordsworthian deafness exposes the universe's own muteness as itself a form of figurative language, "the muteness of a nature" rendered all but indistinguishable from the muteness of the figure: "the picture of the thing and, as such, it is silent, mute as pictures are mute." De Man then turns for corroboration to Wordsworth's own assertion that language of this sort works "unremittingly and *noiselessly*" (80). The italics are de Man's, a form of stage direction that draws our attention to one mute word over another. James's "obscure hurt," by contrast, testifies in the keenness of its temporal tenacity to that other word, "unremittingly," by which language as counter-spirit "work[s] to derange, to subvert, to lay waste, to vitiate, and to dissolve" (Wordsworth, *Selected Prose* [New York: Penguin Books, 1988], 361); and does so unremittingly because language fills what it carves, the well-wrought urn as the daughters of Danaus.

20. Both Wescott's invoking of "extreme tenderness" and his essay's titular "sentiment[ality]" seem indebted to William Hazlitt's estimation of Keats, who "is also dead. He gave the greatest promise of genius of any poet of his day. He displayed extreme tenderness, beauty, originality, and delicacy of fancy; all he wanted was manly strength and fortitude to reject the temptations of singularity in sentiment and expression." *The Collected Works of William Hazlitt*, vol. 5, ed. A. R. Waller and Arnold Glover (London: J.M. Dent & Co., 1902), 378–79.

21. Glenway Wescott, "A Sentimental Contribution," *Hound and Horn* 7 (Spring 1934): 523.

22. Wescott, "A Sentimental Contribution," 533.

23. Henry James, *The Portrait of a Lady* (New York: Norton, 2018), 402.

24. Peter Rawlings, *Henry James and the Abuse of the Past* (New York: Palgrave, 2005), 44.

25. Rawlings, *Henry James*, 54.

26. Rawlings, *Henry James,* xii.

27. Rawlings, *Henry James,* xii. We find an echo of Rawlings's sentiment in Gregory Phipps's suggestion that the "obscurity and lack of any medical verification of the hurt seems to distance it from the very real suffering that had descended on the 'social body.'" Phipps, *Henry James and the Philosophy of Literary Pragmatism* (New York: Palgrave, 2016), 14.

28. Phipps, *Henry James,* 27n19.

29. George Steiner, *On Difficulty and Other Essays* (New York: Oxford University Press, 1980), 69.

30. Our present attention to the qualia of obscurity's communication may protect obscurity—and we who live with it—from an industry of exposure (medical and poetic alike) not perhaps dissimilar in its own salacious covertures from those answering to the name of the repressive hypothesis. See Foucault, *The History of Sexuality,* 15–49.

31. Daniel Tiffany, *Infidel Poetics: Riddles, Nightlife, Substance* (Chicago: University of Chicago Press, 2009), 7.

32. Tiffany, *Infidel Poetics,* 8.

33. Tiffany, *Infidel Poetics,* 8.

34. Samuel Vriezen, "Rituals of Contingency 1," *Theory & Event* 17, no. 4 (2014).

35. Jean-Luc Marion, *Being Given: Toward a Phenomenology of Givenness* (Stanford: Stanford University Press, 2002), 125.

36. Fredric Jameson, *Marxism and Form: Twentieth-Century Dialectical Theories of Literature* (Princeton: Princeton University Press, 1974), 341.

37. Although the above text corresponds to F313 in Franklin's edition of Dickinson's poems, I've chosen to follow the lineation of Dickinson's original manuscript. Cited in Tiffany, *Infidel Poetics,* 80–81. See https://www.edickinson.org/editions/1/image_sets/235534.

38. Anne-Marie Albiach, *Mezza Voce,* trans. Joseph Simas (Sausalito: Post-Apollo Press, 1988), 29.

39. Dickinson, *Poems,* F824.

40. Sharon Cameron, *Choosing Not Choosing: Dickinson's Fascicles (Chicago: University of Chicago Press, 1992),* 64. See also Branka Arsić's thoughtful exposition of Deleuzian masochism as the obviation of pleasure rather than its affirmation (156). Arsić understands masochism's "noneconomical attitude toward pain" in terms of a "literality" (147) that balks at the pleasure principle's will-toward-metaphorization (147). If my account of James likewise insists on the literality of the obscure hurt, it no less believes that the figurative dilations of chronic pain to which his work attests is the rhythm of its literal substance, an animacy that only sometimes lines up with the hydraulics of metaphor, presenting us instead with

what Arsić calls an "endless" process that isn't like so much as "is a spreading of the ocean of impersonal, neutral waves of pain" (158). Arsić, "The Rhythm of Pain: Freud, Deleuze, Derrida," in *Derrida, Deleuze, Psychoanalysis,* ed. Gabriele Schwab (New York: Columbia University Press, 2007), 142–70.

41. Sharon Cameron, *Thinking in Henry James* (Chicago: University of Chicago Press, 1989), 163.

42. Oliver Herford, *Henry James's Style of Retrospect: Late Personal Writings, 1890–1915* (New York: Oxford University Press, 2018), 142.

43. Timothy Lustig, *Henry James and the Ghostly* (Cambridge: Cambridge University Press, 1994), 96.

44. Leon Edel, *Henry James: The Untried Years, 1843–1870* (New York: Lippincott, 1953), 175.

45. Edel, *Henry James,* 175.

46. Edel, *Henry James,* 176.

47. These vicissitudes of consciousness are all the more relevant to our examination given the propensity of critics to treat the "obscure hurt" as a synecdoche for agency and passivity alike. Consider Peter Rawlings's acrimonious claim that "James's theory and practice as a writer, and especially the uses to which he put his accident, everywhere belie the ascription to art of a passive, 'noncombatant', status . . . The self-absorbed centralization of his injury is the means by which he both marginalizes the conflict [i.e., of the Civil War] and seizes on it, in a move he was to make repeatedly in the proximity of soldiers and war, as a delightfully serendipitous convenience" (*Henry James,* 42). See also Sheila Teahan, "Autobiographies and Biographies," in *Henry James in Context,* ed. David McWhirter (New York: Cambridge University Press, 2010), 63; and Andrew Taylor, *Henry James and the Father Question* (Cambridge: Cambridge University Press), 59.

48. Jean Laplanche, *New Foundations for Psychoanalysis,* trans. David Macey (Cambridge, Mass.: Basil Blackwell, 1989), 135.

49. Geoffrey Hartman, *The Geoffrey Hartman Reader,* ed. Geoffrey Hartman and Daniel T. O'Hara (Edinburgh: Edinburgh University Press, 2004), 396.

50. Laplanche, *New Foundations for Psychoanalysis,* 139.

51. Laplanche, *New Foundations for Psychoanalysis,* 130.

52. Inadvertently evoking pain's unhealing textuality, seventeenth-century lexicographer Francis Gouldman defines the Latin *luridus* as "the color of lead or bruised flesh." Gouldman, *A Copious Dictionary in Three Parts* (London: John Field, 1664).

53. Laplanche, *New Foundations for Psychoanalysis,* 45.

54. Edel, *Henry James,* 180. As Edel himself writes of the episode, it is "a queer tale—queer since he has mingled so many elements in it and at the same time thoroughly confused us about the time sequence" (*Henry James,* 175).

55. Edel, *Henry James,* 180.

56. Emerson, *Essays and Lectures,* 290.

57. Branka Arsić, *On Leaving: A Reading in Emerson* (Cambridge: Harvard University Press, 2010), 169.

58. Dickinson, *Poems,* F714.

59. Edel, *Henry James,* 177. It's worth noting how the military argot of "spring[ing] to the colors" aligns Edel (who served in the army during World War II) with those young men who did enlist for the Civil War, as though to mark in passing the camaraderie of the biographer against the effete isolation of his subject.

60. Henry James, *The Turn of the Screw,* ed. Robert Kimbrough (New York: Norton, 1966), 3.

61. James, *The Turn of the Screw,* 1.

62. Elaine Scarry, *The Body in Pain,* 4.

63. "He was there or was not there: not there if I didn't see him. I got hold of this; then, instinctively, instead of returning as I had come, went to the window. It was confusedly present to me that I ought to place myself where he had stood. I did so; I applied my face to the pane and looked, as he had looked, into the room. As if, at this moment, to show me exactly what his range had been" (James, *The Turn of the Screw,* 21).

64. Eli Clare, *Brilliant Imperfection: Grappling with Cure* (Durham: Duke University Press, 2017, 41). If, as Clare writes, diagnosis "at its best . . . affirms our distress, orients us to what's happening in our body-minds, helps make meaning out of chaotic visceral experiences" (41), then the failure of diagnosis—or more pointedly in James's case, the refusal of diagnosis—exacts an especial epistemological violence that surely bleeds into the texture of ontology itself. Were it not the case that so many of us have lived this exact scene of disregard, I would say one could only imagine this experience of despair, so often distended across time to an all but imperceptible fineness, the low-light penumbra of disconcertment's shadow.

65. "Thus it was at any rate that she was able to live more or less in the light of the fact expressed so lucidly by their common comforter—the fact that the Prince was saving up, for some very mysterious but very fine eventual purpose, all the wisdom, all the answers to his questions, all the impressions and generalisations, he gathered; putting them away and packing them down because he wanted his great gun to be loaded to the brim on the day he should decide to fire it off. He wanted first to make sure of the *whole* of the subject that was unrolling itself before him; after which the innumerable facts he had collected would find their use. He knew what he was about—trust him at last therefore to make, and to some effect, his big noise" (Henry James, *The Golden Bowl* [New York: Penguin Books, 1987], 155–56). What, after all, is diagnosis if not, in the words of nineteenth-century immunologist Paul Ehrlich, a magic bullet? See Robert S. Schwartz, "Paul Ehrlich's

Magic Bullets," *New England Journal of Medicine* 350, no. 11 (2004): 1079–80. See also Michael D. Snediker, "Stasis and Verve: Henry James and the Fictions of Patience," *Henry James Review* 27, no. 1 (2006): 38.

66. James, *The Golden Bowl,* 327–28. Maggie's attention to the acoustics of the pagoda's elaborate figurative substance calls to mind an observation made in Alphonse Daudet's *In the Land of Pain:* "At first, a heightened awareness of sound: the noise of the shovel, tongs near the hearth, the screech of doorbells; the ticking watch, a spider's web on which work begins at four in the morning" (Daudet, *In the Land of Pain,* ed. and trans. Julian Barnes [New York: Vintage Books, 2016], 6). James admired Daudet's work, averring that "the tissue of each of his novels is, for all the rest, really pure gold" (*Partial Portraits* [London: MacMillan, 1894], 199).

67. James, *The Golden Bowl,* 329.

68. Michel Foucault, *The Care of the Self,* trans. Robert Hurley (New York: Vintage Books, 1986), 43.

69. Emerson, *Essays and Lectures,* 1105.

70. R. P. Blackmur, one of James's most attentive readers, sounds this Emersonian note in his examination of the *modus vivendi* (in the more general sense) as the means by which "we go about converting energy and momentum into intellect . . . the first and continuing and ever-necessary act of the mind." Blackmur, "Toward a Modus Vivendi," *Kenyon Review* 16, no. 4 (Autumn 1954): 507–8.

71. "But what is pain? Pain rends. It is the rift. But it does not tear apart into dispersive fragments. Pain indeed tears asunder, it separates, yet so that at the same time it draws everything to itself, gathers it to itself. Its rending, as a separating that gathers, is at the same time that drawing which, like the pen-drawing of a plan or sketch, draws and joins together what is held apart in separation. Pain is the joining agent in the rending that divides and gathers. Pain is the joining of the rift. The joining is the threshold. It settles the between, the middle of the two that are separated in it. Pain joins the rift of the difference. Pain is the dif-ference itself." Martin Heidegger, *Poetry, Language, Thought,* trans. Albert Hofstadter (New York: Harper Perennial, 2013), 201–2.

72. Hart Crane, *Complete Poems and Selected Letters* (New York: Library of America, 2006), 3.

73. Gilles Deleuze and Félix Guattari, *A Thousand Plateaus: Capitalism and Schizophrenia,* trans. Brian Massumi (Minneapolis: University of Minnesota Press, 2000), 249.

74. More than *A Thousand Plateaus,* the Deleuzian idiom most responsive to the "obscure hurt" appears in *Francis Bacon: The Logic of Sensation:* "The Figure is no longer simply isolated but deformed, sometimes contracted and aspirated, sometimes stretched and dilated. This is because the movement is no longer that of the material structure curling around the Figure; it is the movement of the Figure

going toward the structure. . . . The Figure is not simply the isolated body, but also the deformed body that escapes from itself. . . . Just as the effort of the body is exerted upon itself, so the deformation is static. An intense movement flows through the whole body, a deformed and deforming movement that at every moment transfers the real image onto the body in order to constitute the Figure" (17–18).

5. IS THE RECTANGLE A GRAVE?

1. Leo Bersani, *The Culture of Redemption* (Cambridge: Harvard University Press, 1990), 144–47. See also Michael D. Snediker, "Melville and Queerness without Character," in *The New Cambridge Companion to Herman Melville*, ed. Robert S. Levine (New York: Cambridge University Press, 2013), 155–68.

2. Leo Bersani, *A Future for Astyanax: Character and Desire in Literature* (New York: Columbia University Press, 1984), 148.

3. Emerson, *Essays and Lectures*, 479.

4. Leo Bersani and Ulysse Dutoit, *Arts of Impoverishment: Beckett, Rothko, Resnais* (Cambridge: Harvard University Press, 1993), 1.

5. Bersani and Dutoit, *Arts of Impoverishment*, 136.

6. Leo Bersani and Ulysse Dutoit, *Forms of Being: Cinema, Aesthetics, Subjectivity* (London: British Film Institute, 2004), 70.

7. Bersani and Dutoit, *Arts of Impoverishment*, 134.

8. Bersani, "Is the Rectum a Grave?," 30.

9. Bersani, "Is the Rectum a Grave?," 8.

10. Bersani and Dutoit, *Arts of Impoverishment*, 145.

11. "In a sense, the question of ascetics, of the whole system of ascesis-exercises, is essentially a question of technique. It can be analyzed as a technical question." Michel Foucault, *The Hermeneutics of the Subject*, ed. Frédéric Gros, trans. Graham Burchell (New York: Palgrave, 2005), 417.

12. Mark Rothko, *The Artist's Reality: Philosophies of Art* (New Haven: Yale University Press, 2004), 47.

13. Bersani and Dutoit, *Arts of Impoverishment*, 127.

14. *Oxford English Dictionary*, s.v. "entertain."

15. Tim Dean, *Unlimited Intimacy: Reflections on the Subculture of Barebacking* (Chicago: University of Chicago Press, 2009), 113.

16. Bersani, "Is the Rectum a Grave?," 24.

17. Leo Bersani, *The Freudian Body: Psychoanalysis and Art* (New York: Columbia University Press, 1986), 3–4.

18. Leo Bersani, *Receptive Bodies* (Chicago: University of Chicago Press, 2018), x.

19. Bersani, *Receptive Bodies*, 47.

20. Thomas Weiskel, *The Romantic Sublime: Studies in the Structure and Psychology of Transcendence* (Baltimore: Johns Hopkins University Press, 1986), 83.

21. Bersani and Dutoit, *Arts of Impoverishment,* 108.

22. Elizabeth Bishop, *The Complete Poems, 1927–1979* (New York: Farrar, Straus, Giroux, 1983), 3.

23. See Lee Edelman, "Aesthetic Value and Literary Language: Bishop and de Man," in *Never Again Would Birds' Song Be the Same: Essays on Early Modern and Modern Poetry in Honor of John Hollander,* ed. Jennifer Lewin (New Haven: Beinecke Library, 2002); and Michael D. Snediker, "Floating into Blossom: Bishop's Poetics of Queer Speculation," in *Elizabeth Bishop in Context,* ed. Angus Cleghorn and Jonathan S. Ellis (Cambridge: Cambridge University Press, in contract).

24. Bersani and Dutoit, *Arts of Impoverishment,* 107.

25. Bersani and Dutoit, *Forms of Being,* 170. Compare to Henry James: "What it had come to was that he wore a mask painted with the social simper, out of the eye-holes of which there looked eyes of an expression not in the least matching the other features. This the stupid world, even after years, had never more than half discovered. It was only May Bartram who had, and she achieved, by an art indescribable, the feat of at once—or perhaps it was only alternately—meeting the eyes from in front and mingling her own vision, as from over his shoulder, with their peep through the apertures." James, "The Beast in the Jungle," in *Tales of Henry James* (New York: Norton, 2003), 315.

26. George Herbert Mead, *The Philosophy of the Present,* ed. Arthur E. Murphy (London: The Open Court Company, 1932), 121.

27. Mead, *Philosophy of the Present,* 125.

28. Henry James, *The Golden Bowl,* 327–28.

29. Bersani, "Is the Rectum a Grave?," 30.

30. Bersani and Dutoit, *Arts of Impoverishment,* 100.

31. Berlant and Edelman, *Sex, or the Unbearable,* 12.

32. Christopher Bollas, "The Spirit of the Object as the Hand of Fate," in *The Shadow of the Object: Psychoanalysis of the Unthought Known* (New York: Columbia University Press, 1987), 15–22.

33. Cary Howie, *Claustrophilia: The Erotics of Enclosure in Medieval Literature* (New York: Palgrave, 2007), 15.

34. Leo Bersani and Adam Phillips, *Intimacies* (Chicago: University of Chicago Press, 2008), viii.

35. Bersani and Dutoit, *Forms of Being,* 6.

36. Bersani and Dutoit, *Forms of Being,* 69. Compare to the abstract expressionism of Henry James's early novel *Roderick Hudson*: "Then at last, suddenly, his climax was a yawn and he declared that he must tumble in. Rowland let him go

alone and sat there late between sea and sky." *Roderick Hudson* (New York: Scribner, 1907), 83.

37. Bersani and Dutoit, *Forms of Being,* 19.

38. Colin Gardner, "Barnett Newman's Zip as Figure," *Deleuze Studies* 6, no. 1 (2012): 53.

39. Roger Mathew Grant, *Peculiar Attunements: How Affect Theory Turned Musical* (New York: Fordham University Press, 2020), 68.

40. Deleuze, *Francis Bacon,* 60.

41. Eve Kosofsky Sedgwick, *Between Men: English Literature and Male Homosocial Desire* (New York: Columbia University Press, 1985), 21.

42. René Girard, *Deceit, Desire, and the Novel: Self and Other in Literary Structure* (Baltimore: Johns Hopkins University, 1976), 52.

43. See Rei Terada's magnificent *Looking Away: Phenomenality and Dissatisfaction, Kant to Adorno* (Cambridge: Harvard University Press, 2009).

44. Michael D. Snediker, *Queer Optimism: Lyric Personhood and Other Felicitous Persuasions* (Minneapolis: University of Minnesota Press, 2009), 10–13.

45. Bersani and Dutoit, *Arts of Impoverishment,* 117.

46. Bersani and Dutoit, *Arts of Impoverishment,* 112.

47. D.H. Lawrence, *Sons and Lovers* (New York: Viking Press, 1971), 152.

48. Rothko, *The Artist's Reality,* 56.

49. Barthes, *The Neutral,* 83, 77.

50. Leo Bersani, "Psychoanalysis and the Aesthetic Subject," in *Is the Rectum a Grave? And Other Essays* (Chicago: University of Chicago Press, 2009), 141.

51. Jacques Lacan, *The Seminar of Jacques Lacan, Book VII: The Ethics of Psychoanalysis,* ed. Jacques-Alain Miller, trans. Dennis Porter (New York: Norton, 1992), 281.

52. Lacan, *The Ethics of Psychoanalysis,* 248.

53. Lacan, *The Ethics of Psychoanalysis,* 247.

54. Bersani and Dutoit, *Arts of Impoverishment,* 128.

55. Bersani, *A Future for Astyanax,* 160.

56. Bersani and Phillips, *Intimacies,* 26.

57. Henry James, *The Sacred Fount,* intro. Leon Edel (New York: New Directions, 1983), 4.

58. Henry James. *Roderick Hudson* (New York: Penguin, 1986), 217.

59. Bersani and Dutoit, *The Forms of Violence,* 81.

60. Bersani and Dutoit, *The Forms of Violence,* 3.

61. Bersani and Dutoit, *The Forms of Violence,* 81.

62. Bersani and Dutoit, *The Forms of Violence,* 80.

63. The absorption that this geometry orchestrates recalls the embouchure of

encroaching surfaces found throughout Walt Whitman's theorizations of interrelation: "The proof of a poet is that his country absorbs him as affectionately as he has absorbed it." Whitman, *Leaves of Grass: The First (1855) Edition,* ed. Malcolm Cowley (New York: Penguin Books, 1986), 24.

64. Bersani and Dutoit, *Arts of Impoverishment,* 4.

65. Bersani and Dutoit, *Arts of Impoverishment,* 142.

66. Emerson, *Essays and Lectures,* 10.

67. Bersani and Dutoit, *Arts of Impoverishment,* 100.

68. Leo Bersani, "Psychoanalysis and the Aesthetic Subject," 139–53.

69. Bersani and Dutoit, *Forms of Being,* 127.

70. Bersani and Dutoit, *Arts of Impoverishment,* 98–99.

71. Sedgwick, *Epistemology of the Closet,* 219.

72. Bersani and Dutoit, *Arts of Impoverishment,* 98.

73. Bersani, "Is the Rectum a Grave?," 23.

74. Bersani and Dutoit, *Arts of Impoverishment,* 106.

75. Leo Bersani, *Homos* (Cambridge: Harvard University Press, 1995), 100.

76. Friedrich Nietzsche, *Daybreak: Thoughts on the Prejudices of Morality,* ed. Maudemarie Clark and Brian Leiter, trans. R. J. Hollingdale (Cambridge: Cambridge University Press, 1997), 74.

77. Bersani and Dutoit, *Arts of Impoverishment,* 100.

78. Bersani and Dutoit, *Forms of Being,* 153.

79. Bersani, "Is the Rectum a Grave?," 23.

80. Bersani, "Is the Rectum a Grave?," 25.

81. Bersani and Dutoit, *Forms of Being,* 129.

82. Bersani and Dutoit, *Forms of Being,* 149.

83. Bersani, *A Future for Astyanax,* 136–37.

84. Henry James, *The Europeans* (New York: Penguin Classics, 1984), 133.

85. Bersani and Dutoit, *Arts of Impoverishment,* 99.

86. Bersani and Dutoit, *Forms of Being,* 147.

87. Bersani and Dutoit, *Forms of Being,* 147.

88. Bersani and Dutoit, *Arts of Impoverishment,* 149.

89. Bersani and Dutoit, *Arts of Impoverishment,* 4.

90. Bersani and Dutoit, *Arts of Impoverishment,* 104.

91. Bersani and Dutoit, *Arts of Impoverishment,* 4.

92. Bersani and Dutoit, *Forms of Being,* 146.

93. Bersani and Dutoit, *Forms of Being,* 142.

94. Bersani and Dutoit, *Forms of Being,* 176.

95. Bersani and Dutoit, *Arts of Impoverishment,* 112.

96. Bersani and Dutoit, *The Forms of Violence,* 81.

97. Bersani and Dutoit, *Forms of Being,* 169–70.

98. Bersani and Dutoit, *Forms of Being,* 164.

99. Bersani and Dutoit, *Forms of Being,* 164.

100. As Witt urges, sounding like *Leaves of Grass,* "Oh my soul, let me be in you now" (Bersani, *Forms of Being,* 168).

101. Bersani and Dutoit, *Forms of Being,* 169.

102. Leo Bersani, *The Freudian Body,* 70.

103. Bersani and Dutoit, *Forms of Being,* 126.

104. Bersani and Dutoit, *The Forms of Violence,* 131.

105. Bersani, *The Freudian Body,* 78.

106. See Michael D. Snediker, "Whitman on the Verge: Or the Desires of Solitude," *Arizona Quarterly* 61, no. 3 (Autumn 2005): 27–56.

107. Leo Bersani and Ulysse Dutoit, *Caravaggio's Secrets* (Cambridge: MIT Press, 1998), 65.

108. Maud Ellmann, "Lessness: The Art Criticism of Leo Bersani and Ulysse Dutoit," *Oxford Literary Review* 20, nos. 1–2 (1998): 40.

109. Bersani and Dutoit, *Caravaggio's Secrets,* 21.

110. Bersani and Dutoit, *Caravaggio's Secrets,* 29.

111. Bersani, "Is the Rectum a Grave?," 29.

112. Bersani and Dutoit, *Caravaggio's Secrets,* 72.

113. Bersani, "Is the Rectum a Grave?," 30.

114. Bersani and Dutoit, *Arts of Impoverishment,* 111.

6. WEAVER'S HANDSHAKE

1. Emerson, *Essays and Lectures,* 7.

2. Paul Grimstad, "Emerson's Adjacencies: Radical Empiricism in *Nature,*" in *The Other Emerson,* ed. Branka Arsić and Cary Wolfe (Minneapolis: University of Minnesota Press, 2010), 251–70.

3. William James, "A World of Pure Experience," *Journal of Philosophy, Psychology, and Scientific Methods* 1, no. 20 (1904): 534.

4. Lacan, *The Ethics of Psychoanalysis,* 61.

5. Michel Foucault, *The Hermeneutics of the Subject: Lectures at the College de France, 1981–1982* (New York: Palgrave, 2005), 14. See also Leo Bersani, "'Ardent Masturbation' (Descartes, Freud, and Others)," *Critical Inquiry* 38 (Autumn 2011): 1–16.

6. Jordy Rosenberg, "The Molecularization of Sexuality: On Some Primitivisms of the Present," *Theory & Event* 17, no. 2 (2014): 6.

7. Rosenberg, "Molecularization of Sexuality," 6.

8. Sedgwick, *Tendencies,* 46.

9. Sedgwick, *Tendencies,* 120–21.

10. Sedgwick, *Tendencies*, 118.

11. In his *New Republic* screed against Sedgwick and queer theory, Lee Siegel treats her (heuristically motivated) disregard for the inauthenticity of this Chatterton-like document as pièce de résistance ("The Gay Science," *New Republic*, November 9, 1998, 30-42). For an efficient account of Siegel's stink, see Vincent Quinn's "Loose Reading: Sedgwick, Austen, Critical Practice," *Textual Practice* 14, no. 2 (2000): 305–26.

12. Daniel Tiffany, *My Silver Planet* (Baltimore: Johns Hopkins University Press, 2014), 65–69.

13. Rosenberg, "Molecularization of Sexuality," 3.

14. Emerson, *Essays and Lectures*, 473.

15. Emerson, *Essays and Lectures*, 46.

16. Emerson, *Essays and Lectures*, 119. Emerson's sensitivity to the evanescing texture of the interface, the nonequivalence of smoothness and textual lack, recalls Sedgwick's fondness for Renu Bora's essay "Outing Texture": "One consequence of Bora's treatment of the concept: however high the gloss, there is no such thing as textual lack" (*Touching Feeling*, 15).

17. "But the best read naturalist who lends an entire and devout attention to truth, will see that there remains much to learn of his relation to the world, and that it is not to be learned by any addition or subtraction or other comparison of known quantities, but is arrived at by untaught sallies of the spirit, by a continual self-recovery, and by entire humility" (Emerson, *Essays and Lectures*, 43).

18. Lacan, *The Ethics of Psychoanalysis*, 59–60.

19. Emerson, *Essays and Lectures*, 456.

20. *drastic* (adj.), 1690s, originally medical, "forceful, vigorous, especially in effect on bowels," from Greek *drastikos*, "effective, efficacious; active, violent," from *drasteon*, "(thing) to be done," from *dran*, "to do, act, perform." Looking ahead to Sedgwick's growing interest in fractals, I think of these new marginal notes beside the older ones in terms of Cole Swensen's observation (in the context of Susan Howe) that the margin is "the dividing line made extra-dimensional, inhabitable." Swensen, *Noise That Stays Noise: Essays* (Ann Arbor: University of Michigan Press, 2011), 33.

21. Henry James, *The Golden Bowl* (New York: Penguin Books, 1987), 538.

22. I'm imagining (if not quite trying to justify) the flagrance of this recollection as a response, in part, to the concluding note of Sedgwick's 1986 essay "A Poem Is Being Written." "Part of the motivation behind my work on it," she writes, "has been a fantasy that readers or hearers would be variously—in anger, identification, pleasure, envy, 'permission,' exclusion—stimulated to write accounts 'like' this one (whatever that means) of their own, and share those" (Sedgwick, *Tendencies*, 214).

23. Sedgwick, *Tendencies,* 79.

24. *Your Dictionary,* s.v. "cacozelia," http://www.yourdictionary.com/caco zelia.

25. "'They had no opportunity of going into society; they formed no *relations.*' This was one of a certain number of words that the Baroness often pronounced in the French manner." Henry James, *The Europeans* (New York: Penguin Classics, 2008), 133.

26. Cited in Jonathan Culler, "Bad Writing and Good Philosophy," *Just Being Difficult? Academic Writing in the Public Arena,* ed. Jonathan Culler and Kevin Lamb (Stanford: Stanford University Press, 2003), 45.

27. Culler and Lamb, "Introduction," 6.

28. Quintilian, *The Institutio Oratoria of Quintilian,* vol. 3, translated with an introduction by H. E. Butler, M.A. (New York: G.P. Putnam's Sons, 1922), 241–43.

29. Sedgwick, *Epistemology of the Closet,* 141–46.

30. Sedgwick, *Touching Feeling,* 38.

31. Sedgwick, *Touching Feeling,* 44.

32. Eve Kosofsky Sedgwick, *A Dialogue on Love* (New York: Beacon Press, 2000), 31.

33. Eve Kosofsky Sedgwick, *Fat Art, Thin Art* (Durham: Duke University Press, 1994), 95.

34. Sedgwick, *Fat Art, Thin Art,* 95.

35. Jonathan Culler, "Reading Lyric," *Yale French Studies,* no. 69, *The Lesson of Paul de Man* (1985): 99.

36. Jonathan Culler, "Lyric Continuities: Speaker and Consciousness," *Neohelicon* 13, no. 1 (1986): 114, 108. Culler quotes "corrosive but magical substance" from Hugo Friedrich's account of Baudelaire in *The Structure of Modern Poetry.*

37. Jacques Lacan, *The Seminar of Jacques Lacan, Book III: The Psychoses, 1955–1956,* ed. Jacques-Alain Miller, trans. Russell Grigg (New York: Norton, 1997), 268.

38. Lacan, *The Psychoses,* 268.

39. Lacan, *The Psychoses,* 100.

40. Eve Kosofsky Sedgwick, *The Weather in Proust,* ed. Jonathan Goldberg (Durham: Duke University Press, 2011), 71.

41. Sedgwick, *Between Men,* 28, 206.

42. Sedgwick, *Between Men,* 206.

43. Emerson, *Essays and Lectures,* 471.

44. Walt Whitman, *Leaves of Grass: The First (1855) Edition,* ed. Malcolm Cowley (New York: Penguin Books, 1986), 86.

45. Henry James, *Complete Stories, 1898–1910* (New York: Library of America, 1996), 513.

46. Henry James, *The Art of the Novel: Critical Prefaces* (Chicago: University of Chicago Press, 2011), 244.

47. James, *The Art of the Novel,* 5.

48. Sedgwick, *Touching Feeling,* 153.

49. Sedgwick, *Touching Feeling,* 153–54.

50. Sedgwick, *Touching Feeling,* 154.

51. Sedgwick, *The Weather in Proust,* 71.

52. Sedgwick, *Tendencies,* 209.

53. Sedgwick, *The Weather in Proust,* 71.

54. Sedgwick, *Tendencies,* 185.

55. Sedgwick, *Tendencies,* 187.

56. Sedgwick, *The Weather in Proust,* 69.

57. Sedgwick, *Fat Art, Thin Art,* 149.

58. Sedgwick, *Tendencies,* 3.

59. Sedgwick, *Tendencies,* 182.

60. Sedgwick, *A Dialogue on Love,* 203.

61. Sedgwick, *Tendencies,* 86.

62. Sedgwick, *Tendencies,* 209.

63. James, *Complete Stories, 1898–1910,* 511.

64. James, *Complete Stories, 1898–1910,* 540.

65. Bersani, *A Future for Astyanax,* 148.

66. Kevin Ohi, *Dead Letters Sent: Queer Literary Transmission* (Minneapolis: University of Minnesota Press, 2015), 164.

67. Sedgwick, *Epistemology of the Closet,* 199, 200.

68. Sedgwick, *Tendencies,* 97.

69. Sedgwick, *Tendencies,* 84.

70. Sedgwick, *Touching Feeling,* 41.

71. James, *The Art of the Novel,* 219–20.

72. Henry James, *The Spoils of Poynton,* ed. David Lodge (New York: Penguin Books, 1987), 82.

73. James, *The Art of the Novel,* 221, 246.

74. James, *The Art of the Novel,* 225.

75. Culler, "Reading Lyric," 99.

76. Sedgwick, *The Weather in Proust,* 79.

77. Sedgwick, *Epistemology of the Closet,* 3.

78. Sedgwick, *Epistemology of the Closet,* 12.

79. Herman Melville, *Billy Budd, Sailor (An Inside Narrative),* ed. Harrison Hayford and Merton M. Sealts, Jr. (Chicago: University of Chicago Press, 1962), 102.

80. Sedgwick, *A Dialogue on Love,* 94.

81. Sedgwick, *The Weather in Proust,* 11.

82. Sedgwick, *The Weather in Proust,* 79.

83. Sedgwick, *The Weather in Proust,* 79.

84. Sedgwick, *The Weather in Proust,* 84.

85. Sedgwick, *The Weather in Proust,* 100–101.

86. James, *Complete Stories, 1898–1910,* 510.

87. Sedgwick, *The Weather in Proust,* 90.

88. Sedgwick, *The Weather in Proust,* 90.

89. Sedgwick, *Tendencies,* 195. Compare to James's speculation on consecutively dimensionalized selves in terms of the jamming of a door. "[And] I was to regard [this experience] . . . as the marked limit of my state of being a small boy. I took on, when I had decently . . . recovered, the sense of being a boy of other dimensions somehow altogether, and even with a new dimension introduced and acquired; a dimension that I was eventually to think of as a stretch in the direction of essential change or of living straight into a part of myself previously quite unvisited and now made accessible as by the sharp forcing of a closed door. The blur of consciousness imaged by my grease-spot was not, I hasten to declare, without its relenting edges and even, during its major insistence, fainter thicknesses; short of which, I see, my picture, the picture I was always so incurably 'after,' would have failed of animation altogether." Henry James, *A Small Boy and Others* (New York: Scribner, 1913), 398–99.

90. Sedgwick, *Fat Art, Thin Art,* 72.

91. Bersani, "The It in the I," *Intimacies,* 1–30.

92. Sedgwick, *Fat Art, Thin Art,* 24.

93. Sedgwick, *Touching Feeling,* 23–24.

94. Sharon Cameron, *Beautiful Work: A Meditation on Pain* (Durham: Duke University Press, 2000), 1.

95. Judith Butler, "Values of Difficulty," in Culler and Lamb, *Just Being Difficult?,* 214.

96. Henry James, *Washington Square, ed. Mark Le Fanu* (New York: Oxford World's Classics, 1998), 8.

97. Sedgwick, *Fat Art, Thin Art,* 75.

Index

aboutness, 4, 14, 21, 31, 35, 37, 39, 40, 46, 62–63, 69, 77, 95, 125, 145, 147
accessible/inaccessible, 9, 13, 23, 31–32, 40, 42, 51, 69, 72, 104, 110, 112, 128, 131, 143, 146–47, 167, 247n89
acedia/inertia, 77–78, 90, 166, 169, 224n41
Adorno, Theodor, 82
Agamben, Giorgio, 224n41
Aida (Verdi), xii
AIDS crisis, 63, 156
Albee, Edward: *Who's Afraid of Virginia Woolf?*, 63
Albiach, Anne-Marie, 136, 235n38
allure, 10, 42, 77, 114, 122, 158
Althusser, Louis, 25. *See also* interpellation
anamorphosis, 174, 205
Annie: The Musical, 192
anthropomorphosis, 61, 73, 113–14, 135, 190, 194, 196, 200, 207, 210
Antigone, 98, 167–68, 178, 180, 228n30
apostrophe, 136–37, 193, 194, 207
Arendt, Hannah, 109, 230n57
Arsić, Branka, 1, 43, 143, 223n17, 235n40, 237n57, 243n2
Ashbery, John (on Gertrude Stein), 21, 71, 218n37, 223n26
attention, xi, xiv, 9, 12, 21, 31, 33, 42–43, 51–52, 56, 59, 70, 76, 86, 89, 95–96, 100–101, 126, 140, 147, 155–81, 196, 203, 207, 212, 216n16, 225n3, 235n30, 238n66
Auerbach, Erich (on *figura*), xvi, 13, 16, 215n13, 218n25, 218n30, 231n88
Austin, J. L., 19

Bacon, Francis, 4, 57, 164, 216n5, 238n74, 241n40
Balfour, Ian, 85, 119, 231n84
Barthes, Roland, xii, 77; and cruising, 2; and death of the author,

xii; *The Grain of the Voice,* 2, 216n3; *A Lover's Discourse,* xii; and the Neutral, 61, 67–68, 72, 76, 81, 82, 117, 128, 167; and punctum, 55, 221n36
Baudelaire, Charles, 113, 245n36
Benjamin, Walter, 24, 167; and collecting, 79–80, 224n45; *Trauerspiel,* 188
Berlant, Lauren, 25, 67–69, 131, 162, 223n13, 223n14, 223n20, 233n16, 240n31; and cruel optimism, 25, 67, 69, 223n13
Bersani, Leo, 62–67, 71–72, 155–81; "Blocked Vision," 156, 157, 160, 165, 168–69, 170, 172, 175, 177; *Caravaggio's Secrets,* 180–81; *Culture of Redemption,* 221n23, 239n1, 221n23; *Forms of Being,* 160, 163, 172; *The Forms of Violence,* 170, 180; *The Freudian Body,* 159, 175, 179–80; *A Future for Astyanax,* 33, 53, 65, 176, 203, 221n33; *Intimacies,* 163–64; *Is the Rectum a Grave? And Other Essays,* 31, 54, 62–67, 71, 72, 82, 219n49; *Receptive Bodies,* xvi, 159, 239n18, 239n19, 251n11
Berubé, Michael, 20, 218n34, 218n35
Bidgood, James, 54
Bingham, Millicent Todd, 112
Bishop, Elizabeth, 160, 240nn22–23
Blackmur, R.P.: *Language as Gesture,* 44, 53, 118, 225n2, 231n86; "Toward a Modus Vivendi," 238n70
Blanchot, Maurice, 29, 30, 76, 80–82, 111, 117, 128, 130, 233n14; and Hawthorne, 82; *The Infinite Conversation,* 233n11, 233n14; *The Space of Literature,* 29–30, 76, 80–82, 111, 117, 128, 130, 233n14
blindness, 5, 39, 87, 88, 93, 105, 128, 155, 158, 167, 168, 170, 171, 173–74, 177, 227n9, 234n19
Bollas, Christopher: *The Shadow of the Object,* 162, 20n32
Bond, Justin Vivian, 53
Brinkema, Eugenie: *Forms of the Affects,* 53–54, 221n34, 221n35
Brown, Nathan, 58, 222n40
Bryant, Levi R., 41, 220n9
Buddhism, 34, 103, 198
Burton, Robert: *Anatomy of Melancholy,* 109–11, 230n56
Butler, Judith, 35, 41, 50, 98, 184–85, 216n4; melancholy, 50–51; performativity, 41; and *Washington Square,* 212

cacozelia, 191–93, 245n24
Cameron, Sharon, 12, 85, 90–94, 212; *Beautiful Work,* 212, 247n94; *Choosing Not Choosing,* 235n40; *Lyric Time,* 85, 90–94; *Thinking in Henry James,* 236n41
Caravaggio, 180, 181, 243n107, 243n109–10, 243n112
Carmody, Todd, 11–12, 218n19

centripetal/centrifugal, 33, 94, 188, 228n14
characterology, 1–5, 7–9, 11, 15–16, 20–21, 31–33, 44–46, 49, 53, 55–58, 72–73, 76, 129, 148, 155, 169, 176, 189, 191, 204–5, 212, 217n15, 225n50
Chase, Cynthia, 217n15
Chen, Mel Y.: *Animacies,* xvi–xvii, 216n15
Clare, Eli: *Brilliant Imperfection,* 145–46, 237n64
closet, xiii, 11, 17, 49, 107, 127, 203, 217n18
constative language, 35; as landlubber language, 37
Crane, Hart, 153, 238n72
cruising, xiii, 2, 173, 190, 222n8
Culler, Jonathan, 69–70, 72, 193–94, 207, 223n19, 223n22, 245nn26–27, 245nn35–36, 246n75, 247n95

Davis, Theo: *Ornamental Aesthetics,* 107, 117–20, 229nn48–49, 230nn74–75, 231n79
Dayan, Colin, 215n12
Dean, Tim, 158, 239n15
Deleuze, Gilles, 4, 48, 121–22, 153, 164, 236nn40–41, 241n38, 241n40; *Difference and Repetition,* 121–22, 232nn93–94; *The Fold,* 48, 221n25; *Francis Bacon: The Logic of Sensation,* 4, 164, 216n5, 241n40; *A Thousand Plateaus,* 153, 238n73
De Man, Paul, 61, 81, 113–15, 133, 194, 200, 222n3, 225n48, 230n66–70, 234n19, 240n23
Derrida, Jacques, 24, 218n26, 219n40, 236n40
Descartes, Rene, 58, 184, 209, 243n5
diagnosis, xiv, 14, 55, 87, 88, 145–47, 151, 199, 200, 203, 237nn64–65
Dickinson, Emily, 4–5, 11, 14, 24, 31–33, 74, 77, 83, 85–123, 136–37, 143, 179, 197, 225nn2–3, 226n4, 226n9, 227n10, 227n13, 229n34, 231n81, 231nn86–87, 235n37; "After great pain a formal feeling comes" (F372), 4–5, 11, 33, 74–75, 77, 81–83, 89, 95, 179, 216n6, 224n35; "Crumbling is not an instant's Act" (F1010), 111; "Further in Summer than the Birds" (F895), 99; "Hope is the thing with feathers" (F314), 100; "I felt a Funeral, in my Brain" (F340), 93; "I got so I could take his name" (F292), 122; "I years had been from Home" (F440), 106; "Like trains of Cars on Tracks of Plush" (F1213), 119; "A nearness to Tremendousness" (F824), 226n3; "No Man can compass a Despair" (F714); "A not admitting / of the wound" (F1188), 122–23; "Opon a Lilac Sea" (F1368), 116–21;

"The Outer – from the Inner" (F450), 104–8, 112; "Pain – expands the Time" (F833), 105; "A Pang is more conspicuous in Spring" (F1545), 98–104, 106, 108, 112–13; "Patience – has a quiet – Outer" (F842), 105; "Publication – is the Auction" (F788), 113; "Surprise is like a thrilling – pungent" (F1324), 118, 231n81; "'Twas like a Maelstrom, with a notch" (F425), 92–95; "We dream – it is good we are dreaming" (F584), 96; "We send the wave to find the wave" (F1643), 95–96; "You see I cannot see – your lifetime" (F313), 136–37, 225n37

Dimock, Wai-Chee, 46, 221n24

disability studies/theory, xvi, 5, 9–15, 19–20, 24–25, 31–32, 35, 44, 45, 49, 58, 62, 69–70, 80, 82, 86, 90, 117, 155–56, 171, 217n11, 217n15, 217n16, 217n18, 218nn21–24, 218nn34–35, 219n41, 220n18, 221n22, 233n14

Douglass, Frederick, 22–23, 219n38

dreams, xv, 5, 16, 25, 28, 37, 69, 73, 92, 98, 102, 121, 123, 145, 149, 150, 152

Dutoit, Ulysse, 156–58, 160–67, 170–78, 180–81

ecology, 10, 86, 106, 112, 137, 162

Edel, Leon, 138–44, 169, 232n7, 236n54, 237n59

Edelman, Lee, 70, 76, 223n14, 223nn24–25, 233n16, 240n23, 240n31

Ellmann, Maud, 180, 243n108

Emerson, Ralph Waldo, 1, 28, 34, 50, 68, 89, 101, 105–6, 109, 122, 125, 143, 150, 155–56, 165, 172, 178, 183–89, 195–96, 198, 204, 207, 223n17, 226n3, 229n34, 244nn16–17; "Beauty," 101, 229n34; "Compensation," 143; *The Conduct of Life,* 150; "Experience," 50, 68, 101, 105, 122, 155, 184, 187–88, 195, 226n3; "Method of Nature," 188; *Nature* (1836), 28, 34, 89, 109, 172, 183, 187–89, 196, 244n17; "The Poet," 189; "Poetry and the Imagination," 106; "Spiritual Laws," 183

empirical, 3, 11, 34, 36, 106, 108, 112, 130, 135, 138, 149, 159, 191

epistemology, 10, 36, 69, 76, 85, 89, 97–98, 107, 127–28, 130, 145–48, 151, 163, 193, 222n9, 237n64

Esch, Deborah: "A Jamesian About-Face," 129, 233

etymology, 3, 39, 40, 43, 61, 76, 100–101, 109, 116, 118, 130, 158, 177, 193, 218n27

excrescence, xvi, 14, 31, 46, 116, 185, 205, 215n12

Fenner, Christopher Smith, 110–11, 230n59
Ferguson, Frances, 27, 66, 219n44, 223n12
Field, Sally, 64–65, 68, 79, 82, 223n10
Flatley, Jonathan, 79, 224n42
Flaubert, Gustave, 190
Foucault, Michel, xi, 3–4, 9, 17, 25, 66, 150, 186, 215n3, 216n4, 223n11, 224n34, 235n30, 238n68, 239n11, 243n5; *The Care of the Self,* 150, 238n68; *Discipline and Punish,* 17, 25; *Herculine Barbin,* 3–4, 9, 216n4; *The Hermeneutics of the Subject,* 239n11, 243n5; *The History of Sexuality,* xi–xii, 66, 186, 215n3, 215n5, 223n11, 224n34, 235n30
François, Anne-Lise: *Open Secrets,* 68, 70, 223n15, 223n21
Frankenstein (Shelley), xiii
Freeman, Elizabeth: *Time Binds,* xiv, 215n6
Freud, Sigmund, 50, 63, 65, 93, 98, 114, 158–60, 169, 172, 175, 179, 236n40; *Civilization and its Discontents,* 63, 179; *Nachträglichkeit,* 65, 114
Friedrich, Caspar David: *Wanderer above the Sea of Fog,* 179
Fuller, Margaret, 125

Galatea, 212
geometry, 33, 153, 155–81, 197, 241n63
gesture, 8, 27–28, 34, 38–39, 66, 90–91, 114, 121–22, 127, 137, 145, 151, 169, 194–95, 198–99, 202, 223, 226n4, 229n34
Glavey, Brian, 224n43
Godard, Jean-Luc: *Contempt,* 163–64
Goffman, Erving: *Stigma,* 9–11, 217nn13–15
Goldilocks, 65–66
Gonzáles-Torres, Felix, 91
Gouldman, Francis, 236n52
Grant, Roger Mathew, 164, 241n39
Grimstad, Paul, 183–84, 243n2
Grossman, Allen, 98, 228n31
Guthrie, James, 227n10, 227n13

Hamacher, Warner, 71, 76, 79, 82, 224n29, 224n36, 224n44
Harman, Graham, 41–42, 220n9, 220n11, 220n14
Hawthorne, Nathaniel, 1–2, 15–20, 27, 30–31, 82, 93, 106, 186, 216n1, 225n49, 225n50; "The Custom-House," 1–2, 20, 27, 82, 93, 186; *The Scarlet Letter,* 15–20
Hawthorne, Sophia, 38
Heidegger, Martin, 80, 238n71
Henry, Michel, 85
Herford, Oliver, 138, 236n42
Hitchcock, Alfred, 54
Holden, Kevin, vii
Holland, Elizabeth, 102–3, 229n36
Holzer, Jenny, 22
Hound and Horn, 133, 234n21

Howie, Cary, 162, 240n33
Huffer, Lynne, 74, 224n34
Hume, David, 58
hyperbaton, 119–20

image repertoire, xiv, 39
imperceptibility/perceptibility, xiii, xvii, 10, 14, 22, 31–32, 80, 90, 102–3, 110–11, 118, 135, 145, 173–74, 188, 237n64
impingement, 3, 33, 4, 89, 99, 108–12, 123, 131, 153, 162, 175
impotance, 70
incessancy, 1, 17, 24, 30, 32, 34, 41, 52, 57, 112, 116–22, 130, 137, 142, 190, 194, 199, 208
interpellation, 25, 54, 65, 93
interstice/horizon, 3, 4, 29, 33, 71–73, 108, 123, 142, 148, 150, 163–69, 161–73, 177–79, 193, 199, 211, 227n10, 229n34

Jackson, Virginia: *Dickinson's Misery,* 107–8, 112–15, 229n50, 230n51, 230n52, 230nn62–65, 230nn71–72
Jakobson, Roman, 65
James, Henry, xii, xv, 32, 33, 53, 61, 65, 125–54; "The Beast in the Jungle," 127, 160, 196, 198, 202–7, 210–12, 240n25; and Civil War, 32, 89, 128, 133–34, 139, 236n47, 237n59; *The Europeans,* 245n25; *The Golden Bowl,* xv–xvi, 33, 148–49, 155, 161, 215n9, 237n65, 238n66, 238n67, 240n28, 244n21; "The Jolly Corner," 129, 233n12; middle distance, 50, 55, 68, 107, 138, 188, 209, 210, 211–12, 238n71; *The New York Edition,* 32, 53, 126, 192, 196–97, 205, 246n46; *Notes on a Son and Brother,* 32, 125–54; and "obscure hurt," 32, 125–54; and queerness, 32, 126, 127, 128, 133, 134, 141, 152, 192, 197, 203, 205, 207, 210, 236n54; *Roderick Hudson,* xv, 169, 197, 215nn7–8, 240n36, 241n58; *A Small Boy and Others,* 126, 247n89; *The Spoils of Poynton,* 205–6, 246n72; *The Turn of the Screw,* xii, 139, 143, 144, 145, 212, 237nn60–61, 237n63; *Washington Square,* 212, 247n96; *What Maisie Knew,* 53; *The Wings of the Dove,* 202, 204–5
James, William, 125, 184, 232n2, 243n3
Jameson, Fredric, 136, 235n36
Johnson, Barbara, 74, 77, 209, 224n33, 224nn39–40
Johnson, Thomas H., 86–87, 116, 226n6, 226n7

Kant, Immanuel, 82, 118, 231n80
Keats, John, 39, 113, 234n20
kitsch/camp, 54, 133, 186, 191, 192, 208
Kohler, Michelle, 227n13

Lacan, Jacques, 167, 168, 179, 180,

184, 189, 215n4, 241nn51–53, 243n4, 244n18, 245nn37–39; and Antigone, 167, 168, 178, 180; *jouissance,* 62, 156, 157, 158, 172, 179, 215n4; quilting point, 21, 194–95, 199
Lacoue-Labarthe, Philippe, 132, 234n18
Laplanche, Jean, 140–41, 236n48, 236nn50–51
Lawrence, D.H.: *Sons and Lovers,* 167, 169, 241n47
Lee, Maurice S., 105–6, 229n39, 229nn42–43
Ligon, Glenn, 29
likeness, xv, 12, 31, 61–85, 220n12
Longinus, 119–20
Louima, Abner, 23–24, 219n39
Love, Heather, 217 n15
Luciano, Dana, 226n4
Lucretius, xvi, 6, 16, 42, 120, 220n12
Lustig, Timothy, 138, 236n43

Malick, Terrence: *The Thin Red Line,* 176–79
Marion, Jean-Luc, 89, 135, 228n15, 235n35
Martin, Agnes, 30, 219n48
materiality, 9, 14, 16, 26, 28, 31, 34, 43, 46, 56, 58–59, 82, 85, 99, 106–9, 115, 120, 122, 139, 148, 184–85, 194, 199, 207–9, 220n16, 226n4, 238n74
Matthiessen, F. O., 139
McRuer, Robert: *Crip Theory,* 12, 218n23
Mead, George Herbert: *The Philosophy of the Present,* 159, 161, 240nn26–27
medical encounter, xiv, 23, 26, 31–32, 35, 87, 88, 109, 141, 145, 199, 227n10
melodrama, 20, 54, 65, 67–68, 162, 165, 203
Melville, Herman, 5, 7, 9, 12, 14, 14, 20, 30–31, 32, 35–60, 72, 75, 79, 93, 119, 155, 208; "Bartleby," xiii, 20, 21, 31, 40, 72, 73, 75–76, 78–79, 83, 121; *Benito Cereno,* 31, 72–74; *Billy Budd,* 74–76, 208, 224n32, 246n79; *Clarel,* 59; domestic violence, 7; "Fragments from a Writing Desk," 5–10; milk bowl, 38–40; *Moby-Dick,* 11, 20, 31, 33, 35–46, 48, 58–60, 155, 165, 217n17, 220n8; *Pierre,* 31, 36, 38–40, 42–44, 46–49, 52–55, 119; queerness, 43–47, 53
Merleau-Ponty, Maurice, 51, 58, 105–6, 109, 220n10, 221n29, 221n39, 227n13, 229nn37–38, 229nn44–45, 229n46
metaphor, 3, 9, 11–15, 39, 41, 44, 52, 76, 93–95, 107, 112; versus figuration, 12–15
metonymy, 17, 32, 55, 76, 97, 115, 140, 164, 231n86
Miller, Cristanne, 102, 116
mimetic/anti-mimetic, xvi, 12, 16, 33, 50, 57, 61, 71, 127, 132, 133, 148, 153, 156, 162, 169–72, 191, 207, 228, 234

Misrach, Richard, 38
Mitchell, David T., 11; and Sharon L. Snyder, 10, 20, 45, 217n16, 218n33, 221n27
modus vivendi, 146, 150, 154, 238n70
moistness, 43, 49, 52–55
Moore, Marianne, 53
Moten, Fred, xvii, 216n16
Mozart, Wolfgang Amadeus, 164, 232n7
Muybridge, Edweard, 104, 150
mysticism, 35, 48, 158

Nancy, Jean-Luc, 62, 125, 218n26, 222n6
neck, xi–xvii, 6, 14, 20, 25, 41, 48, 57, 109, 199, 231n81, 223n14
Nelson, Jennifer L., and Bradley S. Berens, 12, 218n21
Newman, Barnett, 164, 168, 172, 177, 241n38
Newton, Isaac, vii, 110, 230n58
Nietzsche, Friedrich, 61, 65, 68, 115, 175, 222nn1–2, 222n3, 242n76
Noble, Marianne, 225n3, 227n13
Novick, Sheldon, 127, 130, 232nn5–6
Nunokawa, Jeff, 125

object-oriented ontology, 41, 220n9
object relations, xii, xvi–xvii, 8, 28–29, 31, 33, 37, 40–43, 51, 55–56, 64, 66–71, 76–81, 86, 89–92, 96, 101, 107–8, 115, 117–19, 121–22, 128–29, 136, 143, 156, 159, 161, 166, 175, 184–212
Ohi, Kevin, 203–4, 246n66
Oppen, George, 223n17
Orpheus, 25, 187–89
Osborne, Gillian, 120, 121, 231n89, 231nn91–92
Otter, Samuel, 5–9, 217n11

paraphrase, 40, 44, 54, 56, 101, 129, 130, 144, 206, 207, 225n3, 232n6
Parmigianino, xiii
Pater, Walter, 117, 120, 231n78
Peretz, Eyal, 42, 220n13
phenomenology, xiv, xvi, 3, 4, 5, 18, 26, 39, 40, 41, 45, 58, 59, 63, 68, 85, 90, 93, 97, 98, 105, 116, 132, 135, 165, 171, 180, 216, 223n17, 226n4, 227n13, 235n35
Phillips, Adam, 163, 240n34, 241n56
Plato: *Phaedrus,* 55–56, 221n37
plushness, 116, 119, 120, 231n86, 231n87
Poe, Edgar Allen, 6, 8; "Ligeia," 6; "The Philosophy of Composition," 3, 114, 128
Pope, Alexander, xi
pornography, 6, 157
Posnock, Ross, 232n2
posthumanism, 19, 218n31
Poulet, Georges, xiv

Prince and the Pauper, The, 112
prosthesis, 20, 35, 39, 54, 111, 208, 217nn16–17, 218n33
Proust, Marcel, 4, 54, 173, 191
psychoanalysis, 17, 98, 114, 159, 167, 230n54, 236n40, 236n48, 236nn50–51, 236n53, 240n32
Puar, Jasbir: *The Right to Maim,* 24–25, 219nn41–42
Pygmalion, 131, 212
Pyle, Forest, 5, 217n7

queer theory, xiii, 31, 33, 49, 62, 155, 158, 184, 186, 200, 217n15, 244n11
Quintilian, 13, 191, 245n28
quotidian, xvii, 27, 29, 31, 32, 38, 41, 67, 88, 98, 101, 134, 148, 149

Rankine, Claudia: *Don't Let Me Be Lonely,* 21–30, 218n36
Rawlings, Peter, 134–35, 234nn24–27, 236n47
Reed, Anthony, 28, 219n47
Renker, Elizabeth, 7–8, 217n10
resistance, xii, 1, 25, 34, 44, 69, 72, 75, 114, 121, 156, 159, 161, 171, 175, 184, 200, 201, 202, 208, 209, 212
rhythm, xiv, 2, 33, 38, 51, 70, 78, 104, 121, 127, 128, 132, 142, 151, 153, 175, 190, 192, 200, 235, 236n40
Richards, I.A., 3, 52, 221n31
Rosenberg, Jordy: "Molecularization of Sexuality," 184, 187, 243nn6–7
Rothko, Mark, 33, 156–81, 239n12
Roupenian, Kristen, 6, 204n9

Samuels, Ellen, 11–12, 217n18, 218n22
Scarry, Elaine: *The Body in Pain,* xvi, 32, 37, 89, 90, 96, 97, 98, 101, 145, 184, 216n14, 218n32, 220n4, 225n3, 227n14, 228nn26–29, 237n62
Scott, Judith, 211, 212
Sedgwick, Eve Kosofsky, 33–34, 49, 53–54, 69, 70, 78, 107, 127, 128, 131, 165, 173, 183–212; *Between Men,* 165, 241n41; and crafts/textile art, 33, 197, 199, 200, 201, 207, 209; *A Dialogue on Love,* 192–93, 202, 209, 245n3; *Epistemology of the Closet,* 49, 107, 128, 178, 181, 187, 190–92, 207, 221n26, 233n10; *Fat Art, Thin Art,* 34, 193, 196, 201, 211, 212, 245nn33–34; *Tendencies,* 34, 69, 78, 183, 185–86, 193, 200–202, 211, 244n22; *Touching Feeling,* 34, 70, 127, 131, 190, 192, 198, 204–5, 244n16; *The Weather in Proust,* 34, 53–54, 194–95, 201, 209, 245n40
sex, xii, xiii, xiv, 31, 33, 43, 62–67, 71, 82, 126, 156, 158, 161, 162, 175, 176, 185–88, 197

Sex, or the Unbearable (Berlant and Edelman), 68, 131, 162
Shakespeare, William, xi, 132, 198, 234n17
Shaviro, Steven, 42
shibboleth, 34, 195–97
shibori, 34, 209–10
Sisyphus, 25, 86, 150
Sjöholm, Cecilia, 109–10, 230n57
Snediker, Michael D.: "Floating into Blossom," 240n23; "Melville and Queerness without Character," 221n38, 239n1; "Minute Effulgencies," 220n16; "*Pierre* and the Non-Transparencies of Figuration," 221n27; *Queer Optimism,* xiv, 165, 225n3, 227n11, 228n30, 241n44; "Stasis and Verve," 238n65; "Whitman on the Verge," 216n2, 243n106
Sontag, Susan, 9, 44, 58, 221n20
spiritual manspreading, and Dimmesdale, 17
Stein, Gertrude, vii, 70, 71, 75, 77, 79, 82, 99, 107, 215n6, 224nn27–28, 229n47; *Stanzas in Meditation,* 21, 31, 75, 77, 79
Stevens, Wallace, xv, 215n10
Sturgis, Caroline Tappan,125
Sturgis, Howard, 125–27
suminagashi, 34, 209
Swensen, Cole, 244n20
synecdoche, xiii, 28, 93, 151, 236n47
Tate, Allen, 89, 122, 227n11, 232n97
tautology, 42, 113, 115, 133, 142, 169, 209
Terada, Rei, 241n43
Thomson, Rosemarie Garland: *Extraordinary Bodies,* 12–13, 15, 20, 44, 218n24, 218nn28–29
Thoreau, Henry David, 43
throughness, 8, 14, 23, 28, 37, 39, 41, 48–49, 52, 55, 68, 86, 99, 111–12, 119, 122, 141, 152, 158–59, 174, 203, 205, 210, 219n3, 220n16
Tiffany, Daniel, 135, 136, 186, 226n4, 235nn31–33
Todd, Mabel Loomis, 112
Tomkins, Silvan, 70–71, 82, 223n23

Valley Girl, 31, 66, 74, 76, 77
Vendler, Helen, 93, 228n24
Venice, xii
Vincent, John Emil,199
Viola, Bill, 65, 165
Vriezen, Sam, 135, 235n34

wabi-sabi, 207, 209
Warhol, Andy, 78, 79, 224n43
Watson, E. L. Grant, 42–43, 53, 54, 220n15
weather/atmosphere, 15, 26, 27, 33, 44, 53, 54, 90, 95, 101, 128, 137, 142, 150, 167, 170, 177
Weisbuch, Robert, 229n36, 231n87

Wescott, Glenway, 133–34, 139, 234n20, 234n21
White, Edmund, 125, 232n1
Whitman, Walt, 77, 96, 179, 180, 195–96, 197, 198, 216n2, 224n38, 241n63, 243n106
Winnicott, D. O., 108, 109, 161–62, 165–66, 172, 179, 209, 230nn53–54
Wolfe, Cary, 19, 218n31, 243n2
Wordsworth, William, 26–27, 52, 55, 117, 120, 217n15, 219n43, 221n30, 234n19; "We are Seven," 26–27

Zappa, Moon Unit, 31, 77–79
Zip (Barnett Newman), 164, 172, 241n38

Michael D. Snediker is associate professor of English at the University of Houston. He is the author of *Queer Optimism: Lyric Personhood and Other Felicitous Persuasions* (Minnesota, 2008) and two books of poems, *The Apartment of Tragic Appliances* and *The New York Editions.*